Apache Spark Machine Learning Blueprints

Develop a range of cutting-edge machine learning projects with Apache Spark using this actionable guide

Alex Liu

BIRMINGHAM - MUMBAI

Apache Spark Machine Learning Blueprints

First published: May 2016

Production reference: 1250516

Published by Packt Publishing Ltd.
Livery Place
35 Livery Street
Birmingham B3 2PB, UK.

ISBN 978-1-78588-039-1

www.packtpub.com

Credits

Author
Alex Liu

Reviewer
Hao Ren

Commissioning Editor
Dipika Gaonkar

Acquisition Editor
Meeta Rajani

Content Development Editor
Anish Sukumaran

Technical Editors
Dhiraj Chandanshive
Siddhesh Patil

Copy Editor
Shruti Iyer

Project Coordinator
Izzat Contractor

Proofreader
Safis Editing

Indexer
Mariammal Chettiyar

Graphics
Disha Haria

Production Coordinator
Nilesh R. Mohite

Cover Work
Nilesh R. Mohite

About the Author

Alex Liu is an expert in research methods and data science. He is currently one of IBM's leading experts in Big Data analytics and also a lead data scientist, where he serves big corporations, develops Big Data analytics IPs, and speaks at industrial conferences such as STRATA, Insights, SMAC, and BigDataCamp. In the past, Alex served as chief or lead data scientist for a few companies, including Yapstone, RS, and TRG. Before this, he was a lead consultant and director at RMA, where he provided data analytics consultation and training to many well-known organizations, including the United Nations, Indymac, AOL, Ingram Micro, GEM, Farmers Insurance, Scripps Networks, Sears, and USAID. At the same time, he taught advanced research methods to PhD candidates at University of Southern California and University of California at Irvine. Before this, he worked as a managing director for CATE/GEC and as a research fellow for the Asia/Pacific Research Center at Stanford University. Alex has a Ph.D. in quantitative sociology and a master's degree of science in statistical computing from Stanford University.

I would like to thank IBM for providing a great open and innovative environment to learn and practice Big Data analytics. I would especially like to thank my managers, Kim Siegel and Kevin Zachary, for their support and encouragement, without which it would not have been possible to complete this book.

I would also like to thank my beautiful wife, Lauria, and two beautiful daughters, Kate and Khloe, for their patience and support, which enabled me to work effectively. Finally, I would like to thank the Packt staff, especially Anish Sukumaran and Meeta Rajani, for making the writing and editing process smooth and joyful.

About the Reviewer

Hao Ren is data engineer working in Paris for a classified advertising website named leboncoin (`https://www.leboncoin.fr/`), which is the fifth most visited site in France. Three years' work experience of functional programming in Scala, Machine Learning, and distributed systems defines his career. Hao's main speciality is based on machine learning with Apache Spark, such as building a crawler detection system, recommander system, and so on. He has also reviewed a more detailed and advanced book by Packt Publishing, *Machine Learning with Spark*, which is worth a read as well.

www.PacktPub.com

eBooks, discount offers, and more

Did you know that Packt offers eBook versions of every book published, with PDF and ePub files available? You can upgrade to the eBook version at www.PacktPub.com and as a print book customer, you are entitled to a discount on the eBook copy. Get in touch with us at customercare@packtpub.com for more details.

At www.PacktPub.com, you can also read a collection of free technical articles, sign up for a range of free newsletters and receive exclusive discounts and offers on Packt books and eBooks.

https://www2.packtpub.com/books/subscription/packtlib

Do you need instant solutions to your IT questions? PacktLib is Packt's online digital book library. Here, you can search, access, and read Packt's entire library of books.

Why subscribe?

- Fully searchable across every book published by Packt
- Copy and paste, print, and bookmark content
- On demand and accessible via a web browser

Table of Contents

Preface

As data scientists and machine learning professionals, our jobs are to build models for detecting frauds, predicting customer churns, or turning data into insights in a broad sense; for this, we sometimes need to process huge amounts of data and handle complicated computations. Therefore, we are always excited to see new computing tools, such as Spark, and spend a lot of time learning about them. To learn about these new tools, a lot of learning materials are available, but they are from a more computing perspective, and often written by computer scientists.

We, the data scientists and machine learning professionals, as users of Spark, are more concerned about how the new systems can help us build models with more predictive accuracy and how these systems can make data processing and coding easy for us. This is the main reason why this book has been developed and why this book has been written by a data scientist.

At the same time, we, as data scientists and machine learning professionals, have already developed our frameworks and processes as well as used some good model building tools, such as R and SPSS. We understand that some of the new tools, such as MLlib of Spark, may replace certain old tools, but not all of them. Therefore, using Spark together with our existing tools is essential to us as users of Spark and becomes one of the main focuses for this book, which is also one of the critical elements, making this book different from other Spark books.

Overall, this is a Spark book written by a data scientist for data scientists and machine learning professionals to make machine learning easy for us with Spark.

What this book covers

Chapter 1, Spark for Machine Learning, introduces Apache Spark from a machine learning perspective. We will discuss Spark dataframes and R, Spark pipelines, RM4Es data science framework, as well as the Spark notebook and implementation models.

Chapter 2, Data Preparation for Spark ML, focuses on data preparation for machine learning on Apache Spark with tools such as Spark SQL. We will discuss data cleaning, identity matching, data merging, and feature development.

Chapter 3, A Holistic View on Spark, clearly explains the RM4E machine learning framework and processes with a real-life example and also demonstrates the benefits of obtaining holistic views for businesses easily with Spark.

Chapter 4, Fraud Detection on Spark, discusses how Spark makes machine learning for fraud detection easy and fast. At the same time, we will illustrate a step-by-step process of obtaining fraud insights from Big Data.

Chapter 5, Risk Scoring on Spark, reviews machine learning methods and processes for a risk scoring project and implements them using R notebooks on Apache Spark in a special DataScientistWorkbench environment. Our focus for this chapter is the notebook.

Chapter 6, Churn Prediction on Spark, further illustrates our special step-by-step machine learning process on Spark with a focus on using MLlib to develop customer churn predictions to improve customer retention.

Chapter 7, Recommendations on Spark, describes how to develop recommendations with Big Data on Spark by utilizing SPSS on the Spark system.

Chapter 8, Learning Analytics on Spark, extends our application to serve learning organizations like universities and training institutions, for which we will apply machine learning to improve learning analytics for a real case of predicting student attrition.

Chapter 9, City Analytics on Spark, helps the readers to gain a better understanding about how Apache Spark could be utilized not only for commercial use, but also for public use as to serve cities with a real use case of predicting service requests on Spark.

Chapter 10, Learning Telco Data on Spark, further extends what was studied in the previous chapters and allows readers to combine what was learned for a dynamic machine learning with a huge amount of Telco Data on Spark.

Chapter 11, Modeling Open Data on Spark, presents dynamic machine learning with open data on Spark from which users can take a data-driven approach and utilize all the technologies available for optimal results. This chapter is an extension of *Chapter 9, City Analytics on Spark*, and *Chapter 10, Learning Telco Data on Spark*, as well as a good review of all the previous chapters with a real-life project.

What you need for this book

Throughout this book, we assume that you have some basic experience of programming, either in Scala or Python; some basic experience with modeling tools, such as R or SPSS; and some basic knowledge of machine learning and data science.

Who this book is for

This book is written for analysts, data scientists, researchers, and machine learning professionals who need to process Big Data but who are not necessarily familiar with Spark.

Conventions

In this book, you will find a number of text styles that distinguish between different kinds of information. Here are some examples of these styles and an explanation of their meaning.

Code words in text, database table names, folder names, filenames, file extensions, pathnames, dummy URLs, user input, and Twitter handles are shown as follows: "In R, the `forecast` package has an `accuracy` function that can be used to calculate forecasting accuracy."

A block of code is set as follows:

```
df1 = sqlContext.read \
. format("json") \ data format is json
. option("samplingRatio", "0.01") \ set sampling ratio as 1%
. load("/home/alex/data1,json") \ specify data name and location
```

Any command-line input or output is written as follows:

```
sqlContext <- sparkRSQL.init(sc)
```

New terms and **important words** are shown in bold. Words that you see on the screen, for example, in menus or dialog boxes, appear in the text like this: "Users can click on **Create new note**, which is the first line under **Notebook** on the first left-hand side column."

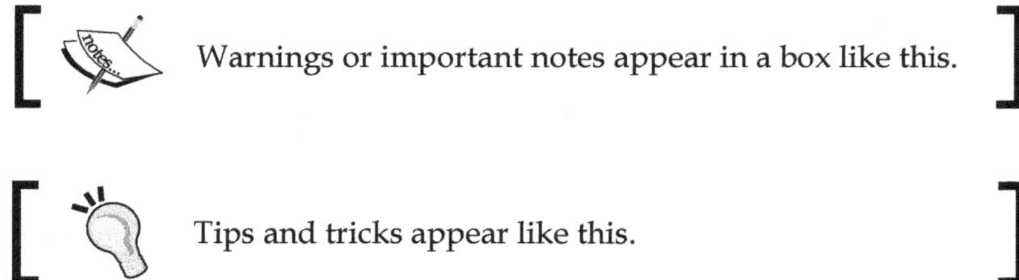

Warnings or important notes appear in a box like this.

Tips and tricks appear like this.

Reader feedback

Feedback from our readers is always welcome. Let us know what you think about this book—what you liked or disliked. Reader feedback is important for us as it helps us develop titles that you will really get the most out of.

To send us general feedback, simply e-mail `feedback@packtpub.com`, and mention the book's title in the subject of your message.

If there is a topic that you have expertise in and you are interested in either writing or contributing to a book, see our author guide at `www.packtpub.com/authors`.

Customer support

Now that you are the proud owner of a Packt book, we have a number of things to help you to get the most from your purchase.

Downloading the color images of this book

We also provide you with a PDF file that has color images of the screenshots/diagrams used in this book. The color images will help you better understand the changes in the output. You can download this file from `http://www.packtpub.com/sites/default/files/downloads/ApacheSparkMachineLearningBlueprints_ColorImages.pdf`.

Errata

Although we have taken every care to ensure the accuracy of our content, mistakes do happen. If you find a mistake in one of our books—maybe a mistake in the text or the code—we would be grateful if you could report this to us. By doing so, you can save other readers from frustration and help us improve subsequent versions of this book. If you find any errata, please report them by visiting `http://www.packtpub.com/submit-errata`, selecting your book, clicking on the **Errata Submission Form** link, and entering the details of your errata. Once your errata are verified, your submission will be accepted and the errata will be uploaded to our website or added to any list of existing errata under the Errata section of that title.

To view the previously submitted errata, go to `https://www.packtpub.com/books/content/support` and enter the name of the book in the search field. The required information will appear under the **Errata** section.

Piracy

Piracy of copyrighted material on the Internet is an ongoing problem across all media. At Packt, we take the protection of our copyright and licenses very seriously. If you come across any illegal copies of our works in any form on the Internet, please provide us with the location address or website name immediately so that we can pursue a remedy.

Please contact us at `copyright@packtpub.com` with a link to the suspected pirated material.

We appreciate your help in protecting our authors and our ability to bring you valuable content.

Questions

If you have a problem with any aspect of this book, you can contact us at `questions@packtpub.com`, and we will do our best to address the problem.

1
Spark for Machine Learning

This chapter provides an introduction to Apache Spark from a **Machine Learning** (**ML**) and data analytics perspective, and also discusses machine learning in relation to Spark computing. Here, we first present an overview of Apache Spark, as well as Spark's advantages for data analytics, in comparison to MapReduce and other computing platforms. Then we discuss five main issues, as below:

- Machine learning algorithms and libraries
- Spark RDD and dataframes
- Machine learning frameworks
- Spark pipelines
- Spark notebooks

All of the above are the most important topics that any data scientist or machine learning professional is expected to master, in order to fully take advantage of Apache Spark computing. Specifically, this chapter will cover all of the following six topics.

- Spark overview and Spark advantages
- ML algorithms and ML libraries for Spark
- Spark RDD and dataframes
- ML Frameworks, RM4Es and Spark computing
- ML workflows and Spark pipelines
- Spark notebooks introduction

Spark overview and Spark advantages

In this section, we provide an overview of the Apache Spark computing platform and a discussion about some advantages of utilizing Apache Spark, in comparison to using other computing platforms like MapReduce. Then, we briefly discuss how Spark computing fits modern machine learning and Big Data analytics.

After this section, readers will form a basic understanding of Apache Spark as well as a good understanding of some important machine learning benefits from utilizing Apache Spark.

Spark overview

Apache Spark is a computing framework for the fast processing of Big Data. This framework contains a distributed computing engine and a specially designed programming model. Spark was started as a research project at the AMPLab of the University of California at Berkeley in 2009, and then in 2010 it became fully open sourced as it was donated to the Apache Software Foundation. Since then, Apache Spark has experienced exponential growth, and now Spark is the most active open source project in the Big Data field.

Spark's computing utilizes an in-memory distributed computational approach, which makes Spark computing among the fastest, especially for iterative computation. It can run up to 100 times faster than Hadoop MapReduce, according to many tests that have been performed.

Apache Spark has a unified platform, which consists of the Spark core engine and four libraries: Spark SQL, Spark Streaming, MLlib, and **GraphX**. All of these four libraries have Python, Java and Scala programming APIs.

Besides the above mentioned four built-in libraries, there are also tens of packages available for Apache Spark, provided by third parties, which can be used for handling data sources, machine learning, and other tasks.

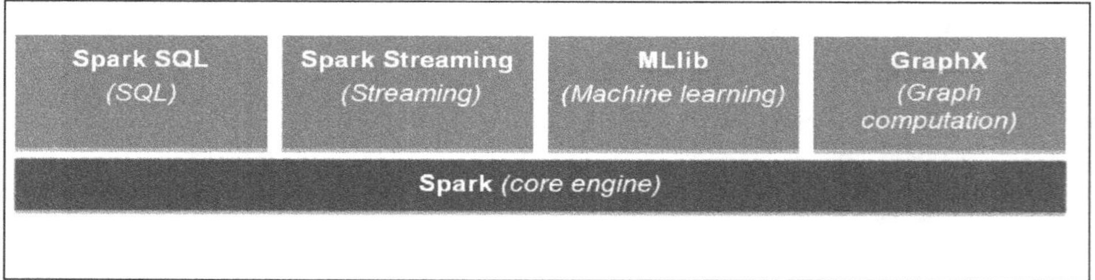

Apache Spark has a 3 month circle for new releases, with Spark version 1.6.0 released on January 4 of 2016. Apache Spark release 1.3 had DataFrames API and ML Pipelines API included. Starting from Apache Spark release 1.4, the R interface (SparkR) is included as default.

To download Apache Spark, readers should go to `http://spark.apache.org/downloads.html`.

To install Apache Spark and start running it, readers should consult its latest documentation at `http://spark.apache.org/docs/latest/`.

Spark advantages

Apache Spark has many advantages over MapReduce and other Big Data computing platforms. Among them, the distinguished two are that it is fast to run and fast to write.

Overall, Apache Spark has kept some of MapReduce's most important advantages like that of scalability and fault tolerance, but extended them greatly with new technologies.

In comparison to MapReduce, Apache Spark's engine is capable of executing a more general **Directed Acyclic Graph** (**DAG**) of operators. Therefore, when using Apache Spark to execute MapReduce-style graphs, users can achieve higher performance batch processing in Hadoop.

Apache Spark has in-memory processing capabilities, and uses a new data abstraction method, **Resilient Distributed Dataset** (**RDD**), which enables highly iterative computing and reactive applications. This also extended its fault tolerance capability.

At the same time, Apache Spark has made complex pipeline representation easy with only a few lines of code needed. It is best known for the ease with which it can be used to create algorithms that capture insight from complex and even messy data, and also enable users to apply that insight in-time to drive outcomes.

As summarized by the Apache Spark team, Spark enables:

- Iterative algorithms in Machine Learning
- Interactive data mining and data processing
- Hive-compatible data warehousing that can run 100x faster
- Stream processing
- Sensor data processing

To a practical data scientist working with the above, Apache Spark easily demonstrates its advantages when it is adopted for:

- Parallel computing
- Interactive analytics
- Complex computation

Most users are satisfied with Apache Spark's advantages in speed and performance, but some also noted that Apache Spark is still in the process of maturing.

`http://svds.com/post/use-cases-apache-spark` has some examples of materialized Spark benefits.

Spark computing for machine learning

With its innovations on RDD and in-memory processing, Apache Spark has truly made distributed computing easily accessible to data scientists and machine learning professionals. According to the Apache Spark team, Apache Spark runs on the Mesos cluster manager, letting it share resources with Hadoop and other applications. Therefore, Apache Spark can read from any Hadoop input source like HDFS.

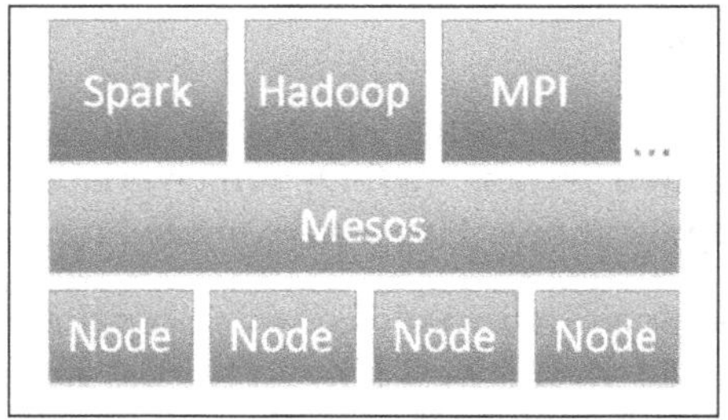

For the above, the Apache Spark computing model is very suitable to distributed computing for machine learning. Especially for rapid interactive machine learning, parallel computing, and complicated modelling at scale, Apache Spark should definitely be utilized.

According to the Spark development team, Spark's philosophy is to make life easy and productive for data scientists and machine learning professionals. Due to this, Apache Spark has:

- Well documented, expressive API's
- Powerful domain specific libraries

- Easy integration with storage systems
- Caching to avoid data movement

Per the introduction by Patrick Wendell, co-founder of Databricks, Spark is especially made for large scale data processing. Apache Spark supports agile data science to iterate rapidly, and Spark can be integrated with IBM and other solutions easily.

Machine learning algorithms

In this section, we review algorithms that are needed for machine learning, and introduce machine learning libraries including Spark's MLlib and IBM's SystemML, then we discuss their integration with Apache Spark.

After reading this section, readers will become familiar with various machine learning libraries including Spark's MLlib, and know how to make them ready for machine learning.

To complete a Machine Learning project, data scientists often employ some classification or regression algorithms to develop and evaluate predictive models, which are readily available in some Machine Learning tools like R or MatLab. To complete a machine learning project, besides data sets and computing platforms, these machine learning libraries, as collections of machine learning algorithms, are necessary.

For example, the strength and depth of the popular R mainly comes from the various algorithms that are readily provided for the use of Machine Learning professionals. The total number of R packages is over 1000. Data scientists do not need all of them, but do need some packages to:

- Load data, with packages like `RODBC` or `RMySQL`
- Manipulate data, with packages like `stringr` or `lubridate`
- Visualize data, with packages like `ggplot2` or `leaflet`
- Model data, with packages like `Random Forest` or `survival`
- Report results, with packages like `shiny` or `markdown`

According to a recent ComputerWorld survey, the most downloaded R packages are:

PACKAGE	# of DOWNLOADS
Rcpp	162778
ggplot2	146008
plyr	123889
stringr	120387
colorspace	118798
digest	113899
reshape2	109869
RColorBrewer	100623
scales	92448
manipulate	88664

For more info, please visit http://www.computerworld.com/article/2920117/business-intelligence/most-downloaded-r-packages-last-month.html

MLlib

MLlib is Apache Spark's machine learning library. It is scalable, and consists of many commonly-used machine learning algorithms. Built-in to MLlib are algorithms for:

- Handling data types in forms of vectors and matrices
- Computing basic statistics like summary statistics and correlations, as well as producing simple random and stratified samples, and conducting simple hypothesis testing
- Performing classification and regression modeling
- Collaborative filtering
- Clustering
- Performing dimensionality reduction
- Conducting feature extraction and transformation
- Frequent pattern mining
- Developing optimization
- Exporting PMML models

The Spark MLlib is still under active development, with new algorithms expected to be added for every new release.

In line with Apache Spark's computing philosophy, the MLlib is built for easy use and deployment, with high performance.

MLlib uses the linear algebra package `Breeze`, which depends on `netlib-java`, and `jblas`. The packages `netlib-java` and `jblas` also depend on native Fortran routines. Users need to install the `gfortran` runtime library if it is not already present on their nodes. MLlib will throw a linking error if it cannot detect these libraries automatically.

For MLlib use cases and further details on how to use MLlib, please visit: `http://spark.apache.org/docs/latest/mllib-guide.html`.

Other ML libraries

As discussed in previous part, MLlib has made available many frequently used algorithms like regression and classification. But these basics are not enough for complicated machine learning.

If we wait for the Apache Spark team to add all the needed ML algorithms it may take a long time. For this, the good news is that many third parties have contributed ML libraries to Apache Spark.

IBM has contributed its machine learning library, SystemML, to Apache Spark.

Besides what MLlib provides, SystemML offers a lot more additional ML algorithms like the ones on missing data imputation, SVM, GLM, ARIMA, and non-linear optimizers, and some graphical modelling and matrix factonization algorithms.

As developed by the IBM Almaden Research group, IBM's SystemML is an engine for distributed machine learning and it can scale to arbitrary large data sizes. It provides the following benefits:

- Unifies the fractured machine learning environments
- Gives the core Spark ecosystem a complete set of DML
- Allows a data scientist to focus on the algorithm, not the implementation
- Improves time to value for data science teams
- Establishes a de facto standard for reusable machine learning routines

SystemML is modeled after R syntax and semantics, and provides the ability to author new algorithms via its own language.

Through a good integration with R by SparkR, Apache Spark users also have the potential to utilize thousands of R packages for machine learning algorithms, when needed. As will be discussed in later sections of this chapter, the SparkR notebook will make this operation very easy.

For more about IBM SystemML, please visit `http://researcher.watson.ibm.com/researcher/files/us-ytian/systemML.pdf`

Spark RDD and dataframes

In this section, our focus turns to data and how Apache Spark represents data and organizes data. Here, we will provide an introduction to the Apache Spark RDD and Apache Spark dataframes.

After this section, readers will master these two fundamental Spark concepts, RDD and Spark dataframe, and be ready to utilize them for Machine Learning projects.

Spark RDD

Apache Spark's primary data abstraction is in the form of a distributed collection of items, which is called **Resilient Distributed Dataset** (**RDD**). RDD is Apache Spark's key innovation, which makes its computing faster and more efficient than others.

Specifically, an RDD is an immutable collection of objects, which spreads across a cluster. It is statically typed, for example RDD[T] has objects of type T. There are RDD of strings, RDD of integers, and RDD of objects.

On the other hand, RDDs:

- Are collections of objects across a cluster with user controlled partitioning
- Are built via parallel transformations like `map` and `filter`

That is, an RDD is physically distributed across a cluster, but manipulated as one logical entity. RDDs on Spark have fault tolerant properties such that they can be automatically rebuilt on failure.

New RDDs can be created from Hadoop Input Formats (such as HDFS files) or by transforming other RDDs.

To create RDDs, users can either:

- Distribute a collection of objects from the driver program (using the parallelize method of the Spark context)
- Load an external dataset
- Transform an existing RDD

Spark's team call the above two types of RDD operations *action* and *transformation*.

RDDs can be operated by *actions*, which return values, or by *transformations*, which return pointers to new RDDs. Some examples of RDD actions are `collect`, `count` and `take`.

Transformations are lazy evaluations. Some examples of RDD transformations are `map`, `filter`, and `join`.

RDD actions and transformations may be combined to form complex computations.

To learn more about RDD, please read the article at `https://www.cs.berkeley.edu/~matei/papers/2012/nsdi_spark.pdf`

Spark dataframes

A Spark dataframe is a distributed collection of data as organized by columns, actually a distributed collection of data as grouped into named columns, that is, an RDD with a schema. In other words, Spark dataframe is an extension of Spark RDD.

Data frame = *RDD* where columns are named and can be manipulated by name instead of by index value.

A Spark dataframe is conceptually equivalent to a dataframe in R, and is similar to a table in a relational database, which helped Apache Spark to be quickly accepted by the machine learning community. With Spark dataframes, users can directly work with data elements like columns, which are not available when working with RDDs. With data scheme knowledge on hand, users can also apply their familiar SQL types of data re-organization techniques to data. Spark dataframes can be built from many kinds of raw data such as structured relational data files, Hive tables, or existing RDDs.

Apache Spark has built a special dataframe API and a Spark SQL to deal with Spark dataframes. The Spark SQL and Spark dataframe API are both available for Scala, Java, Python, and R. As an extension to the existing RDD API, the DataFrames API features:

- Ability to scale from kilobytes of data on a single laptop to petabytes on a large cluster
- Support for a wide array of data formats and storage systems
- State-of-the-art optimization and code generation through the Spark SQL Catalyst optimizer
- Seamless integration with all Big Data tooling and infrastructure via Spark

The Spark SQL works with Spark DataFrame very well, which allows users to do ETL easily, and also to work on subsets of any data easily. Then, users can transform them and make them available to other users including R users. Spark SQL can also be used alongside HiveQL, and runs very fast. With Spark SQL, users write less code as well, a lot less than working with Hadoop, and also less than working directly on RDDs.

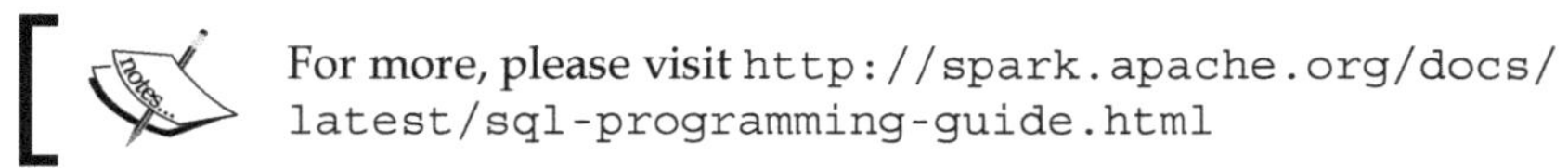

For more, please visit `http://spark.apache.org/docs/latest/sql-programming-guide.html`

Dataframes API for R

A dataframe is an essential element for machine learning programming. Apache Spark has made a dataframe API available for R as well as for Java and Python, so that users can operate Spark dataframes easily in their familiar environment with their familiar language. In this section, we provide a simple introduction to operating Spark dataframes, with some simple examples for R to start leading our readers into actions.

The entry point into all relational functionality in Apache Spark is its `SQLContext` class, or one of its descendents. To create a basic `SQLContext`, all users need is a SparkContext command as below:

```
sqlContext <- sparkRSQL.init(sc)
```

To create a Spark dataframe, users may perform the following:

```
sqlContext <- SQLContext(sc)
df <- jsonFile(sqlContext, "examples/src/main/resources/people.json")
# Displays the content of the DataFrame to stdout
showDF(df)
```

For Spark dataframe operations, the following are some examples:

```
sqlContext <- sparkRSQL.init(sc)
# Create the DataFrame
df <- jsonFile(sqlContext, "examples/src/main/resources/people.json")
# Show the content of the DataFrame
showDF(df)
## age  name
## null Michael
## 30   Andy
## 19   Justin

# Print the schema in a tree format
printSchema(df)
## root
## |-- age: long (nullable = true)
## |-- name: string (nullable = true)

# Select only the "name" column
showDF(select(df, "name"))
## name
## Michael
## Andy
## Justin

# Select everybody, but increment the age by 1
showDF(select(df, df$name, df$age + 1))
## name    (age + 1)
## Michael null
## Andy    31
## Justin  20

# Select people older than 21
showDF(where(df, df$age > 21))
## age name
## 30  Andy
```

```
# Count people by age
showDF(count(groupBy(df, "age")))
## age  count
## null 1
## 19   1
## 30   1
```

For more info, please visit http://spark.apache.org/docs/latest/sql-programming-guide.html#creating-dataframes

ML frameworks, RM4Es and Spark computing

In this section, we discuss machine learning frameworks with RM4Es as one of its examples, in relation to Apache Spark computing.

After this section, readers will master the concept of machine learning frameworks and some examples, and then be ready to combine them with Spark computing for planning and implementing machine learning projects.

ML frameworks

As discussed in earlier sections, Apache Spark computing is very different from Hadoop MapReduce. Spark is faster and easier to use than Hadoop MapReduce. There are many benefits to adopting Apache Spark computing for machine learning.

However, all the benefits for machine learning professionals will materialize only if Apache Spark can enable good ML frameworks. Here, an ML framework means a system or an approach that combines all the ML elements including ML algorithms to make ML most effective to its users. And specifically, it refers to the ways that data is represented and processed, how predictive models are represented and estimated, how modeling results are evaluated, and are utilized. From this perspective, ML Frameworks are different from each other, for their handling of data sources, conducting data pre-processing, implementing algorithms, and for their support for complex computation.

There are many ML frameworks, as there are also various computing platforms supporting these frameworks. Among the available ML frameworks, the frameworks stressing iterative computing and interactive manipulation are considered among the best, because these features can facilitate complex predictive model estimation and good researcher-data interaction. Nowadays, good ML frameworks also need to cover Big Data capabilities or fast processing at scale, as well as fault tolerance capabilities. Good frameworks always include a large number of machine learning algorithms and statistical tests ready to be used.

As mentioned in previous sections, Apache Spark has excellent iterative computing performance and is highly cost-effective, thanks to in-memory data processing. It's compatible with all of Hadoop's data sources and file formats and, thanks to friendly APIs that they are available in several languages, it also has a faster learning curve. Apache Spark even includes graph processing and machine-learning capabilities. For these reasons, Apache Spark based ML frameworks are favored by ML professionals.

However, Hadoop MapReduce is a more mature platform and it was built for batch processing. It can be more cost-effective than Spark, for some Big Data that doesn't fit in memory and also due to the greater availability of experienced staff. Furthermore, the Hadoop MapReduce ecosystem is currently bigger thanks to many supporting projects, tools, and cloud services.

But even if Spark looks like the big winner, the chances are that ML professionals won't use it on its own, ML professionals may still need HDFS to store the data and may want to use HBase, Hive, Pig, Impala, or other Hadoop projects. For many cases, this means ML professionals still need to run Hadoop and MapReduce alongside Apache Spark for a full Big Data package.

RM4Es

In a previous section, we have had some general discussion about machine learning frameworks. Specifically, a ML framework covers how to deal with data, analytical methods, analytical computing, results evaluation, and results utilization, which RM4Es represents nicely as a framework. The **RM4Es (Research Methods Four Elements)** is a good framework to summarize Machine Learning components and processes. The RM4Es include:

- **Equation**: Equations are used to represent the models for our research
- **Estimation**: Estimation is the link between equations (models) and the data used for our research
- **Evaluation**: Evaluation needs to be performed to assess the fit between models and the data

- **Explanation**: Explanation is the link between equations (models) and our research purposes. How we explain our research results often depends on our research purposes and also on the subject we are studying

The RM4Es are the key four aspects that distinguish one machine learning method from another. The RM4Es are sufficient to represent an ML status at any given moment. Furthermore, using RM4Es can easily and sufficiently represent ML workflows.

Related to what we discussed so far, Equation is like ML libraries, Estimation represents how computing is done, Evaluation is about how to tell whether a ML is better, and, as for iterative computer, whether we should continue or stop. Explanation is also a key part for ML as our goal is to turn data into insightful results that can be used.

Per the above, a good ML framework needs to deal with data abstraction and data pre-processing at scale, and also needs to deal with fast computing, interactive evaluation at scale and speed, as well as easy results interpretation and deployment.

The Spark computing framework

Earlier in the chapter, we discussed how Spark computing supports iterative ML computing. After reviewing machine learning frameworks and how Spark computing relates to ML frameworks, we are ready to understand more about why Spark computing should be selected for ML.

Spark was built to serve ML and data science, to make ML at scale and ML deployment easy. As discussed, Spark's core innovation on RDDs enables fast and easy computing, with good fault tolerance.

Spark is a general computing platform, and its program contains two programs: a driver program and a worker program.

To program, developers need to write a driver program that implements the high-level control flow of their application and also launches various operations in parallel. All the worker programs developed will run on cluster nodes or in local threads, and RDDs operate across all workers.

As mentioned, Spark provides two main abstractions for parallel programming: resilient distributed datasets and parallel operations on these datasets (invoked by passing a function to apply on a dataset).

In addition, Spark supports two restricted types of shared variables:

- **Broadcast variables**: If a large read-only piece of data (e.g., a lookup table) is used in multiple parallel operations, it is preferable to distribute it to the workers only once instead of packaging it with every closure.
- **Accumulators**: These are variables that workers can only *add* to using an associative operation, and that only the driver can read. They can be used to implement counters as in MapReduce and to provide a more imperative syntax for parallel sums. Accumulators can be defined for any type that has an *add* operation and a *zero* value. Due to their *add-only* semantics, they are easy to make fault-tolerant.

With all the above, the Apache Spark computing framework is capable of supporting various machine learning frameworks that need fast parallel computing with fault tolerance.

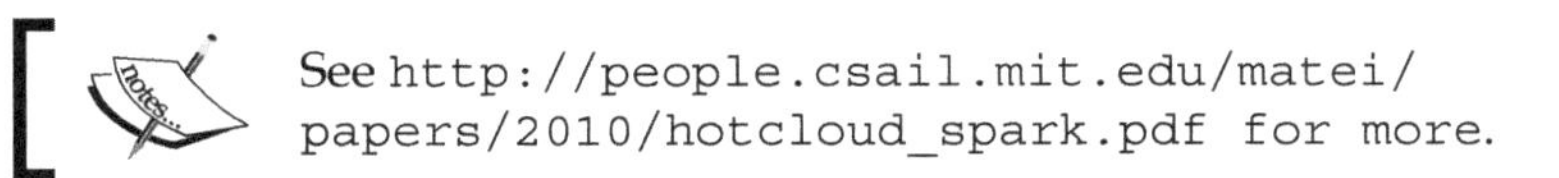

See `http://people.csail.mit.edu/matei/papers/2010/hotcloud_spark.pdf` for more.

ML workflows and Spark pipelines

In this section, we provide an introduction to machine learning workflows, and also Spark pipelines, and then discuss how Spark pipeline can serve as a good tool of computing ML workflows.

After this section, readers will master these two important concepts, and be ready to program and implement Spark pipelines for machine learning workflows.

ML as a step-by-step workflow

Almost all ML projects involve cleaning data, developing features, estimating models, evaluating models, and then interpreting results, which all can be organized into some step by step workflows. These workflows are sometimes called analytical processes.

Some people even define machine learning as workflows of turning data into actionable insights, for which some people will add business understanding or problem definition into the workflows as their starting points.

In the data mining field, **Cross Industry Standard Process for Data Mining** (**CRISP-DM**) is a widely accepted workflow standard, which is still widely adopted. And many standard ML workflows are just some form of revision to the CRISP-DM workflow.

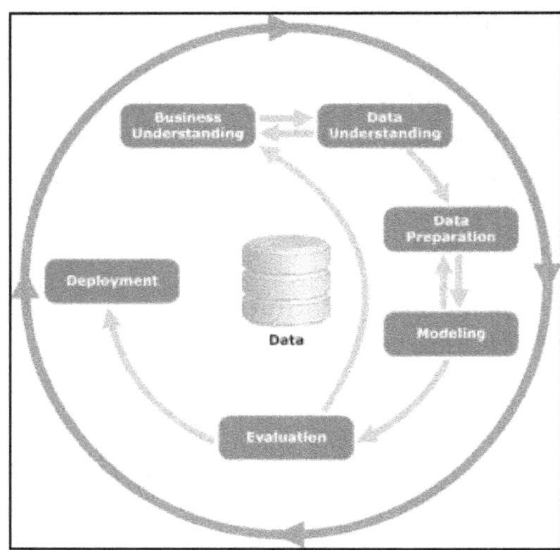

As illustrated in the above picture, for any standard CRISP-DM workflow, we need all the following 6 steps:

1. Business understanding
2. Data understanding
3. Data preparation
4. Modeling
5. Evaluation
6. Deployment

To which some people may add analytical approaches selection and results explanation, to make it more complete. For complicated machine learning projects, there will be some branches and feedback loops to make workflows very complex.

In other words, for some machine learning projects, after we complete model evaluation, we may go back to the step of modeling or even data preparation. After the data preparation step, we may branch out for more than two types of modeling.

ML workflow examples

To further understand machine learning workflows, let us review some examples here.

In the later chapters of this book, we will work on risk modelling, fraud detection, customer view, churn prediction, and recommendation. For many of these types of projects, the goal is often to identify causes of certain problems, or to build a causal model. Below is one example of a workflow to develop a causal model.

1. Check data structure to ensure a good understanding of the data:
    - Is the data a cross sectional data? Is implicit timing incorporated?
    - Are categorical variables used?
2. Check missing values:
    - Don't know or forget as an answer may be recoded as neutral or treated as a special category
    - Some variables may have a lot of missing values
    - To recode some variables as needed
3. Conduct some descriptive studies to begin telling stories:
    - Use comparing means and crosstabulations
    - Check variability of some key variables (standard deviation and variance)
4. Select groups of `ind` variables (exogenous variables):
    - As candidates of causes
5. Basic descriptive statistics:
    - Mean, standard deviaton, and frequencies for all variables
6. Measurement work:
    - Study dimensions of some measurements (efa exploratory factor analysis may be useful here)
    - May form measurement models
7. Local models:
    - Identify sections out from the whole picture to explore relationship
    - Use crosstabulations
    - Graphical plots
    - Use logistic regression
    - Use linear regression

8. Conduct some partial correlation analysis to help model specification.
9. Propose structural equation models by using the results of (8):
    - Identify main structures and sub structures
    - Connect measurements with structure models
10. Initial fits:
    - Use *spss* to create data sets for *lisrel* or *mplus*
    - Programming in lisrel or mplus
11. Model modification:
    - Use SEM results (mainly model fit indices) to guide
    - Re-analyze partial correlations
12. Diagnostics:
    - Distribution
    - Residuals
    - Curves
13. Final model estimation may be reached here:
    - If not repeat step 13 and 14
14. Explaining the model (causal effects identified and quantified).

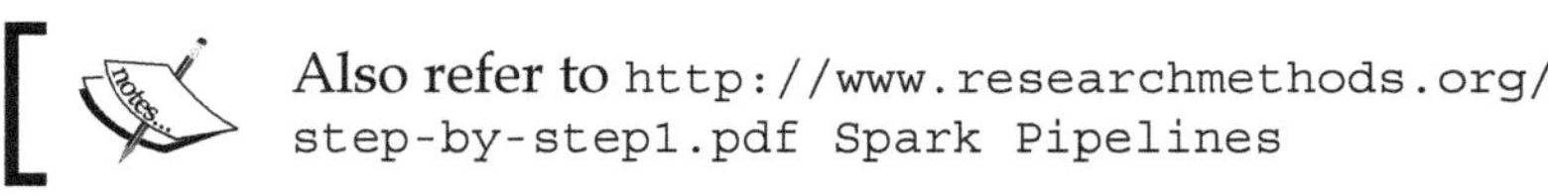

Also refer to `http://www.researchmethods.org/step-by-step1.pdf` `Spark Pipelines`

The Apache Spark team has recognized the importance of machine learning workflows and they have developed Spark Pipelines to enable good handling of them.

Spark ML represents a ML workflow as a pipeline, which consists of a sequence of *PipelineStages* to be run in a specific order.

PipelineStages include Spark Transformers, Spark Estimators and Spark Evaluators.

ML workflows can be very complicated, so that creating and tuning them is very time consuming. The Spark ML Pipeline was created to make the construction and tuning of ML workflows easy, and especially to represent the following main stages:

1. Loading data
2. Extracting features

3. Estimating models
4. Evaluating models
5. Explaining models

With regards to the above tasks, Spark Transformers can be used to extract features. Spark Estimators can be used to train and estimate models, and Spark Evaluators can be used to evaluate models.

Technically, in Spark, a Pipeline is specified as a sequence of stages, and each stage is either a Transformer, an Estimator, or an Evaluator. These stages are run in order, and the input dataset is modified as it passes through each stage. For Transformer stages, the `transform()` method is called on the dataset. For estimator stages, the `fit()` method is called to produce a Transformer (which becomes part of the PipelineModel, or fitted Pipeline), and that Transformer's `transform()` method is called on the dataset.

The specifications given above are all for linear Pipelines. It is possible to create non-linear Pipelines as long as the data flow graph forms a **Directed Acyclic Graph** (**DAG**).

For more info on Spark pipeline, please visit: `http://spark.apache.org/docs/latest/ml-guide.html#pipeline`

Spark notebooks

In this section, we first discuss about notebook approaches for machine learning. Then we provide a full introduction to R Markdown as a mature notebook example, and then introduce Spark's R notebook to complete this section.

After this section, readers will master these notebook approaches as well as some related concepts, and be ready to use them for managing and programming machine learning projects.

Notebook approach for ML

Notebook became a favored machine learning approach, not only for its dynamics, but also for reproducibility.

Most notebook interfaces are comprised of a series of code blocks, called cells. The development process is a discovery type, for which a developer can develop and run codes in one cell, and then can continue to write code in a subsequent cell depending on the results from the first cell. Particularly when analyzing large datasets, this interactive type of approach allows machine learning professionals to quickly discover patterns or insights into data. Therefore, notebook-style development processes provide some exploratory and interactive ways to write code and immediately examine results.

Notebook allows users to seamlessly mix code, outputs, and markdown comments all in the same document. With everything in one document, it makes it easier for machine learning professionals to reproduce their work at a later stage.

This notebook approach was adopted to ensure reproducibility, to align analysis with computation, and to align analysis with presentation, so to end the copy and paste way of research management.

Specifically, using notebook allows users to:

- Analyze iteratively
- Report transparently
- Collaborate seamlessly
- Compute with clarity
- Assess reasoning, not only results
- The note book approach also provides a unified way to integrate many analytical tools for machine learning practice.

For more about adopting an approach for reproducibility, please visit `http://chance.amstat.org/2014/09/reproducible-paradigm/R Markdown`

R Markdown is a very popular tool helping data scientists and machine learning professionals to generate dynamic reports, and also making their analytical workflows reproducible. R Markdown is one of the pioneer notebook tools.

According to RStudio

> *"R Markdown is a format that enables easy authoring of reproducible web reports from R. It combines the core syntax of Markdown (an easy-to-write plain text format for web content) with embedded R code chunks that are run so their output can be included in the final document".*

Therefore, we can use R and the Markdown package plus some other dependent packages like `knitr`, to author reproducible analytical reports. However, utilizing RStudio and the `Markdown` package together makes things easy for data scientists.

Using the Markdown is very easy for R users. As an example, let us create a report in the following three simple steps:

Step 1: Getting the software ready

1. Download R studio at : `http://rstudio.org/`
2. Set options for R studio: **Tools** > **Options** > Click on **Sweave** and choose **Knitr** at **Weave Rnw files using Knitr**.

Step 2: Installing the Knitr package

1. To install a package in RStudio, you use **Tools** > **Install Packages** and then select a CRAN mirror and package to install. Another way to install packages is to use the function `install.packages()`.
2. To install the `knitr` package from the Carnegi Mellon Statlib CRAN mirror, we can use: `install.packages("knitr", repos = "http://lib.stat.cmu.edu/R/CRAN/")`

Step 3: Creating a simple report

1. Create a blank R Markdown file: **File** > **New** > **R Markdown**. You will open a new `.Rmd` file.
2. When you create the blank file, you can see an already-written module. One simple way to go is to replace the corresponding parts with your own information.

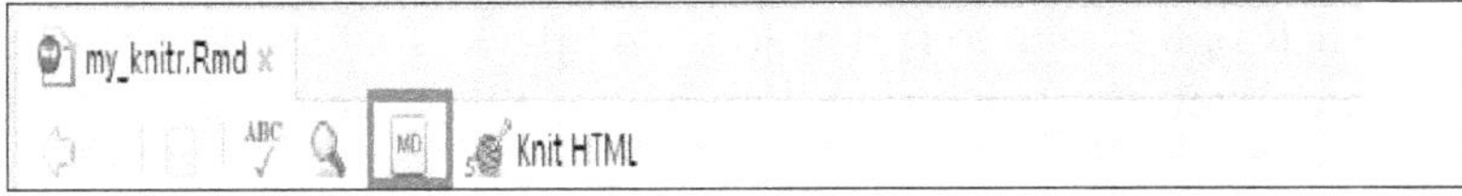

3. After all your information is entered, click **Knit HTML**.

4. Now you will see that you have generated an `.html` file.

Spark notebooks

There are a few notebooks compatible with Apache Spark computing. Among them, Databricks is one of the best, as it was developed by the original Spark team. The Databricks Notebook is similar to the R Markdown, but is seamlessly integrated with Apache Spark.

Besides SQL, Python, and Scala, now the Databricks notebook is also available for R, and Spark 1.4 includes the SparkR package by default. That is, from now on, data scientists and machine learning professionals can effortlessly benefit from the power of Apache Spark in their R environment, by writing and running R notebooks on top of Spark.

In addition to SparkR, any R package can be easily installed into the Databricks R notebook by using `install.packages()`. So, with the Databricks R notebook, data scientists and machine learning professionals can have the power of R Markdown on top of Spark. By using SparkR, data scientists and machine learning professionals can access and manipulate very large data sets (e.g. terabytes of data) from distributed storage (e.g. Amazon S3) or data warehouses (e.g. Hive). Data scientists and machine learning professionals can even collect a SparkR DataFrame to local data frames.

Visualization is a critical part of any machine learning project. In R Notebooks, data scientists and machine learning professionals can use any R visualization library, including R's base plotting, `ggplot`, or Lattice. Like R Markdown, plots are displayed inline in the R notebook. Users can apply Databricks' built-in `display()` function on any R DataFrame or SparkR DataFrame. The result will appear as a table in the notebook, which can then be plotted with one click. Similar to other Databricks notebooks like the Python notebook, data scientists can also use `displayHTML()` function in R notebooks to produce any HTML and Javascript visualization.

Databricks' end-to-end solution also makes building a machine learning pipeline easy from ingest to production, which applies to R Notebooks as well: Data scientists can schedule their R notebooks to run as jobs on Spark clusters. The results of each job, including visualizations, are immediately available to browse, making it much simpler and faster to turn the work into production.

To sum up, R Notebooks in Databricks let R users take advantage of the power of Spark through simple Spark cluster management, rich one-click visualizations, and instant deployment to production jobs. It also offers a 30-day free trial.

Please visit: `https://databricks.com/blog/2015/07/13/introducing-r-notebooks-in-databricks.html`

Summary

This chapter covers all the basics of Apache Spark, which all machine learning professionals are expected to understand in order to utilize Apache Spark for practical machine learning projects. We focus our discussion on Apache Spark computing, and relate it to some of the most important machine learning components, in order to connect Apache Spark and machine learning together to fully prepare our readers for machine learning projects.

First, we provided a Spark overview, and also discussed Spark's advantages as well as Spark's computing model for machine learning.

Second, we reviewed machine learning algorithms, Spark's MLlib libraries, and other machine learning libraries.

In the third section, Spark's core innovations of RDD and DataFrame has been discussed, as well as Spark's DataFrame API for R.

Fourth, we reviewed some ML frameworks, and specifically discussed a RM4Es framework for machine learning as an example, and then further discussed Spark computing frameworks for machine learning.

Fifth, we discussed machine learning as workflows, went through one workflow example, and then reviewed Spark's pipelines and its API.

Finally, we studied the notebook approach for machine learning, and reviewed R's famous notebook Markdown, then we discussed a Spark Notebook provided by Databricks, so we can use Spark Notebook to unite all the above Spark elements for machine learning practice easily.

With all the above Spark basics covered, the readers should be ready to start utilizing Apache Spark for some machine learning projects from here on. Therefore, we will work on data preparation on Spark in the next chapter, then jump into our first real life machine learning projects in *Chapter 3, A Holistic View on Spark.*

2
Data Preparation for Spark ML

Machine learning professionals and data scientists often spend 70% or 80% of their time preparing data for their machine learning projects. Data preparation can be very hard work, but it is necessary and extremely important as it affects everything to follow. Therefore, in this chapter, we will cover all the necessary data preparation parts for our machine learning, which often runs from data accessing, data cleaning, datasets joining, and then to feature development so as to get our datasets ready to develop ML models on Spark. Specifically, we will discuss the following six data preparation tasks mentioned before and then end our chapter with a discussion of repeatability and automation:

- Accessing and loading datasets
  - Publicly available datasets for ML
  - Loading datasets into Spark easily
  - Exploring and visualizing data with Spark
- Data cleaning
  - Dealing with missing cases and incompleteness
  - Data cleaning on Spark
  - Data cleaning made easy
- Identity matching
  - Dealing with identity issues
  - Data matching on Spark
  - Data matching made better

- Data reorganizing
  - Data reorganizing tasks
  - Data reorganizing on Spark
  - Data reorganizing made easy
- Joining data
  - Spark SQL to join datasets
  - Joining data with Spark SQL
  - Joining data made easy
- Feature extraction
  - Feature extraction challenges
  - Feature extraction on Spark
  - Feature extraction made easy
- Repeatability and automation
  - Dataset preprocessing workflows
  - Spark pipelines for preprocessing
  - Dataset preprocessing automation

Accessing and loading datasets

In this section, we will review some publicly available datasets and cover methods of loading some of these datasets into Spark. Then, we will review several methods of exploring and visualizing these datasets on Spark.

After this section, we will be able to find some datasets to use, load them into Spark, and then start to explore and visualize this data.

Accessing publicly available datasets

As there is an open source movement to make software free, there is also a very active open data movement that made a lot of datasets freely accessible to every researcher and analyst. At a worldwide scale, most governments make their collected datasets open to the public. For example, on `http://www.data.gov/`, there are more than 140,000 datasets available to be used freely, which are spread over agriculture, finance, and education.

Besides open data coming from various governmental organizations, many research institutions also collect a lot of very useful datasets and make them available for public use. For our use in this book, the following is a list:

- A very rich click dataset is provided by University of Indiana with 53.5 billion HTTP requests. To access this data, go to `http://cnets.indiana.edu/groups/nan/webtraffic/click-dataset/`.
- The well known UC Irvine Machine Learning Repository archive offers more than 300 datasets for exploration. To access their datasets, go to `https://archive.ics.uci.edu/ml/datasets.html`.
- Project Tycho® at University of Pittsburgh provides data from all weekly notifiable disease reports in the United States dating back to 1888. To access their datasets, go to `http://www.tycho.pitt.edu/`.
- ICPSR has many datasets that are not very big but are of good quality for research. To access their data, go to `http://www.icpsr.umich.edu/index.html`.
- The airline performance data from 1987 to 2008 is a well-known dataset and is also very big, with 120 million records, as it has been used in many researches and a few competitions. To access this data, go to `http://stat-computing.org/dataexpo/2009/the-data.html`.

Loading datasets into Spark

There are many ways of loading datasets into Spark or directly connecting to a data source for Spark. As Apache Spark develops with new releases once every three weeks, newer and easier methods are expected to become available to users as well as ways of representing imported data.

For example, `JdbcRDD` was the preferred way to connect with a relational data source and transfer data elements to RDD up until Spark 1.3. However, from Spark 1.4 onwards, there is an built in Spark datasource API available to connect to a JDBC source using DataFrames.

Loading data is not a simple task as it often involves converting or parsing raw data and dealing with data format transformation. The Spark datasource API allows users to use libraries based on the Data Source API to read and write dataframes between various formats from various systems. Also Spark's datasource API's data access is very efficient as it is powered by the Spark SQL query optimizer.

To load datasets in as a DataFrame, it is best to use `sqlContext.load`, for which we need to specify the following:

- **Data source name**: This is the source that we load from
- **Options**: These are parameters for a specific data source—for example, the path of data

For example, we can use the following code:

```
df1 = sqlContext.read  \
     . format("json")  \  data format is json
     . option("samplingRatio", "0.01") \ set sampling ratio as 1%
     . load("/home/alex/data1,json")   \ specify data name and
location
```

To export data sets, users can use `dataframe.save` or `df.write` to save the processed DataFrame to a source; for this, we need to specify the following:

- **Data source name**: The source that we are saving to
- **Save mode**: This is what we should do when the data already exists
- **Options**: These are the parameters for a specific data source—for example, the path of data

The `creatExternalTable` and `SaveAsTable` commands are also very useful.

For more information on using the Spark DataSource API, go to: `https://databricks.com/blog/2015/01/09/spark-sql-data-sources-api-unified-data-access-for-the-spark-platform.html`

Exploring and visualizing datasets

Within Apache Spark, there are many ways to conduct some initial exploration and visualization of the datasets loaded with various tools. Users may use Scala or Python direct with Spark shells. Alternatively, users can take a notebook approach, which is to use the R or Python notebook in a Spark environment, similar to that of DataBricks Workspace. Another option is to utilize Spark's MLlib.

Alternatively, users can directly use Spark SQL and its associated libraries, such as the popular Panda library, for some simple data exploration.

If datasets are already transformed into Spark DataFrames, users may use `df.describe().show()` to obtain some simple statistics with values of total count of cases, mean, standard deviation, min, and max for all the columns (variables).

If DataFrame has a lot of columns, users should specify columns in `df.describe(column1, column2, …).show()` to just obtain simple descriptive statistics of the columns they are interested in. You may also just use this command to select the statistics you need:

```
df.select([mean('column1'),min('column1'),max('column1')]).show()
```

Beyond this, some commonly used commands for covariance, correlation, and cross-tabulation tables are as follows:

```
df.stat.cov('column1', 'column2')
df.stat.corr('column1', 'column2')
df.stat.crosstab("column1", "column2").show()
```

If using the DataBricks workspace, users can create an R notebook; then they will be back to the familiar R environment with access to all the R packages and can take advantage of the notebook approach for an interactive exploration and visualization of datasets. Take a look at the following:

```
> summary(x1)
   Min. 1st Qu.  Median    Mean 3rd Qu.    Max.
  0.000   0.600   2.000   2.667   4.000   8.000
> plot(x1)
```

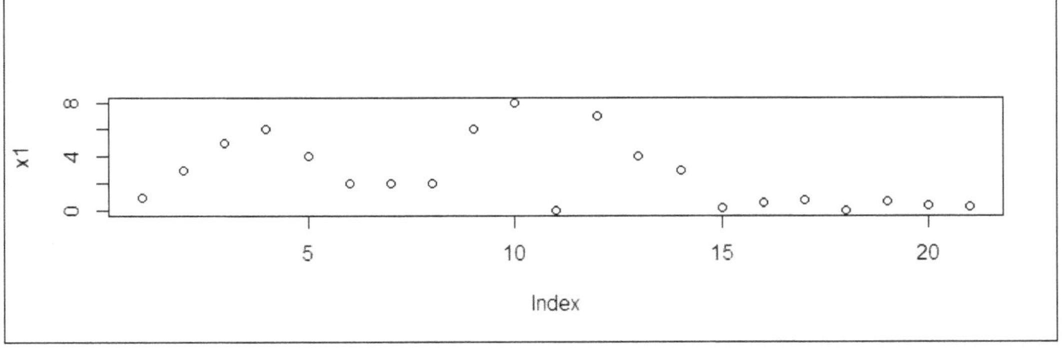

As we will start using the DataBricks Workspace a lot from now on, it is recommended for users to sign up at `https://accounts.cloud.databricks.com/registration.html#signup` for a trial test. Go to its main menu to its upper-left corner and set up some clusters, as follows:

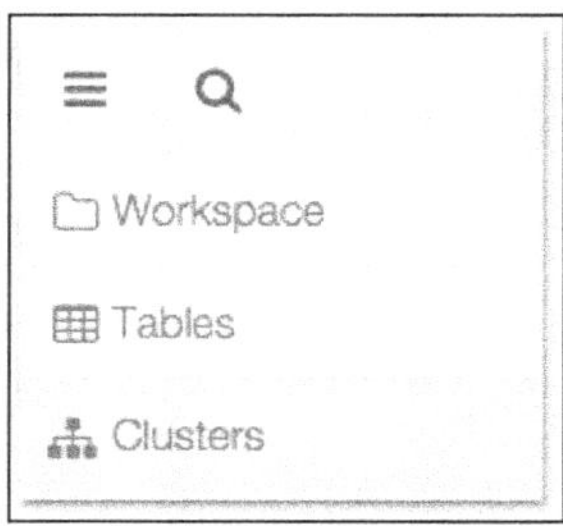

Then, users can go to the same main menu, click on the down arrow on the right-hand side of **Workspace** and navigate to **Create | New Notebook** as follows to create a notebook:

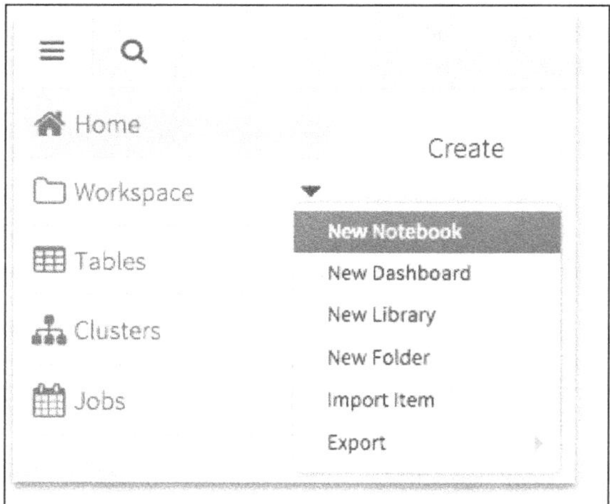

When the **Create Notebook** dialog appears, you need to perform the following:

- Enter a unique *name* for your notebook
- For *language*, click on the drop-down menu and select R
- For *cluster*, click on the drop-down menu and select the cluster you previously created

Data cleaning

In this section, we will review some methods for data cleaning on Spark with a focus on data incompleteness. Then, we will discuss some of Spark's special features for data cleaning and also some data cleaning solutions made easy with Spark.

After this section, we will be able to clean data and make datasets ready for machine learning.

Dealing with data incompleteness

For machine learning, the more the data the better. However, as is often the case, the more the data, the dirtier it could be—that is, the more the work to clean the data.

There are many issues to deal with data quality control, which can be as simple as data entry errors or data duplications. In principal, the methods of treating them are similar—for example, utilizing data logic for discovery and subject matter knowledge and analytical logic to correct them. For this reason, in this section, we will focus on missing value treatment so as to illustrate our usage of Spark for this topic. Data cleaning covers data accuracy, completeness, uniqueness, timeliness, and consistency.

Treating missing values and dealing with incompleteness is not an easy task, though it may sound simple. It involves many issues and often requires the following steps:

1. Counting the missing percentage.

   If the percentage is lower than 5% or 10% then, depending on the studies, we may not need to spend time on it.

2. Studying the missing patterns.

   There are two patterns of missing data: completely at random or not at random. If they are missing completely at random, we can ignore this issue.

3. Deciding the methods to deal with missing patterns.

   There are several commonly used methods to deal with missing cases. Filling with mean, deleting the missing cases, and imputation are among the main ones.

4. Performing filling for missing patterns.

   To work with missing cases and incompleteness, data scientists and machine learning professionals often utilize their familiar SQL tools or R programming. Fortunately, within the Spark environment, there are Spark SQL and R notebooks for users to continue their familiar paths, for which we will have detailed reviews in the following two sections.

There are also other issues with data cleaning, such as treating data entry errors and outliers.

Data cleaning in Spark

In the preceding section, we discussed working with data incompleteness.

With Spark installed, we can easily use the Spark SQL and R notebook on DataBricks Workspace for the data cleaning work described in the previous section.

Especially, the `sql` function on `sqlContext` enables applications to run SQL queries programmatically and return the result as a DataFrame.

For example, with R notebook, we can use the following to perform SQL commands and turn the results into a `data.frame`:

```
sqlContext <- sparkRSQL.init(sc)
df <- sql(sqlContext, "SELECT * FROM table")
```

Data cleaning is a very tedious and time-consuming work and, in this section, we would like to bring your attention to SampleClean, which can make data cleaning, and especially distributed data cleaning, easy for machine learning professionals.

SampleClean is a scalable data cleaning library built on AMPLab **Berkeley Data Analytics Stack (BDAS)**. The library uses Apache Spark SQL 1.2.0 and above as well as Apache Hive to support distributed data cleaning operations and related query processing on dirty data. SampleClean implements a set of interchangeable and composable physical and logical data cleaning operators, which makes quick construction and adaptation of data cleaning pipelines possible.

To get our work started, let's first import Spark and SampleClean with the following commands:

```
import org.apache.spark.SparkContext
import org.apache.spark.SparkContext._
import org.apache.spark.SparkConf
import sampleclean.api.SampleCleanContext
```

To begin using `SampleClean`, we need to create an object called `SampleCleanContext`, and then use this context to manage all of the information for working sessions and provide the API primitives to interact with the data. `SampleCleanContext` is constructed with a `SparkContext` object, as follows:

```
new SampleCleanContext(sparkContext)
```

Data cleaning made easy

With SampleClean and Spark together, we can make data cleaning easy, which is to write less code and utilize less data.

Overall, SampleClean employs a good strategy; it uses asynchrony to hide latency and sampling to hide scale. Also, SampleClean combines all the three (*Algorithms*, *Machines*, and *People*) in one system to become more efficient than others.

For more information on using `SampleClean`, go to: `http://sampleclean.org/guide/` and `http://sampleclean.org/release.html`.

For the purposes of illustration, let's imagine a machine learning project with four data tables:

- `Users(userId INT, name String, email STRING, age INT, latitude: DOUBLE, longitude: DOUBLE, subscribed: BOOLEAN)`
- `Events(userId INT, action INT, Default)`
- `WebLog(userId, webAction)`
- `Demographic(memberId, age, edu, income)`

To clean this dataset, we need to:

- Count how many are missing for each variable, either with the SQL or R commands
- Fill in the missing cases with the mean value if this is the strategy we agree to

Even though the preceding are very easy to implement, it could be very time consuming if our data is huge. Therefore, for efficiency, we may need to divide the data into many subsets and complete the previous steps in parallel, for which Spark becomes the best computing platform to use.

In the Databricks R notebook environment, we can first create notebooks with the R command `sum(is.na(x))` to count the missing cases.

To replace the missing cases with the mean, we can use the following code:

```
for(i in 1:ncol(data)){
  data[is.na(data[,i]), i] <- mean(data[,i], na.rm = TRUE)
}
```

In Spark, we can easily schedule to implement R notebooks in all the data clusters.

Identity matching

In this section, we will cover one important data preparation topic, which is about identity matching and related solutions. We will discuss some of Spark's special features for solving identity issues and also some data matching solutions made easy with Spark.

After this section, we will be capable of taking care of some common data identity problems with Apache Spark.

Identity issues

For data preparation, we often need to deal with some data elements that belong to the same person or units, but which do not look similar to them. For example, we may have purchased some data for customer Larry Z. and web activity data for L. Zhang. Is Larry Z a same person as L. Zhang? Are there many identity variations in the data?

Matching entities is a big challenge for machine learning data preparation as these types of entity variation are very common and could be caused by many different reasons, such as duplications, errors, name variants, and intentional aliasing. Sometimes, it could be very difficult to complete the matching or even just to find the linking, and this work is definitely very time consuming. However, it is necessary and extremely important as any kind of mismatching will produce a lot of errors, and no matching will produce biases. At the same time, a correct matching also has additional values as an aid to group detection, such as with terror cells and drug cartels.

Some new methods, such as fuzzy matching, have been developed to attack this issue. However, in this section, we will focus on some commonly used methods. These commonly used approaches include:

- Manual search with SQL queries.

  This is a labor intensive with few discoveries but good accuracy.

- Automated data cleansing.

  This type of approach often adopts a few rules that use the most informative attributes.

- Lexical similarity.

  This approach is rational and useful but can generate many false alarms.

- Feature and relationship statistics.

  This approach is a good one but does not address nonlinear effects.

The accuracy of any of the preceding methods often depends on the sparseness and size of the data and also on whether these tasks are to resolve duplications, errors, variants, or aliases.

Identity matching on Spark

Similarly to the previous section, we would like to review some methods utilizing SampleClean to deal with entity matching issues even though the most commonly used tools are `SparkSQL` or R.

Entity resolution

SampleClean provides an easy-to-use interface for some basic entity matching tasks. It provides the `EntityResolution` class that wraps some common deduplication programming patterns.

A basic `EntityResolution` class involves the following steps:

1. Identifying a column of inconsistent categorical attributes.
2. Linking together similar attributes.
3. Selecting a single canonical representation of the linked attributes.
4. Applying changes to the data.

Short string comparison

Here, we have a column of short strings that are inconsistently represented (for example, United States, United States). The `EntityResolution.shortAttributeCanonicalize` function takes as input the current context, the name of the working set to clean, the column to fix, and a threshold in [0,1] (0 merges all, and 1 merges only the exact matches). It uses `EditDistance` as its default similarity metric. The following is a coding example:

```
val algorithm = EntityResolution.
shortAttributeCanonicalize(scc,workingSetName,columnName,threshold)
```

Long string comparison

Here, we have a column of long strings, such as addresses, that are close but not exact. The basic strategy is to tokenize these strings and compare the set of words rather than the whole string. It uses the `WeightedJaccard` similarity metric as default. The following is a coding example:

```
longAttributeCanonicalize(scc,workingSetName,columnName,threshold)
```

Record deduplication

A more advanced deduplication task is when records, rather than individual columns, are inconsistent. That is, there are multiple records that refer to the same real entity. `RecordDeduplication` uses *Long Attribute* similarity metrics as default. The following is a coding example:

```
RecordDeduplication.deduplication(scc, workingSetName,
columnProjection, threshold)
```

For more information on the `SampleClean` guide, visit `http://sampleclean.org/guide/`.

Identity matching made better

Similarly to data cleaning, with SampleClean and Spark together we can make things easy—that is write less code and utilize less data—as demonstrated in the previous section. As discussed, automated cleaning is easy and fast, but its accuracy may not be good. A common approach to make things better is to utilize more people for labor-intensive approval based on crowd sourcing.

Here, SampleClean combines Algorithms, Machines, and People, all in its crowd-sourced deduplication.

Crowdsourced deduplication

As crowdsourcing scales poorly to very large datasets, the SampleClean system asks the crowd to deduplicate only a sample of the data and then train predictive models to generalize the crowd's work to the entire dataset. In particular, SampleClean applies Active Learning to sample points that lead to a good model quickly.

Configuring the crowd

To clean data using crowd workers, SampleClean uses the open source AMPCrowd service to support multiple crowd platforms and provide automated quality control. Thus, users must have a running installation of AMPCrowd. In addition, crowd operators must be configured to point to the AMPCrowd server by passing the `CrowdConfiguration` objects.

Using the crowd

SampleClean currently provides one main crowd operator: ActiveLearningMatcher. This is an add-on step to an existing `EntityResolution` algorithm that trains a crowd-supervised model to predict duplicates. Take a look at the following code:

```
createCrowdMatcher(scc:SampleCleanContext, attribute:String,
workingSetName:String)
val crowdMatcher = EntityResolution.createCrowdMatcher(scc,attribute,w
orkingSetName)
```

Make sure to configure the matcher here, as follows:

```
crowdMatcher.alstrategy.setCrowdParameters(crowdConfig)
```

To add this matcher to existing algorithms, use the following function:

```
addMatcher(matcher:Matcher)
algorithm.components.addMatcher(crowdMatcher)
```

Dataset reorganizing

In this section, we will cover dataset reorganization techniques. Then, we will discuss some of Spark's special features for data reorganizing and also some of R's special methods for data reorganizing that can be used with the Spark notebook.

After this section, we will be able to reorganize datasets for various machine learning needs.

Dataset reorganizing tasks

Reorganizing datasets sounds easy but could be very challenging and also often very time consuming.

Two common data reorganizing tasks are—firstly, to obtain a subset of the data for modeling and, secondly, to aggregate data to a higher level. For example, we have students' data, but we need to have a dataset at the classroom level. For this, we will need to calculate some attributes for students and then reorganize it into new data.

To work with data reorganizing, data scientists and machine learning professionals often utilize their familiar SQL or R programming tools. Fortunately within the Spark environment, there are Spark SQL and R notebooks for users to continue their familiar paths; we will have detailed reviews in the following two sections for this.

Overall, we recommend using SparkSQL to reorganizing datasets. However, for the learning purpose, in this section, our focus will be on the utilization of R Notebook from Databricks Workspace.

R and Spark nicely complement each other for several important use cases in statistics and data science. The Databricks R notebooks include the SparkR package by default so that data scientists can effortlessly benefit from the power of Apache Spark in their R analyses. In addition to SparkR, any R package can be easily installed into the notebook. In this blog post, I will highlight a few of the features in our R notebooks.

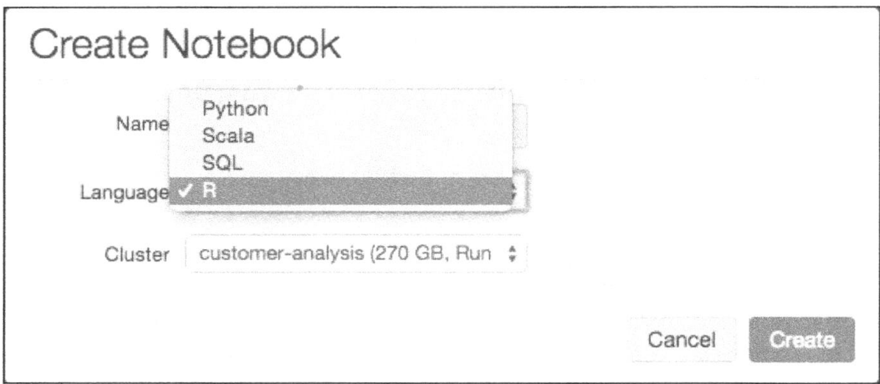

To get started with R in Databricks, simply choose R as the language when creating a notebook. Since SparkR is a recent addition to Spark, remember to attach the R notebook to any cluster running Spark version 1.4 or higher. The SparkR package is imported and configured by default. You can run Spark queries in R.

Dataset reorganizing with Spark SQL

In the last section, we discussed using SparkSQL to reorganize datasets.

SQL can be a powerful tool to perform complex aggregations with many familiar examples to machine learning professionals.

`SELECT` is a command to obtain some data subsets.

For data aggregation, machine learning professionals may use some of SpartSQL's `simple.aggregate` or window functions.

For more information about SparkSQL's various aggregation functions, go to `https://spark.apache.org/docs/1.4.0/api/scala/index.html#org.apache.spark.sql.functions$`.

For more information on SparkSQL's window functions, go to `https://databricks.com/blog/2015/07/15/introducing-window-functions-in-spark-sql.html`.

Dataset reorganizing with R on Spark

R has a subset command to create subsets with the following formats:

```
# using subset function
newdata <- subset(olddata, var1 >= 20, select=c(ID, var2))
```

Also, we may use the aggregate command from R, as follows:

```
aggdata <-aggregate(mtcars, by=list(cyl,vs),
  FUN=mean, na.rm=TRUE)
```

However, data often has multiple levels of grouping (nested treatments, split plot designs, or repeated measurements) and typically requires investigation at multiple levels. For example, from a long-term clinical study, we may be interested in investigating relationships over time or between times or patients or treatments. To make your job even more difficult, the data probably has been collected and stored in a way optimized for ease and accuracy of collection and in no way resembles the form you need for statistical analysis. You need to be able to fluently and fluidly reshape the data to meet your needs, but most software packages make it difficult to generalize these tasks, and new code needs to be written for each new case.

Especially, R has a `reshape` package that was specially designed for data reorganization. The package `reshape` uses a paradigm of *melting and casting*, where the data is *melted* into a form which distinguishes measured and identifying variables and then "casts" it into a new shape, whether it be a data frame, list, or highly dimensional array.

As we may recall, in section *Data cleaning made easy*, we had four tables for the purposes of illustration:

- `Users(userId INT, name String, email STRING, age INT, latitude: DOUBLE, longitude: DOUBLE, subscribed: BOOLEAN)`
- `Events(userId INT, action INT, Default)`
- `WebLog(userId, webAction)`
- `Demographic(memberId, age, edu, income)`

For this example, we often need to obtain a subset from the first data and aggregate the fourth data.

Dataset joining

In this section, we will cover dataset joining techniques. We will also discuss some of Spark's special features for data joining plus some data joining solutions made easy with Spark.

After this section, we will be able to join data for various machine learning needs.

Dataset joining and its tool – the Spark SQL

In preparing datasets for a machine learning project, we often need to combine data from multiple datasets. For relational tables, the task is to join tables through a primary and foreign key relationship.

Joining two or more datasets together sounds easy, but can be very challenging and time consuming. In SQL, `SELECT` is the most frequently used command. As an example, the following is a typical SQL code to perform a join:

```
SELECT column1, column2, …
FROM table1, table2
WHERE table1.joincolumn = table2.joincolumn
AND search_condition(s);
```

To work with the table joining tasks mentioned before, data scientists and machine learning professionals often utilize their familiar SQL tools. Within the Spark environment, the Spark SQL was created for this task.

The Spark SQL lets users query structured data inside Spark programs using either SQL or a familiar DataFrame API, which is usable in the R notebook as well. The Spark SQL reuses the Hive frontend and metastore, giving full compatibility with existing Hive data and queries.

The Spark SQL includes a cost-based optimizer, columnar storage, and code generation to make queries fast. At the same time, it scales to thousands of nodes and multihour queries using the Spark engine, which provides full mid-query fault tolerance.

The two main components when using the Spark SQL are **DataFrame** and **SQLContext**.

As discussed before, DataFrame is a distributed collection of data organized into named columns. It is based on the data frame concept in R language and is similar to a database table in a relational database. The Spark SQL provides SQLContext to encapsulate all relational functionality in Spark.

Dataset joining in Spark

Here, with some concrete examples, we will demonstrate some methods and related processes of using Spark SQL.

For the purposes of illustration, imagine an application with the following four tables:

- `Users(userId INT, name String, email STRING, age INT, latitude: DOUBLE, longitude: DOUBLE, subscribed: BOOLEAN)`
- `Events(userId INT, action INT, Default)`
- `WebLog(userId, webAction)`
- `Demographic(memberId, age, edu, income)`

At least, we need to join the `User` and `Events` tables together; we can do this with the following code:

```
val trainingDataTable = sql("""
  SELECT e.action
         u.age,
         u.latitude,
         u.logitude
  FROM Users u
  JOIN Events e
  ON u.userId = e.userId""")
```

As the results of the Spark SQL are also stored in RDDs, interfacing with other Spark libraries is trivial. The returned results from the preceding can be directly used for machine learning.

In the preceding example, the Spark SQL made it easy to join various datasets, preparing them for the machine learning algorithm. Furthermore, the Spark SQL allows developers to close the loop by making it easy to manipulate and join the output of these algorithms, producing the desired final result.

For more information about using the Spark SQL, please go to:

`http://spark.apache.org/docs/1.0.0/sql-programming-guide.html`

Dataset joining with the R data table package

The Spark technology has made data work faster and data analytics easier than before.

According to the Spark development team, the Spark SQL was created for:

- Writing less code
- Reading less data
- Passing the hard work to optimizer

This was achieved by utilizing DataFrames and the Spark SQL commands, `sqlContext.read` and `df.write`.

Besides Spark SQL, users may also use R to join tables, for which the `data.table` R package is very powerful and should be used. The `data.table` package is created for:

- Fast aggregation of large data (for example, 100 GB in RAM) and fast ordered joins
- Fast adding/modifying/deleting of columns by group, using no copies at all
- Listing columns and a fast file reader (`fread`)

This package offers a natural and flexible syntax for faster development as well.

To use `data.table` for joining, you need to create a `data.frame` first, which is easy.

Then, just use `X[Y]` to join two tables.

This is also known as **Last Observation Carried Forward** (**LOCF**) or a rolling join.

`X[Y]` is a join between `data.table X` and `data.table Y`. If `Y` has two columns, the first column is matched to the first column of the key of `X`, and the second column is matched to the second. An *equi-join* is performed by default, meaning that the values must be equal.

Instead of an equi-join, a rolling join is as follows:

```
X[Y,roll=TRUE]
```

As before, the first column of `Y` is matched to `X`, where the values are equal. However, the last join column in `Y`, the second one in this example, is treated specially. If no match is found, then the row before is returned, provided the first column still matches.

Further controls are rolling forwards, rolling backwards, rolling to the nearest, and limited staleness.

For example, type the following and follow the output at the prompt:

```
example(data.table)
```

The R `data.table` package provides an enhanced version of `data.frame`, including:

- Fast aggregation of large data—for example, 100 GB in RAM (take a look at the benchmarks on up to two billion rows)
- Fast ordered joins—for example, rolling forwards, rolling backwards, rolling to the nearest, and limited staleness
- Fast overlapping range joins—for example, GenomicRanges

As we may recall, in section *Data cleaning made easy*, we had four tables for the purposes of illustration, as follows:

- `Users(userId INT, name String, email STRING, age INT, latitude: DOUBLE, longitude: DOUBLE, subscribed: BOOLEAN)`
- `Events(userId INT, action INT, Default)`
- `WebLog(userId, webAction)`
- `Demographic(memberId, age, edu, income)`

For this example, we obtained a subset from the first data and aggregated the fourth data in last section. Now, we need to join them together. As per the preceding section, mixing the Spark SQL with R on the R notebook could make data joining very easy.

Feature extraction

In this section, we will turn our focus to feature extraction, which is to develop new features or variables from the available features or information of working datasets. At the same time, we will discuss some of Apache Spark's special capabilities for feature extraction as well as some related feature solutions made easy with Spark.

After this section, we will be able to develop and organize features for various machine learning projects.

Feature development challenges

For most Big Data machine learning projects, with many Big Datasets, we often cannot use them immediately. For example, when we take in some web log data, it is very messy and often in a form such as a collection of random text, from which we need to extract useful information and draw out useful features ready for machine learning. For example, we need to extract *number of clicks* and *number of impressions* out from web log data, for which many text mining tools and algorithms are ready to be used.

With any feature extraction, machine learning professionals need to decide:

- What information to use and what features to create
- What methods and algorithms to use

What feature to extract depends on the following:

- Data availability and also data properties, such as how easy it is to handle missing cases
- The available algorithms, as there are a lot of algorithms available for the numeric combination of data elements but less on text manipulation
- The domain knowledge as the explained ability of features is often concerned

Overall, there are a few commonly used techniques to track features:

- Data description
- Data aggregation
- Time series transformations
- Geographical
- PCA

Another task for feature preparation is to select features from hundreds or perhaps thousands of available features and then make them available for our ML projects. In machine learning, specifically in supervised learning, the general problem at hand is always to predict an outcome from a set of predictive features. At first glance, in our Big Data era, it is tempting to say that the more features we have, the better our predictions will be. However, there are problems that arise as the number of features increases, such as an increase in computing time, which may cause difficulties in interpreting results.

In most cases, for the feature preparation stage, machine learning professionals often use feature selection methods and algorithms, which are associated with regression modeling.

Feature development with Spark MLlib

Feature extraction could be implemented with the Spark SQL, while Spark's MLlib also has some special functions for this task, such as TF-IDF and Word2Vec.

Both MLlib and R have packages for principal component analysis, which are often employed for feature development.

As we may recall, in section *Data cleaning made easy*, we have four data tables to work with for the purpose of illustration:

- `Users(userId INT, name String, email STRING, age INT, latitude: DOUBLE, longitude: DOUBLE, subscribed: BOOLEAN)`
- `Events(userId INT, action INT, Default)`
- `WebLog(userId, webAction)`
- `Demographic(memberId, age, edu, income)`

Here, we can apply our feature extraction techniques to the third data and then apply feature selection to the final merged (joined) dataset.

With Spark MLlib, we can apply TF-IDF with the following commands:

```
val hashingTF = new HashingTF()
val tf: RDD[Vector] = hashingTF.transform(documents)
```

Alternatively, we can apply `Word2Vec` as illustrated by the following example. The following example (in Scala) first loads a text file, parses it as an RDD of `Seq[String]`, constructs a `Word2Vec` instance, and then fits `Word2VecModel` with the data. Then, we can display the top 40 synonyms of the specified word. Here, we will assume that the extracted file named `text8` is in same directory as you run the Spark shell. Run the following code:

```
import org.apache.spark._
import org.apache.spark.rdd._
import org.apache.spark.SparkContext._
import org.apache.spark.mllib.feature.{Word2Vec, Word2VecModel}

val input = sc.textFile("text8").map(line => line.split(" ").toSeq)

val word2vec = new Word2Vec()

val model = word2vec.fit(input)

val synonyms = model.findSynonyms("china", 40)
```

```
for((synonym, cosineSimilarity) <- synonyms) {
  println(s"$synonym $cosineSimilarity")
}

// Save and load model
model.save(sc, "myModelPath")
val sameModel = Word2VecModel.load(sc, "myModelPath")
```

For more information about using Spark MLlib for feature extraction, go to:

`http://spark.apache.org/docs/latest/mllib-feature-extraction.html`

Feature development with R

As for the four tables mentioned before, take a look at the following:

- `Users(userId INT, name String, email STRING, age INT, latitude: DOUBLE, longitude: DOUBLE, subscribed: BOOLEAN)`
- `Events(userId INT, action INT, Default)`
- `WebLog(userId, webAction)`
- `Demographic(memberId, age, edu, income)`

As discussed, we can apply our feature extraction techniques to the third data and then apply feature selection to the final merged (joined) data set.

If we implement them in R, with the R notebook in Spark, we need to utilize some of the R packages. If we use `ReporteRs`, we can execute the following commands:

```
## Not run:
doc = docx( title = "My example", template = file.path(
  find.package("ReporteRs"), "templates/bookmark_example.docx") )
text_extract( doc )
text_extract( doc, header = FALSE, footer = FALSE )
text_extract( doc, bookmark = "author" )

## End(Not run)
```

For more information on the `ReporteRs` R package, go to `https://cran.r-project.org/web/packages/ReporteRs/ReporteRs.pdf`.

Repeatability and automation

In this section, we will discuss some methods of organizing datasets, preprocessing into workflows, and then use the Apache Spark pipeline to represent as well as implement these workflows. Then, we will review data preprocessing automation solutions.

After this section, we will be able to use Spark pipelines to represent and implement datasets preprocessing workflows and understand some automation solutions made available by Apache Spark.

Dataset preprocessing workflows

Our data preparation work from *Data cleaning to Identity matching* to *Data re-organization to Feature extraction* were organized in a way to reflect our step-by-step orderly process of preparing datasets for machine learning. In other words, all the data preparation work can be organized into a workflow.

Organizing data cleaning into workflows can help achieve repeatability and also possible automation, which is often the most valuable for machine learning professionals as ML professionals and data scientists often spend 80% of their time on data cleaning and preprocessing.

For most ML projects, including the ones to be discussed in later chapters, data scientists need to split their data into training, testing, and validation sets; here, the same preprocessing of the training set needs to be repeated on the testing and validation sets. For this reason alone, utilizing workflows to repeat will save ML professionals a lot of time and also help avoiding many mistakes.

Using Spark to represent and implement data preprocessing workflows has special advantages, which include:

- Seamless Data Flow Integration between different sources.

  This is the first but very important step.

- Availability of data processing libraries MLlib and GraphX.

  As we can note from the previous sections, the libraries built on MLIB and GraphX make data cleaning easy.

- Avoiding slow offline Table Joins.

  Spark SQL is faster than SQL.

- The significantly quicker execution of operations that could be naturally parallelized.

  Parallelized computation is what is naturally offered by Apache Spark; also, optimization is another advantage offered by Spark.

The Spark pipeline API makes it especially easy to develop and deploy data cleaning and data preprocessing workflows.

Spark pipelines for dataset preprocessing

As an example, SampleClean was used as one of the systems for data preprocessing—specifically for the work of cleaning and entity analytics.

For learning purposes, we encourage users to combine SampleClearn with the R notebook and then utilize Apache Spark Pipeline to organize workflows.

As discussed in previous sections, to complete a data preprocessing and make it available, we need at least the following steps:

1. Data cleaning to deal with missing cases.
2. Entity analytics to resolve entity problems.
3. Reorganizing data to cover subsetting and aggregating data.
4. Joining some data together.
5. Developing new features from the existing features.

For some of the most basic preprocessing, we may be able to organize the workflow with a few R codes, including the following:

```
df$var[is.na(df$var)] <- mean(df$var, na.rm = TRUE)
```

We will then use the R functions, `subset`, `aggregate`, and `merge`, to reorganizing and join datasets.

The preceding R work on the R Notebook in combination with SampleClean and feature development should complete our workflow.

However, in reality, the preprocessing workflows can be a lot more complicated and may involve feedbacks as well.

Dataset preprocessing automation

Spark's new pipelines are good to represent workflows.

Once all the data preprocessing steps get organized into workflows, automation becomes easy.

Databricks is an end-to-end solution to make building a data pipeline easier—from ingest to production. The same concept applies to R notebooks as well: You can schedule your R notebooks to run as jobs on existing or new Spark clusters. The results of each job run, including visualizations, are available to browse, making it much simpler and faster to turn the work of data scientists into production.

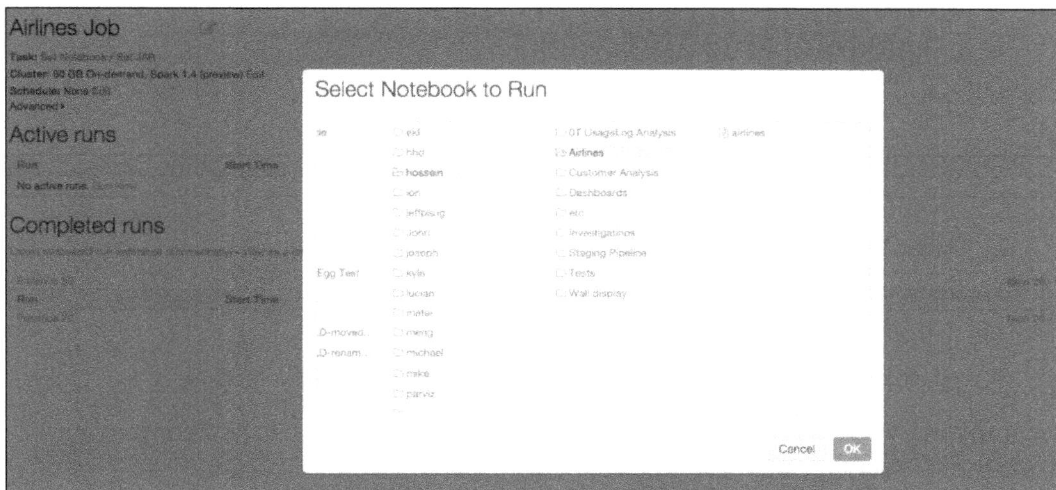

An important point here is that the data preparation will turn its outputs into DataFrames. Then, this can be easily combined with machine learning pipelines to automate all together.

For example, the most common advanced analytic tasks can be specified using the new pipeline API in MLlib. For example, the following code creates a simple text classification pipeline consisting of a tokenizer, a hashing term frequency feature extractor, and logistic regression:

```
tokenizer = Tokenizer(inputCol="text", outputCol="words")
hashingTF = HashingTF(inputCol="words", outputCol="features")
lr = LogisticRegression(maxIter=10, regParam=0.01)
pipeline = Pipeline(stages=[tokenizer, hashingTF, lr])
```

Once the pipeline is set up, we can use it to train on a DataFrame directly:

```
df = context.load("/path/to/data")
model = pipeline.fit(df)
```

For the preceding code, we will discuss more in later chapters.

As we may recall, in section *Data cleaning made easy*, we had four tables for the purposes of illustration, as follows:

- `Users(userId INT, name String, email STRING, age INT, latitude: DOUBLE, longitude: DOUBLE, subscribed: BOOLEAN)`
- `Events(userId INT, action INT, Default)`
- `WebLog(userId, webAction)`
- `Demographic(memberId, age, edu, income)`

For this group of datasets, we performed:

1. Data cleaning.
2. Identity matching.
3. Datasets reorganizing.
4. Datasets joining.
5. Feature extraction, then data joining, and then feature selection.

To implement the preceding, we can use an R notebook to organize them into a workflow for automation and also Spark Pipeline for help.

With all the preceding completed, we are now ready for machine learning.

Summary

Machine learning professionals and data scientists often spend 80% or more of their time on data preparation, which makes data preparation the most important task to perform even though it could be the most boiling task.

In this chapter, after discussing locating datasets and loading them into Apache Spark, we covered the methods of completing the six critical data preparation tasks, which include:

- Treating dirty data with a focus on missing cases
- Resolving entity problems to match datasets
- Reorganizing datasets, with creating subsets and aggregating data as examples
- Joining tables together
- Developing features
- Organizing data preparation workflows and automating them

In covering these, we studied the Spark SQL and R as two primary tools in combination with some special Spark packages, such as SampleClean, and some R packages, such as `reshape`. We also explored ways of making data preparation easy and fast.

After this chapter, we should master all the necessary data preparation methods plus a few advanced methods and become capable of cleaning datasets, such as the four used as examples in this chapter. From now on, we should be able to complete data preparation tasks fast with a workflow approach and be ready for practical machine learning tasks.

3
A Holistic View on Spark

After setting the Apache Spark system up as per *Chapter 1, Spark for Machine Learning*, and completing our data preparation work according to what we discussed in *Chapter 2, Data Preparation for Spark ML*, we will now move to a new stage of utilizing Apache Spark-based systems to turn data into insight.

According to the research done by Gartner and others, many organizations lost a large amount of value simply due to the lack of a holistic view of their business. In this chapter, we will review machine learning methods and processes of obtaining a holistic view of business. Then, we will discuss how Apache Spark fits in to making the related computing easy and fast and, at the same time, illustrate this process of developing holistic views from data using Apache Spark computing with one real-life example step by step.

- Spark for a holistic view
- Methods for a holistic view
- Feature preparation
- Model estimation
- Model evaluation
- Results explanation
- Deployment

Spark for a holistic view

Spark is very suitable for machine learning projects, such as obtaining a holistic view of business, as it enables us to process huge amounts of data fast and code complicated computations easily. In this section, we will first describe a real business case and then how to prepare Spark computing for our project.

The use case

The company IFS sells and distributes thousands of IT products and has a lot of data on marketing, training, team management, promotion, and products. The company wants to understand how various kinds of actions, such as those in marketing and training, affect the sales team's success. In other words, IFS is interested in finding out how much impact marketing, training, or promotion generates separately.

In the past, IFS has done a lot of analytical work, but all of it was completed by individual departments on soloed datasets. That is, they have analytical results about how marketing affects sales from using marketing data alone and how training affects sales from analyzing training data alone.

When the decision makers collect all the results together and prepare to make use of them, they find that some of the results contradict each other. For example, when they add all the effects together, the total impact is beyond what is intuitively imagined.

This is a typical problem every organization faces. A soloed approach with soloed data will produce not only an incomplete view, but also often a biased view or even conflicting views. To solve this problem, the analytical team needs to take a holistic view of all the company data and gather it in one place and then utilize new machine learning approaches to gain a holistic view of the business.

To do so, companies also need to care for:

- The completeness of causes
- Advanced analytics to account for the complexity of relationships
- Computing complexity related to subgroups and a large number of products or services

For this example, we have eight datasets that include one for marketing with 48 features, one for training with 56 features, and one data set for team administration with 73 features; the following table is a complete summary:

Category	Number of Features
Team	73
Marketing	48
Training	56
Staffing	103
Product	77
Promotion	43
Total	400

In this company, researchers understood that pooling all the datasets together and building a complete model was the solution, but they were not able to achieve it for several reasons. Besides organizational issues inside the corporation, the tech capability to store all the data, process it quickly with the right methods, and present all the results in the right ways with reasonable speed are other challenges.

At the same time, the company has more than 100 products to offer, for which data was pooled together to study the impacts of company interventions. That is, calculated impacts are average impacts, but variations among products are too large to ignore. If we need to assess the impact of each product, parallel computing is preferred and needs to be implemented at good speed. Without utilizing a good computing platform such as Apache Spark, meeting the requirements described previously is a big challenge for this company.

In the sections that follow, we will use modern machine learning over Apache Spark to attack this business use case and help the company gain a holistic view of their business. In order to help you learn machine learning in Spark effectively, discussions in the following sections are all based on work about this real business use case. However, we left some details out to protect the company's privacy and also to keep everything brief.

As discussed in the previous section, parallel computing is needed for our project; for this, we should set up clusters and worker notes. Then we can use the driver program and cluster manager to manage the computing to be done in each worker node.

We discussed preparing Spark in *Chapter 1, Spark for Machine Learning*, and for more information you may refer to `http://spark.apache.org/docs/latest/configuration.html`.

As an example, assume that we choose to work within the Databricks environment; then we can perform the following steps to set up the clusters:

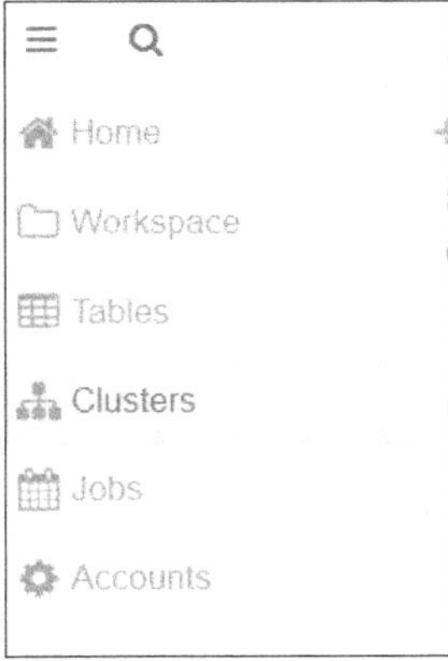

Go to the preceding main menu, click on **Clusters** and then a window will open for users to create a name for the cluster. Here, select a version of Spark and then specify the number of workers.

Once clusters are created, we can go to the preceding illustrated main menu, click on the down arrow on the right-hand side of **Tables**, and then select **Create Tables** to import our datasets that are cleaned and prepared as per the *Chapter 2, Data Preparation for Spark ML*, discussion, as shown in the following screenshot:

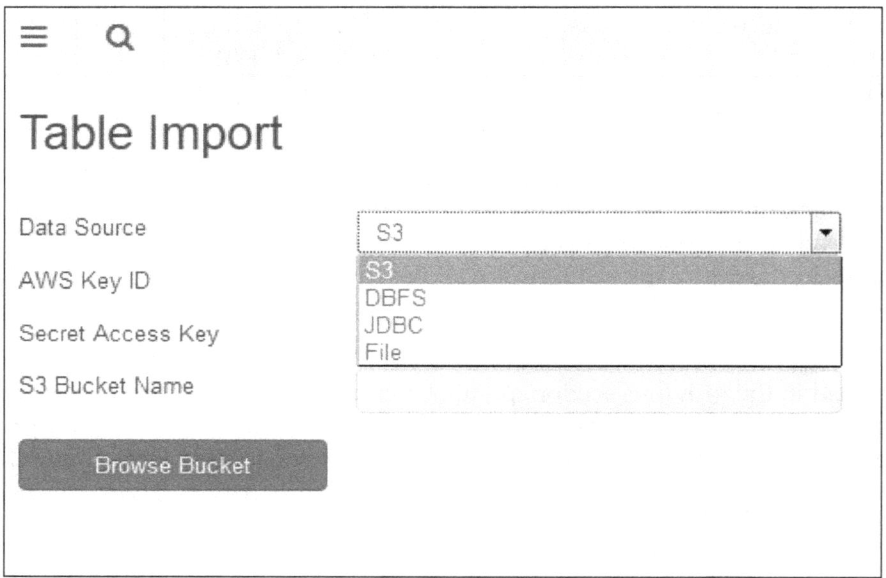

For the data source, the options include S3, DBFS, JDBC, and Files (for local fields). As described in *Chapter 2, Data Preparation for Spark ML*, our data is separated into two subsets—one for training and one to test for each product—as we need to train a few models per product.

In Apache Spark, we need to direct workers to complete the computation on each node; for this, on Databricks, we will use a scheduler to get the Notebook computation completed and collect the results back, which will be discussed in the *Model estimation* section.

Fast and easy computing

One of the most important advantages of utilizing Apache Spark is to make coding easy, for which several approaches are available.

Here, for this project, we will focus our efforts on the notebook approach; specifically, we will use R notebooks to develop and organize code. At the same time, with an effort to illustrate the Spark technology more thoroughly, we will also use MLlib directly to code some of our needed algorithms as MLlib is seamlessly integrated with Spark.

In the Databricks environment, setting up notebooks requires the following steps:

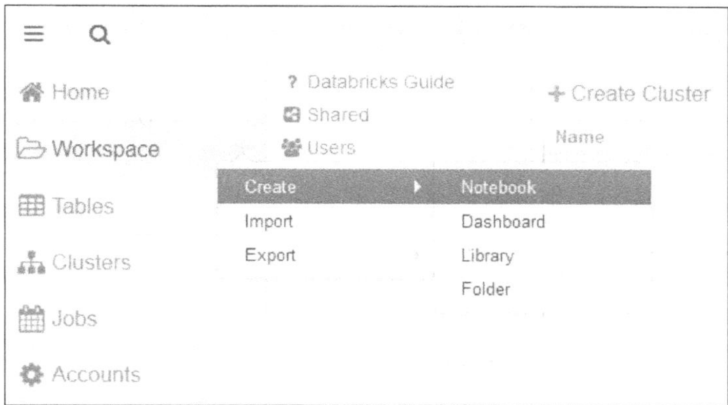

As shown in the preceding screenshot, users can go to the Databricks main menu, click on the down arrow on the right-hand side of **Workspace**, and select **Create** -> **Notebook** to create a new notebook. For this, a table will pop up for users to create a name and also select a language (R, Python, Scala, or SQL).

In order to make our work repeatable and also easy to be understood, we will adopt a workflow approach consistent with the RM4Es framework described in *Chapter 1, Spark for Machine Learning*. Also, we will adopt Spark's ML Pipeline tools to represent our workflows whenever possible. Specifically, for the training dataset, we need to estimate the models, evaluate them, and then maybe reestimate them before we can finalize them. So we need to use Spark's Transformer, Estimator, and Evaluator to organize an ML pipeline for this project. In practice, we can also organize these workflows within the R notebook environment.

For more information about pipeline programming, go to `http://spark.apache.org/docs/latest/ml-guide.html#example-pipeline` and `http://spark.apache.org/docs/latest/ml-guide.html`.

Once our computing platform gets set up and our framework is made clear, everything becomes clear too. In the following sections, we will move forward step by step. That is, we will use our RM4Es framework and related processes discussed in *Chapter 1, Spark for Machine Learning*, first to identify equations or methods and prepare features, second to complete model estimations, third to evaluate models, fourth to explain our results, and finally to deploy the models.

Methods for a holistic view

As discussed in the previous section, in this section, we need to select our analytical methods or models (equations) to complete the task of mapping our business use case to machine learning methods.

To assess the impact of various factors on the sales team's success, there are many suitable models for us to use. As an exercise, we will select (a) regression models, (b) structural equation models, and (c) decision trees, mainly for their ease of interpretation as well as their implementablility on Spark.

Once we finalize our decision for analytical methods or models, we will need to prepare the dependent variable and also prepare for coding; we will discuss these one by one in the following section.

Regression modeling

To get ready for regression modeling on Spark, there are three issues for us to take care of:

- Linear regression or logistic regression.

  Regression is the most mature and also the most widely used model to represent the impact of various factors on one dependent variable. Whether to use linear regression or logistic regression depends on whether the relationship is linear or not. Here, we are not sure, so we will adopt both and then compare their results to decide on which to deploy.

- Preparing the dependent variable.

  In order to use logistic regression, we need to recode the target variable or dependent variable (the sales team's success variable, now with a rating from 0 to 100) to be 0 versus 1 by separating it with the medium value.

- Preparing coding.

  In MLlib, we can use the following code for regression modeling, as we will use Spark MLlib's **Linear Regression with Stochastic Gradient Descent (LinearRegressionWithSGD)**:

  ```
  val numIterations = 90
  val model = LinearRegressionWithSGD.train(TrainingData,
  numIterations)
  ```

  For Logistic regression, we use the following code:

  ```
  val model = new LogisticRegressionWithSGD()
    .setNumClasses(2)
    .run(training)
  ```

For more information about using MLlib for regression modeling, you can go to:

`http://spark.apache.org/docs/latest/mllib-linear-methods.html#linear-least-squares-lasso-and-ridge-regression.`

In R, we can use the `lm` function for linear regression, and the `glm` function for logistic regression with `family=binomial()`.

The SEM approach

To get ready for **Structural Equation Modeling (SEM)** on Spark, there are also three issues for us to take care of:

- SEM introduction specification.

  SEM may be considered an extension of regression modeling as it consists of several linear equations similar to regression equations. However, this method estimates all the equations at the same time with regard to their internal relations, so it is less biased than regression modeling. SEM consists of both structural modeling and latent variable modeling; however, we will only use structural modeling.

- Preparing the dependent variable.

  We can just use the sales team's success scale (with a rating of 0 to 100) as our target variable here.

- Preparing the coding.

  We will adopt R notebook within the Databricks environment, for which we should use the `SEM` R package. There are also other SEM packages, such as `lavaan`, available for use; however, for this project, we will use the `sem` package for its ease of learning.

To load an SEM package into the R notebook, we will use `install.packages("sem", repos="http://R-Forge.R-project.org")`. Then, we need to execute the R code, `library(sem)`.

After this, we need to use the `specify.model()` function to write some code to specify the models into our R notebook, for which the following code is needed:

```
mod.no1 <- specifyModel()
s1 <- x1, gam31
s1 <- x2, gam32
```

Decision trees

To get ready for the decision tree modeling on Spark, there are again three issues for us to take care of:

- Decision tree selection

  Decision trees aim to model classifying cases, which is about classifying them into successful or not successful for our use case in sequence. It is also one of the most mature and widely used methods. It could even lead to overfitting, which requires methods such as afterward regularization. For this exercise, we will only use the simple linear decision tree and not venture into any more complicated trees such as random forests.

- Preparing the dependent variable

  To use the decision tree model here, we will separate the sales team ratings into two categories—SUCCESS and NOT—as we did for logistic regression.

- Preparing the coding

  For MLlib, we can use the following code:

```
val numClasses = 2
val categoricalFeaturesInfo = Map[Int, Int]()
val impurity = "gini"
val maxDepth = 6
val maxBins = 32
val model = DecisionTree.trainClassifier(trainingData, numClasses,
categoricalFeaturesInfo,
  impurity, maxDepth, maxBins)
```

For more information on using MLlib for decision trees, go to `http://spark.apache.org/docs/latest/mllib-decision-tree.html`.

As for the R notebook on Spark, we need to use the `rpart` R package and then the `rpart` functions for all the calculation. For `rpart`, we need to specify the classifier and also all the features to be used.

Feature preparation

In the previous section, we selected our models and also prepared our dependent variable for our supervised machine learning. In this section, we need to move forward to prepare our independent variables, which are all the features representing the factors impacting our dependent variable: the sales team success. Specifically, for this important work, we need to reduce our four hundred of features to a reasonable group for final modeling. For this, we will employ PCA, utilize some subject knowledge, and then perform some feature selection tasks.

PCA

PCA is a very mature and also commonly used feature reduction method that is often used to find a small set of variables that counts for most of the variance. Technically, the goal of PCA is to find a low dimensional subspace that captures as much of the variance of a dataset as possible.

If you are using MLlib, `http://spark.apache.org/docs/latest/mllib-dimensionality-reduction.html#principal-component-analysis-pca` has a few example codes that users may adopt and modify to run PCA on Spark. For more on MLlib, go to `https://spark.apache.org/docs/1.2.1/mllib-dimensionality-reduction.html`.

Here for this project, we will use R only for its richness of PCA algorithms. In R, there are at least five functions to compute PCAs, which are as follows:

- `prcomp()` (stats)
- `princomp()` (stats)
- `PCA()` (FactoMineR)
- `dudi.pca()` (ade4)
- `acp()` (amap)

The `prcomp` and `princomp` from the basic package stats are commonly used, and we also have good functions for the results summary and plots. Therefore, we will use these two functions.

Grouping by category to use subject knowledge

As is always the case, if some subject knowledge can be used the feature reduction results can be improved greatly.

For our example, data categories are good to start with. They are:

- Marketing
- Training
- Promotion
- Team administration
- Staffing
- Products

So, we will execute six PCA algorithms, one for each data category. For example, for the Team category, we need to run a PCA algorithm on 73 features or variables to identify factors or dimensions that can fully represent the information we have about TEAM. As for this exercise, we found two dimensions for the Team category's 73 features.

Also, for the Staffing category, we need to execute a PCA algorithm on 103 features or variables to identify the factors or dimensions that can fully represent the information we have about Staffing. As for this exercise, we also found two dimensions for the Staffing category's 103 features. Take a look at the following table:

Category	Number of Factors	Factor Names
Team	2	T1, T2
Marketing	3	M1, M2, M3
Training	3	Tr1, Tr2, Tr3
Staffing	2	S1, S2
Product	4	P1, P2, P3, P4
Promotion	3	Pr1, Pr2, Pr3
Total	17	

At the end of this PCA exercise, we obtained two to four features for each category, as summarized in the preceding table.

Feature selection

Feature selection is often used to remove redundant or irrelevant features but is often used at least for the following reasons:

- Making models easier to understand
- Creating fewer chances for overfitting
- Saving time and space for model estimation

In MLlib, we can use the `ChiSqSelector` algorithm, as follows:

```
// Create ChiSqSelector that will select top 25 of 400 features
val selector = new ChiSqSelector(25)
// Create ChiSqSelector model (selecting features)
val transformer = selector.fit(TrainingData)
```

In R, we can use some R packages to make computation easy. Among the available packages, `CARET` is one of the commonly used packages.

First, as an exercise, we performed feature selection on all the 400 features.

Then, we started with all the features selected from our PCA work. We also performed feature selection so that we could keep all of them.

Therefore, at the end, we have 17 features to use, which are as follows:

Features
T1, T2 for Team
M1, M2, M3 for Marketing
Tr1, Tr2, Tr3 for Training
S1, S2 for Staffing
P1, P2, P3, P4 for Product
Pr1, Pr2, Pr3 for Promotion

For more about feature selection on Spark, go to `http://spark.apache.org/docs/latest/mllib-feature-extraction.html`.

Model estimation

Once feature sets get finalized in our last section, what follows is to estimate the parameters of the selected models, for which we can use either MLlib or R here, and we need to arrange the distributed computing.

To simplify, we can utilize Databricks' Job feature. Specifically, within the Databricks environment, we can go to **Jobs** and then create jobs, as shown in the following image:

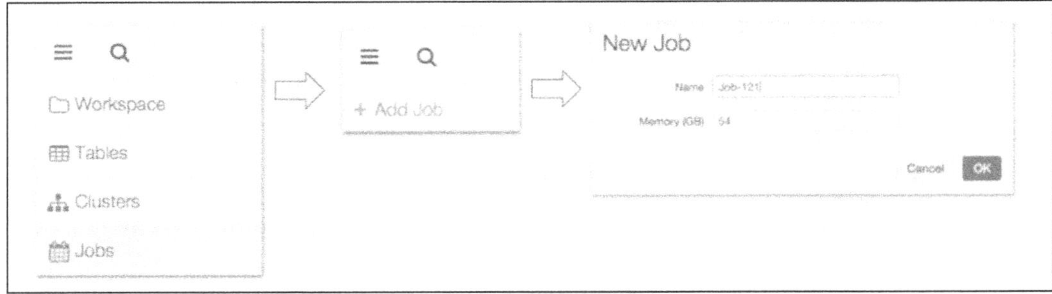

Then, users can select notebooks to run, specify clusters, and schedule jobs. Once scheduled, users can also monitor the running and then collect the results.

In section, *Methods for a holistic view*, we prepared some codes for each of the three models selected. Now, we need to modify them with the final set of features selected in the last section so as to create our final notebooks.

In other words, we have one dependent variable prepared and 17 features selected out from our PCA and feature selection work. Therefore, we need to insert all them into the codes developed in section II to finalize our notebook. Then we will use the Spark Job feature to get these notebooks implemented in a distributed way.

MLlib implementation

First, we need to prepare our data with the s1 dependent variable for linear regression and s2 dependent variable for logistic regression or decision tree. Then, we need to add the selected 17 features into them to form the datasets ready for our use.

For linear regression, we will use the following code:

```
val numIterations = 90
val model = LinearRegressionWithSGD.train(TrainingData, numIterations)
```

For logistic regression, we will use the following code:

```
val model = new LogisticRegressionWithSGD()
  .setNumClasses(2)
```

For decision tree, we will use the following code:

```
val model = DecisionTree.trainClassifier(trainingData, numClasses,
categoricalFeaturesInfo,
  impurity, maxDepth, maxBins)
```

The R notebooks' implementation

For better comparison, it is a good idea to write linear regression and SEM into an R notebook and also write logistic regression and decision tree into the same R notebook.

Then, the main task left here is to schedule the estimation for each worker and then collect the results using the JOB feature mentioned before in the Databricks environment.

- For linear regression and SEM, execute the following code:

```
lm.est1 <- lm(s1 ~ T1+T2+M1+ M2+ M3+ Tr1+ Tr2+ Tr3+ S1+ S2+ P1+
P2+ P3+ P4+ Pr1+ Pr2+ Pr3)
mod.no1 <- specifyModel()
s1 <- x1, gam31
s1 <- x2, gam32
```

- For logistic regression and decision tree, run the following script:

```
logit.est1 <- glm(s2~ T1+T2+M1+ M2+ M3+ Tr1+ Tr2+ Tr3+ S1+ S2+ P1+
P2+ P3+ P4+ Pr1+ Pr2+ Pr3,family=binomial())

 dt.est1 <- rpart(s2~ T1+T2+M1+ M2+ M3+ Tr1+ Tr2+ Tr3+ S1+ S2+ P1+
P2+ P3+ P4+ Pr1+ Pr2+ Pr3, method="class")
```

After we get all the models estimated as per each product, for simplicity, we will focus on one product to complete our discussion on model evaluation and deployment.

Model evaluation

In the last section, we completed our model estimation task. Now, it is time for us to evaluate the estimated models to see whether they meet our model quality criteria so that we can either move to our next stage for the results explanation or go back to some previous stages to refine our models.

To perform our model evaluation, in this section, we will focus our effort on utilizing **RMSE (Root-Mean-Square Error)** and **ROC (Receiver Operating Characteristic)** curves to assess the quality of fit for our models. To calculate RMSEs and ROC curves, we need to use our test data rather than training data used to estimate our models.

Quick evaluations

Many packages have already included some algorithms for users to assess models quickly. For example, both MLlib and R have algorithms to return confusion matrix for logistic regression models and even get false positive numbers calculated.

Specifically, MLlib has the `confusionMatrix` and `numFalseNegatives()` functions for us to use and even some algorithms to calculate MSE quickly, as follows:

```
MSE = valuesAndPreds.(lambda (v, p): (v - p)**2).mean()
print("Mean Squared Error = " + str(MSE))
```

Also, R has the `confusion.matrix` function for us to use. In R, there are even many tools to produce some quick graphical plots that can be used to gain a quick evaluation of models.

For example, we can perform plots of predicted versus actual values and also residuals on predicted values.

Intuitively, the methods of comparing predicted versus actual values are easiest to understand and give us a quick model evaluation. The following is a calculated confusion matrix for one of the company products, which shows a reasonable fit of our model. Take a look at the following table:

Success or not	Predicted as Success	Predicted as NOT
Actual Success	83%	17%
Actual Not	9%	91%

RMSE

In MLlib, we can use the following codes to calculate RMSE:

```
val valuesAndPreds = test.map { point =>
    val prediction = new_model.predict(point.features)
    val r = (point.label, prediction)
    r
    }
```

```
val residuals = valuesAndPreds.map {case (v, p) => math.pow((v - p),
2)}
val MSE = residuals.mean();
val RMSE = math.pow(MSE, 0.5)
```

Besides the preceding, MLlib also has some functions in the `RegressionMetrics` and `RankingMetrics` classes for us to use for RMSE calculation.

In R, we can compute RMSE, as follows:

```
RMSE <- sqrt(mean((y-y_pred)^2))
```

Before this, we need to obtain the predicted values with the following commands:

```
> # build a model
> RMSElinreg <- lm(s1 ~ . ,data= data1)
>
> #score the model
> score <- predict(RMSElinreg, data2
```

After obtaining the RMSE values for all the estimated models, we will compare them to evaluate the linear regression model with the logistic regression model and the decision tree model. For our case, the linear regression model turned out to be the best.

Then we will also compare the RMSE values across products and send back some product models for refinement.

For another example of obtaining RMSE, go to `http://www.cakesolutions.net/teamblogs/spark-mllib-linear-regression-example-and-vocabulary`.

ROC curves

As an example, we will calculate ROC curves to assess our logistic models.

In MLlib, we can use the MLlib function `metrics.areaUnderROC()` to calculate ROC once we apply our estimated model to our test data and get labels to test cases.

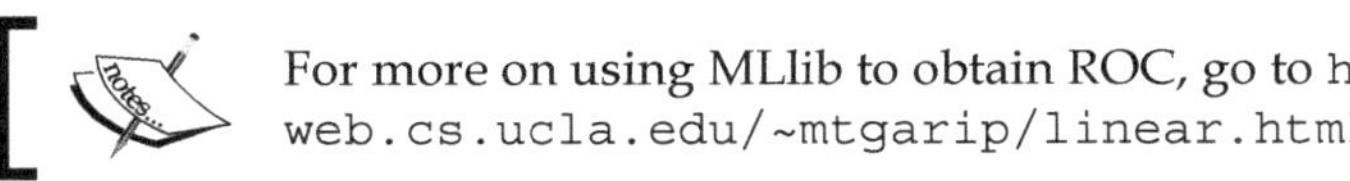

For more on using MLlib to obtain ROC, go to `http://web.cs.ucla.edu/~mtgarip/linear.html`.

In R, using the `pROC` package, we can run the following to calculate and plot the ROC curves:

```
mylogit <- glm(s2 ~ ., family = "binomial")
summary(mylogit)
prob=predict(mylogit,type=c("response"))
```

```
testdata1$prob=prob
library(pROC)
g <- roc(s2 ~ prob, data = testdata1)
plot(g)
```

As discussed, once the ROC curves get calculated, we can use them to compare our logistic models against decision tree models or compare models across products. For our case, logistic models perform better than decision tree models:

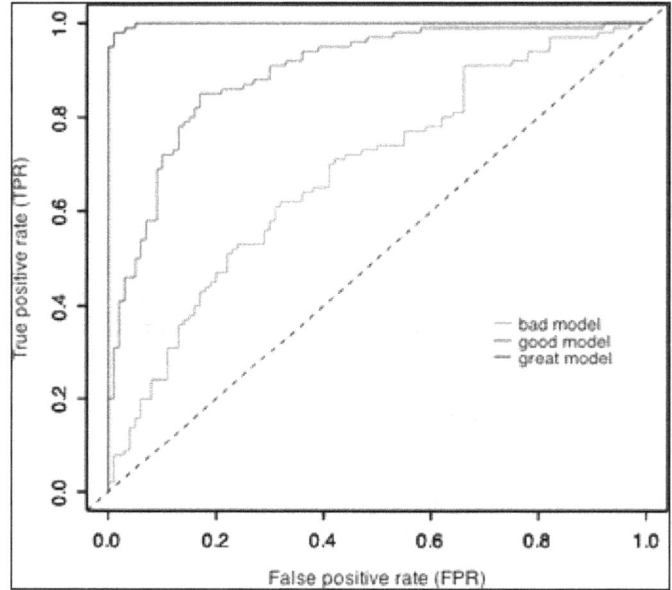

Results explanation

Once we pass our model evaluation and decide to select the estimated model as our final model, we need to interpret the results to the company executives and also their technicians.

In the following, we discuss some commonly used ways of interpreting our results, one using tables and another using graphs, with our focus on impact assessment.

Some users may prefer to interpret our results in terms of ROIs, for which the cost and benefit data is needed. Once we have the cost and benefit data, our results here can be easily expanded to cover the ROI issues. Also, some optimization may need to be applied for real decision making.

Impact assessments

As discussed in section, *Spark for a holistic view*, the main purpose of this project is to gain a holistic view of sales team success. For example, the company wishes to understand the impact of marketing on sales success in comparison to training and other factors.

As we have our linear regression model estimated, one easy way of comparing impacts is to summarize the variance explained by each feature group using ANOVA, with the results as shown by the following table:

Feature Group	%
Team	8.5
Marketing	7.6
Training	5.7
Staffing	12.9
Product	8.9
Promotion	14.6
Total	58.2

Also, the following image is another example of using graphs to display the results discussed:

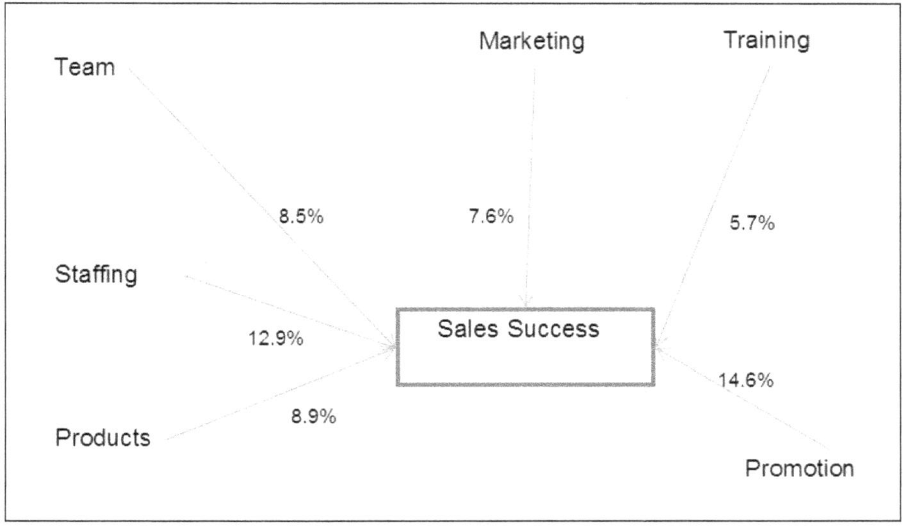

Deployment

Some users may have some deployment systems in place already for which exporting the developed models to users' desired forms could be good enough.

For linear regression and logistic regression, MLlib supports model exporting to **Predictive Model Markup Language** (**PMML**).

For more information about exporting to PMML from MLlib, visit `https://spark.apache.org/docs/latest/mllib-pmml-model-export.html`.

For the R notebook, it can be run on another environment directly. Also, with the R package PMML, R models can be exported.

For more information on the R package PMML, go to `http://journal.r-project.org/archive/2009-1/RJournal_2009-1_Guazzelli+et+al.pdf`.

It is also possible to deploy the models for decision making directly on Apache Spark and make the results easily available to users.

Two commonly used methods of deploying results are (1) dashboard and (2) rule-based decision making. Which one to select depends on who we will supply our result to.

Here, we will discuss them only briefly as a full deployment for decision making will need optimization that is not covered in this chapter. In later chapters, we will spend a little more time on deployment for readers to learn more.

Dashboard

For real-time analytical dashboard, most users use Spark Streaming together with other tools.

For our work here, we will take an easy dashboard approach, which is to use graphs and tables to quickly present our analytical results to consumers. All the dashboards are interactive as every plot depends on one or more features. When these features get updated, the algorithms behind each plot can be automatically reexecuted, and the plot will be regenerated.

Starting from our R notebooks, we can use the `shiny` and `shinydashboard` R packages to quickly build a dashboard.

For more information about using the `shinydashboard` package, go to `https://rstudio.github.io/shinydashboard/`.

Databricks' new version also has a dashboard builder. To use it, just go to **Workspace** -> **Create** -> **Dashboard**.

This Databricks dashboard builder is very powerful and intuitive. Once built, users can then publish a dashboard just with the click of a button to other employees in the organization or to their customers.

Rules

To turn all the modeling results into rules is easy as many tools are available. Especially for R results, there are several tools to help extract rules from developed predictive models.

For decision tree models, we should use the `rpart.utils` R package, which can extract rules and export them in various formats, including RODBC.

For more information about the `rpart.utils` R package, go to `https://cran.r-project.org/web/packages/rpart.utils/rpart.utils.pdf`.

For a discussion on extracting rules from MLlib, go to:

`http://stackoverflow.com/questions/31782288/how-to-extract-rules-from-decision-tree-spark-mllib`.

Summary

In this chapter, we went through a step-by-step process from data to a holistic view of business, from which we processed a large amount of data on Spark and then built a model to produce a holistic view of the sales team's success for the IFS company.

Specifically, we first selected models as per business needs after we prepared Spark computing and loaded in preprocessed data. Second, we prepared and reduced features. Third, we estimated model coefficients. Fourth, we evaluated the estimated models. Then, we interpreted the analytical results. And finally, we deployed our estimated models.

The preceding process is similar to the process of working with small data. However, in dealing with Big Data, we need parallel computing, for which Apache Spark is utilized. Also, during the previously described process, Apache Spark makes things easy and fast.

After this chapter, readers will have gained a full understanding of how Apache Spark can be utilized to make our work easier and faster in obtaining a holistic view of business. At the same time, readers should become familiar with the RM4Es modeling processes of processing large amounts of data and developing predictive models and especially become capable of producing their own holistic view of business.

4
Fraud Detection on Spark

In *Chapter 1, Spark for Machine Learning*, we discussed how to get the Apache Spark system ready, and in *Chapter 2, Data Preparation for Spark ML*, we listed detailed instructions for data preparation. Now, in chapters 4 to 6, we will move to a new stage of utilizing Apache Spark-based systems to turn data into insights for some specific projects, which is fraud detection for this chapter; risk modeling for *Chapter 5, Risk Scoring on Spark*; and churn prediction for *Chapter 6, Churn Prediction on Spark*.

Specifically, in this chapter, we will review machine learning methods and analytical processes for a fraud detection project, and also discuss how Apache Spark makes them easy and fast. At the same time, with a real-life fraud detection example, we will illustrate our step-by-step process of obtaining fraud insight from Big Data.

- Spark for fraud detection
- Methods of fraud detection
- Feature preparation
- Model estimation
- Model evaluation
- Result explanation
- Deploying fraud detection

Spark for fraud detection

In this section, we will start with a real business case of fraud detection to further illustrate our step-by-step machine learning process and then describe how to prepare Spark for this fraud detection project.

The use case

The ABC Corporation is a billion-dollar company that processes payments for thousands of clients in many industries, including real estate and vacation travel. Many kinds of frauds happened to this company and cost a lot. Most of the frauds happened online.

In order to prevent frauds from happening, the company collected a lot of data on its clients relating to payment processing transactions and also about past online activities for each client. Also, the company purchased a lot of data from third parties about the computer devices and bank accounts their clients use.

As for this project, our unit of analysis can be an individual company or person (ABC's client). Our unit of analysis can also be a payment transaction. In real practice, we performed modeling on both. However, as for the practice here, we will focus on analytics and transactions. Therefore, in terms of data and features, for each transaction online, we have web log data, data about its owner/user, and also data on the computer devices and bank accounts used.

In practice, the ABC company hopes to quickly score each transaction as per the likelihood of fraud and hopes to immediately stop a transaction if it is highly suspicious. Also, the company hoped to identify suspicious clients before the company approved them. In other words, the company needs to utilize the fraud detection systems for underwriting as well as for real-time transaction monitoring. As for this exercise, we will focus on scoring transactions with a suspicious score or fraud likelihood score and use this score to monitor all the transactions so the ABC corporation can take actions to stop potential frauds.

To sum up, for this project we have a target variable of fraud and web log data for each transaction, plus account, computing device, and user data.

Through some preliminary analysis, the company understands some of its data challenges, as follows:

- Data is not ready to use; the web log data especially needs to be extracted into features ready for modeling
- There are many kinds of fraud cases per payment transaction service with very different behaviors
- Less information exists for some new and less active clients

Distributed computing

Similarly to the previous chapter, for our project, parallel computing is needed due to the many kinds of frauds for which we should set up clusters and worker notes as before.

Let's assume we continue to work within the Databricks environment:

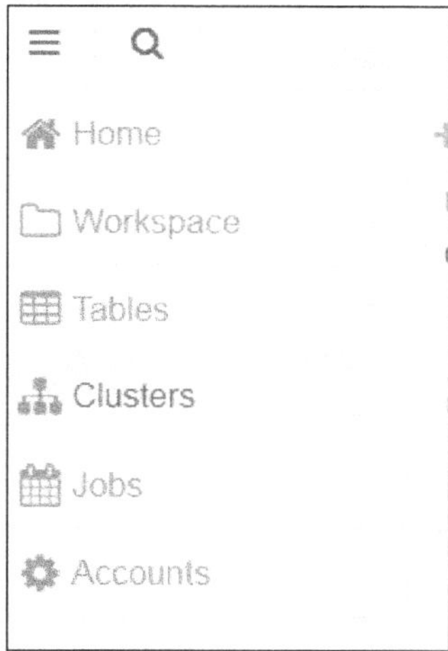

Then, we will need to go to the preceding main menu, click on Clusters, then create a name for the cluster, select the newest version of Spark, and then specify the number of workers.

Once the clusters are created, we can go to the preceding illustrated main menu, click on the down arrow to the right of **Tables**, and select **Create Tables** to import all of our cleaned and prepared datasets, as per the instructions discussed in *Chapter 2, Data Preparation for Spark ML*.

For this project, we will need to import a lot of web log data, structured data about the individual users or companies, the computer device used, and also on the bank accounts used.

As before, in Apache Spark, we need to direct workers to complete the computation on each note, for which we will use a scheduler on Databricks to get our R Notebook computation completed, and then collect results.

Also here, we will continue to take an R notebook approach.

In the Databricks environment, setting up notebooks will need us to go into the following menu:

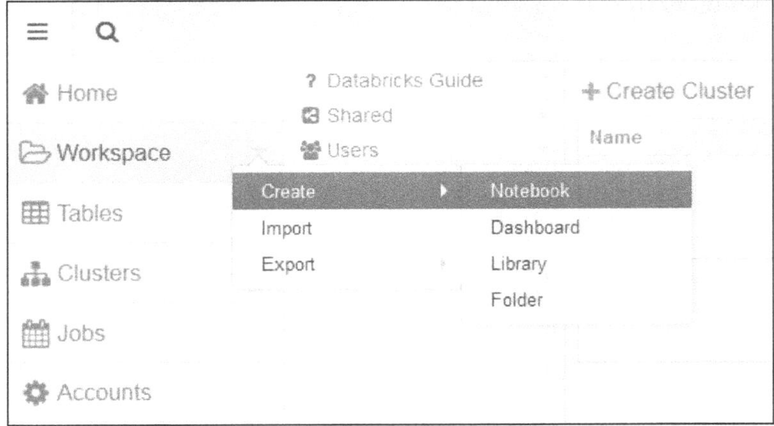

In the preceding main menu, click on the down arrow to the right of **Workspace** and select **Create** -> **New Notebook** to create a notebook.

If users do not want to use the R notebook provided by Databricks, one option is to use Zepperlin. To build a free notebook on Spark using Zeppelin, go to:

`http://hortonworks.com/blog/introduction-to-data-science-with-apache-spark/`.

Methods for fraud detection

In the previous section, we described our business use case and also prepared our Spark computing platform as well as our datasets. In this section, we need to select our analytical methods or predictive models (equations) for this fraud detection project, which is to complete a task of mapping our business use case to machine learning methods.

For fraud detection, both supervised machine learning and unsupervised machine learning are commonly used. However, for this case, we will perform a supervised machine learning because we do have good data for our target variable of fraud and also because our practical goal is to reduce frauds while continuing business transactions.

To model and predict frauds, there are many suitable models, including logistic regression and the decision tree. Selecting one among them can sometimes become extremely difficult as it depends on the data to be used. One solution is to first run all the models and then select the best ones using model evaluation indices. As in many situations, after applying evaluation methods, there may be no one best model but many best models. In this case, we will ensemble all of them to improve our model's performance.

To adopt the preceding mentioned strategy, we will need to develop a few models of neural network, logistic regression, SVM, and decision trees. However, for this exercise, we will focus our effort on Random forest and decision trees, as to demonstrate machine learning on Apache Spark and also to demonstrate their usefulness to meet the special needs of this use case.

As always, once we finalize our decision for analytical methods or models, we will need to prepare the related dependent variable and also prepare for coding.

Random forest

Random forest is a quite popular machine learning method because its interpretation is very intuitive, and it usually leads to good results. There are many algorithms developed in R, Java, and others to get Random forest implemented, so the preparation is relatively easy.

- **Random forest**: Random forest is an ensemble learning method for classification and regression that builds hundreds or even more decision trees at the training stage and then combines their output for the final prediction.
- **Preparing the dependent variable**: To use Random forest, we need to recode the variable to be 0 versus 1 by transforming FRAUD to 1 and NOT FRAUD to 0.
- **Preparing coding**: In MLlib, we can use the following codes for Random forest:

```
// To train a RandomForest model.
val treeStrategy = Strategy.defaultStrategy("Classification")
val numTrees = 300
val featureSubsetStrategy = "auto" // Let the algorithm choose.
val model = RandomForest.trainClassifier(trainingData,
  treeStrategy, numTrees, featureSubsetStrategy, seed = 12345)
```

For a good example of using MLlib for Random forest, go to `https://databricks.com/blog/2015/01/21/random-forests-and-boosting-in-mllib.html`.

In R, we need to use the R package Random forest.

For a good example of running random forest on Spark, go to `https://spark-summit.org/2014/wp-content/uploads/2014/07/Sequoia-Forest-Random-Forest-of-Humongous-Trees-Sung-Chung.pdf`.

Decision trees

Random forest comes from a set of trees with good functions to produce scores and rank independent variables by their impact on a target variable.

However, the mean results of hundreds of trees somehow cover details so that a decision tree explanation can still be very intuitive and valuable, as follows:

- **Decision tree introduction**: Decision tree aims to model classifying cases, which is about classifying into fraud or not fraud for our use case, in sequence
- **Prepare dependent variable**: Our target variable has already been coded as fraud or not, which is ready for our machine learning
- **Prepare coding**: As before, within MLlib, we can use the following codes:

```
val numClasses = 2
val categoricalFeaturesInfo = Map[Int, Int]()
val impurity = "gini"
val maxDepth = 6
val maxBins = 32
val model = DecisionTree.trainClassifier(trainingData, numClasses,
categoricalFeaturesInfo,
  impurity, maxDepth, maxBins)
```

As for the R notebook on Spark, we will continue to use the package `rpart` and then the `rpart` function for all the calculation. For `rpart`, we need to specify the classifier and also all the features to be used.

Feature preparation

In section, *Feature extraction*, of *Chapter 2, Data Preparation for Spark ML*, we reviewed a few methods for feature extraction and discussed their implementation on Apache Spark. All the techniques discussed there can be applied to our data here, especially the ones utilizing time series and feature comparison to create new features.

For this project, feature extraction is one of the most important tasks because all the fraud happens online and the web log is the most important and most recent data to predict frauds, which needs extraction to produce features ready for modeling.

Also, as we have features for transactions, users, bank accounts, and computer devices, a lot of work is needed to merge all these features together to form a complete data file ready for machine learning.

Feature extraction from LogFile

Log files are always unstructured, similarly to a collection of random symbols and numbers. One example of this is as follows:

```
May 23 12:19:11 elcap siu: 'siu root' succeeded for tjones on /dev/
ttyp0 www.abccorp.com/pay w
```

Parsing them and making sense of them needs a lot of work as well as some subject knowledge. Most people will work manually with some sample data and then use the patterns discovered to develop codes in R or others to parse and turn extracted information into features.

For this project, our strategy is not to parse all the log files into as many features as possible but only to extract a few features useful for our machine learning.

Through some special programming in **SparkSQL** and R for this project, we were able to extract a few good features from the log file. These features include the number of clicks, the time between clicks, type of clicks, and others.

After feature extraction, we will perform some feature selection work on LogFile features as well as on other features from other datasets, which result in a selection of features, as summarized by the following table:

Category	**Number of Features**
Web Log	3
Account	4
Computer devise	3
User	5
Business	3
Total	18

Data merging

As discussed in section, *Spark for fraud detection*, we have five datasets for web log, accounts, computer devices, users, and business. In other words, for each transaction, there is always a user using one computer device to complete a payment transaction for a business to an account.

In the previous section, we extracted features from web logs and then selected features for each dataset.

Now, we need to merge all the data together to form a table with each feature organized together with the target variable, so we can build predictive models on them.

To merge them together, let's follow what was discussed in section, *Joining data sets* of *Chapter 2, Data Preparation for Spark ML*, for which we can use SparkSQL or the `data.table` R package.

After data gets merged, we can create some new features by comparison between features in different datasets. For example, we can do a comparison between addresses and computer device languages to form new features. Therefore, for this case, we added three more features to form a set of 21 features. Then, we can perform some feature reduction and selection to explore our feature space.

After the preceding, we will split the data into the training and test sets.

Model estimation

Once feature sets get finalized in our last section, what follows is to estimate the parameters of the selected models, for which we can use either MLlib or R. As before, we need to arrange distributed computing.

To simplify, we can utilize Databricks' Job feature. Specifically, within the Databricks environment, we can go to **Jobs** to create jobs.

Then, users can select R notebooks to run specific clusters, and then schedule jobs. Once scheduled, users can also monitor the running and then collect the results.

In section, *Methods for fraud detection*, we prepared some codes for each of the three models selected. Now, we need to modify them with the final set of features, so we can create notebooks.

For now, we have one target variable prepared and 18 features, so we need to insert all of them into the code developed in section, *Methods for fraud detection* to finalize our notebook. Then, we will use Spark's distributed computing to get the notebook implemented in a distributed way.

MLlib implementation

Besides the preceding R notebook approach, another option is to use MLlib, which is a built-in ML library for Apache Spark. With MLlib, we can use the following code for Random forest:

```
// Train a RandomForest model.
val treeStrategy = Strategy.defaultStrategy("Classification")
val numTrees = 300
val featureSubsetStrategy = "auto" // Let the algorithm choose.
val model = RandomForest.trainClassifier(trainingData,
  treeStrategy, numTrees, featureSubsetStrategy, seed = 12345)
```

For decision trees, we use:

```
val model = DecisionTree.trainClassifier(trainingData, numClasses,
categoricalFeaturesInfo,
  impurity, maxDepth, maxBins)
```

R notebooks implementation

Now, the main task here is to schedule the estimation for each worker and then collect the results using the JOB feature mentioned before in the Databricks environment:

- **Random forest**: The following codes are needed for the R notebook:

  ```
  library(randomForest)
  randomForest((fraud~ ., data=NULL, ..., subset, na.action=na.fail))
  ```

- **Decision tree**: The following codes are needed for the R notebook to estimate decision trees:

  ```
  f.est1 <- rpart(fraud~ r1 + … + r21, method="class")
  ```

After we get all the models estimated as per each fraud type and customer group, we will need to calculate some averages and other statistics. However, for simplicity, we will focus on one group for discussion in the following sections.

Model evaluation

In the last section, we completed our model estimation. Now, it is the time for us to evaluate these estimated models to see whether they fit our client's criteria so that we can either move to results explanation or go back to some previous stages to refine our predictive models.

To perform our model evaluation, in this section, we will focus on utilizing confusion matrix and FalsePositive numbers to assess the goodness of fit for our models. To calculate them, we need to use our test data rather than training data.

A quick evaluation

As discussed before, both MLlib and R have algorithms to return a confusion matrix and even false positive numbers.

MLlib has `confusionMatrix` and `numFalseNegatives()` to use.

The following code calculates error ratios:

```
// Evaluate model on test instances and compute test error
val testErr = testData.map { point =>
  val prediction = model.predict(point.features)
  if (point.label == prediction) 1.0 else 0.0
}.mean()
println("Test Error = " + testErr)
println("Learned Random Forest:n" + model.toDebugString)
```

To visualize the performance of our classifiers, we can use the R package ROCR. For more information on using ROCR, readers may visit `https://rocr.bioinf.mpi-sb.mpg.de/`.

Confusion matrix and false positive ratios

In MLlib, we can use the following code to produce a confusion matrix and related false positive ratios:

```
// compute confusion matrix
val metrics = new MulticlassMetrics(predictionsAndLabels)
println(metrics.confusionMatrix)
```

In R, we can produce a confusion matrix and related false positive ratios with the following code:

```
model$confusion
```

For the fraud type social engineering, we produced the following confusion matrix, which shows a good result:

Type of Fraud	Predicted as Fraud	Predicted as NOT
Actual Fraud	81%	19%
Actual Not	12%	88%

For this project, the preceding table is the most important evaluation as the company wants to increase the ratio in the upper-left cell, which is to catch fraud as much as possible. However, they also need to reduce the ratio in the lower-left cell, which is to reduce the false positive ratio as much as possible.

As discussed earlier, the low ratio in the upper-left cell means that many frauds will not be caught, which may lead to big losses.

The high false positive ratio often leads to wasted labor on the company's side and also incovenience to customers, which could lead to low customer satisfaction and even loss of customers.

Results explanation

After we passed our model evaluation stage and decided to select the estimated and evaluated model as our final model, our next task is to interpret results to the company executives and technicians.

Here, we will work on results explanation with a focus on large influencing variables.

Big influencers and their impacts

As we briefly discussed before, quality and freshness are very different for each dataset. Each data has its own weakness, as summarized in the following:

Category	Weakness
Web Log	incomplete
Account	old
Computer device	incomplete
User	old
Business	Incomplete and old

Due to the preceding issues, we often do not have enough data to score each transaction or score it with good accuracy, and we can only score it later. Because of this, the company hopes to identify some special signals or insights that can be used to take action quickly and easily.

The following briefly summarizes some of the result samples that we use some functions from `randomForest` and decision tree to produce.

With the `randomForest` package in R, a simple code of `estimatedModel$importance` will return a ranking of variables by their importance in determining frauds.

Tables for Impact Assessment:

Feature	**Impacts**
Click speed	1
Account	2
ComputerDevice	3

Here, obtaining variable importance through the `randomForest` functions needs a full model estimated and will complete all data. So, it does not really solve our problems.

What customers really needed is actually to use a partial set of available features to estimate a model with limited variables and then assess how good this partial model is, which is to tell the fraud catching and false positive ratio. To complete this task, Apache Spark's advantage of fast computing is utilized, which helps get results.

Deploying fraud detection

As discussed before, MLlib supports model exporting to **Predictive Model Markup Language** (**PMML**). For the R notebook, it could run on other environments as well as, and with the PMML R package, R models could be exported. Also, it is possible to deploy models for decision making directly on Apache Spark and make results easily available to users. Therefore, we do export some developed models to PMML for this project.

However, in practice, the users of this project will be more interested in rule-based decision making to use some of our insights and also in score-based decision making to prevent frauds.

Here, we will discuss each one of them only briefly as a full deployment for decision making will need an optimization that is not covered in this chapter.

Turning estimated models into rules and scores is not very challenging and could be done under nonSpark platforms. However, Apache Spark makes things easy and fast. The advantage of utilizing Apache Spark is to allow us to quickly produce new rules and scores when data and customer requirements get changed.

Rules

As discussed before, for R results, there are several tools to help extract rules out from developed predictive models.

For the decision tree model we developed, we should use the `rpart.utils` R package, which can extract rules and export them in various formats, such as RODBC.

The `rpart.rules.table(model1)    *` package returns an unpivoted table of variable values (factor levels) associated with each branch.

However, for this project, partially due to the issue of data incompleteness, we will need to utilize some insights to derive rules directly. That is, we need to use insights discussed in the last section. For example, we can do the following:

- If the online click speed is dramatically different from the past, contact the user by phone
- If the bank account is not a real bank account or just a debit card or the bank account is very new, some actions are needed

From an analytical perspective, we face the same issue here to minimize false positives while catching enough frauds.

The company had a high false positive ratio from their past rules, and as a result of this, too many alerts were sent out that became a burden for manual inspection and also caused a lot of customer complaints.

Therefore, by taking advantage of Spark's fast computing, we carefully produced rules and, for each rule, we supplied false positive ratios that helped the company utilize the rules.

Scoring

From the coefficients of our predictive models, we can derive a suspicious score for fraud, but that takes some work.

In R, `model$predicted` will return the case class as FRAUD or NOT. However, `prob=predict(model,x,type="prob")` will produce a probability value, which can be used directly as a score.

However, in order to use the score, we need to select a cutting-out score. For example, we can decide to take actions when the suspicious score is over 80.

Different score cutting points will produce different fraud positive ratios and also the ratios of catching frauds; for this, users need to make a decision about how to balance the results here.

By taking advantage of Spark's fast computing, results can be calculated quickly, which allows the company to select cutting points instantly and make changes any time when needed.

Another way to deal with this issue is to use the `OptimalCutpoints` R package.

Summary

In this chapter, we went through a step-by-step process, from Big Data to a rapid development of fraud detection systems from which we processed data on Spark and then built several models to predict frauds. With this, we then developed rules and scores to help the ABC company prevent frauds.

Specifically, we first selected a supervised machine learning approach with a focus on Random forest and decision trees as per business needs, after we prepared Spark computing and loaded preprocessed data. Second, we worked on feature extraction and selection. Third, we estimated model coefficients. Fourth, we evaluated these estimated models using a confusion matrix and false positive ratios. Then, we interpreted our machine learning results. Finally, we deployed our machine learning results, with a focus on scoring but also used insights to develop rules.

The preceding process is similar to the process of working with small data. However, in dealing with Big Data, we need parallel computing, which Apache Spark is utilized for. Also, during the process described before, Apache Spark makes things easy and fast so that we are able to solve a few difficult problems, such as incomplete data. This means that we could take advantage of Apache Spark's fast computing to meet ABC Corporation's special analytical needs.

After this chapter, you will have gained a full understanding of how Apache Spark can be utilized to make our work easier and faster in conducting supervised machine learning, and developing fraud detection systems. Also, you now understand how fast computing can turn into analytical capabilities.

5
Risk Scoring on Spark

Starting with this chapter, we will go deep into some technologies for using Apache Spark for machine learning. While this chapter focuses on notebooks for Spark, *Chapter 6, Churn Prediction on Spark* will focus on machine learning libraries including MLlib, and *Chapter 7, Recommendations on Spark*, will focus on SPSS with Spark.

Specifically, in this chapter, we will review machine learning methods and analytical processes for a risk scoring project, and get them implemented by R notebooks on Apache Spark in a special DataScientistWorkbench environment. We will also discuss how Apache Spark notebooks help to get everything well-organized and easy. The following topics will be covered in this chapter:

- Spark for risk scoring
- Methods for risk scoring
- Data and feature preparation
- Model estimation
- Model evaluation
- Results explanation
- Deployment of risk scoring

Spark for risk scoring

In this section, we will start with a real business case, and then describe how to prepare an Apache Spark environment to use R notebooks to work on this real life risk scoring project.

The use case

XST Corp provides loans and other financial assistance to millions of individuals who need the cash either to continue their business or to take care of some emergent personal needs. This company accepts applications online and then makes instant decisions on most of the received applications. For this purpose, they use the data collected from the online applications and data collected in the past in their data warehouse, along with additional data provided by third parties.

Their online applications provide identity data and some financial data of the applicants. The company's compiled data consists of information related to location, economy, and others. The third-party data has a lot of rich data related to past credit, current employment, and others.

This company works in a fast-changing industry with many competitors. So they are constantly looking for better risk scoring models that can enable them to outperform their competitors. Specifically, the model should predict defaults more accurately than their competitors, and should be easily deployed to allow the company to approve more applicants, with low default risks on the approved applicants.

With these three sets of data, the company has more than two thousand features (variables) to use for their machine learning. Therefore, feature selection is a big task, and so is data preparation, because the data quality is not as good as it should be, with a lot of missing values.

The company has clear ideas about evaluating their models by following the industry standards as well as by meeting their own goal of approving more applicants with low risk. It is also clear on how to deploy their models. But all these tasks need to be completed in the minimum amount of time, or even be automated if possible, to enable their instant decision-making needs and their need for constantly refining models. For this reason, a notebook approach is ideal, as notebook facilitates replication and iterative computing with options for quick modification. At the same time, new data comes in frequently, so the models need to be refined very often just to accommodate the new data.

As for the machine learning part, for this project, we do have a target variable of loan default, and applicant data from online applications along with credit data, consumer data, public record data, and social media data from the three data sources mentioned earlier.

Apache Spark notebooks

As mentioned in the previous section, for this project, we will need to organize our machine learning for replication and possibly automation. For this, we will use notebooks to organize all the code, and then get them implemented on Apache Spark. Notebooks facilitate replication, and also provide a good foundation for future automation.

Most R users are familiar with the R package `Markdown`, which makes it easy to create R notebooks that enable easy creation of dynamic documents, analytics, presentations, and reports from R.

> Readers unfamiliar with Markdown may visit the following web links to gain a quick understanding, and also view an example of an R notebook:
>
> `http://rmarkdown.rstudio.com/` and `http://ramnathv.github.io/rNotebook/`

To prepare notebooks on Apache Spark, one option is to use Zeppelin, which is an open source product, and has been used widely. For building a notebook on Spark by using Zeppelin, the following two links explain everything very clearly:

- `http://blog.sparkiq-labs.com/2015/11/16/interactive-data-science-with-r-in-apache-zeppelin-notebook/`
- `http://hortonworks.com/blog/introduction-to-data-science-with-apache-spark/`

But this will take a lot of coding and system configuration work and, for R notebook, you will even need to use an R interpreter.

You can also use R on the `Jupyter` notebook, for which you can find clear instructions at the following website:

`http://blog.revolutionanalytics.com/2015/09/using-r-with-jupyter-notebooks.html.`

There have been many successful efforts at using the `Jupyter` notebook to organize R programming, with one example at `http://nbviewer.ipython.org/github/carljv/Will_it_Python/blob/master/MLFH/CH2/ch2.ipynb`.

Like Zeppelin, using `Jupyter` also needs a lot of work on coding and system configuration. If you want to avoid too much coding and configuration work, you can use the Databricks environment as described in the previous chapters, where R notebooks can be easily implemented on Apache Spark and data clusters.

Besides Databricks, another option is to utilize the IBM Data Scientist Workbench at `https://datascientistworkbench.com/`.

The DataScientistWorkbench has Apache Spark installed, and also has an integrated data-cleaning system, OpenRefine, so that our data preparation work can be made easier and more organized.

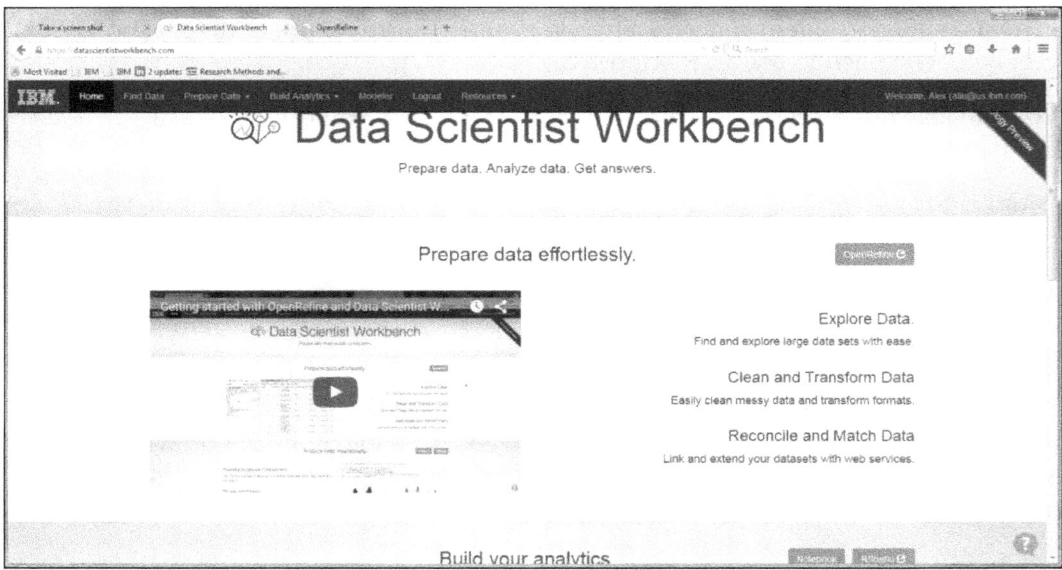

For this project, we will use the DataScientistWorkbench for data cleaning, R notebook creation, and Apache Spark implementation. For this setup, some of the Apache Spark techniques described in the previous chapters may apply.

Methods of risk scoring

Having described our business use case, and prepared our Apache Spark computing platform, in this section, we need to select our analytical methods or predictive models (equations) for this machine learning project for risk scoring, which is to complete a task of mapping our risk modelling case to machine learning methods.

To model and predict loan defaults, logistic regression and decision tree are among the most utilized methods. For our exercise, we will use both. But we will focus on logistic regression, because logistic regression, if well developed in combination with decision trees, can outperform most of the other methods.

As always, once we finalize our decision for analytical methods or models, we will need to prepare our coding, which will be in R for this chapter.

Logistic regression

Logistic regression measures the relationship between one categorical dependent variable and one or more independent variables by estimating probabilities using a logistic function, which is the cumulative logistic distribution. Logistic regression can be seen as a special case of **Generalized Linear Model** (**GLM**), and thus, it is analogous to linear regression.

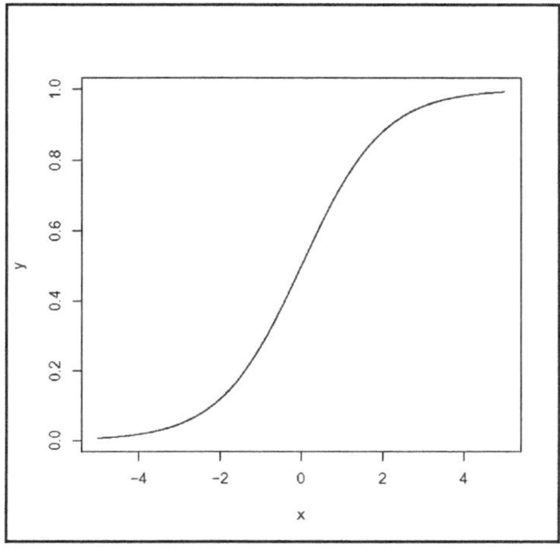

We have chosen to focus on logistic regression for this real life use case mainly for two reasons besides the performance as mentioned previously:

- Logistic regression can be interpreted easily with some simple calculations
- Most financial corporations have implemented logistic regression in the past; so it becomes easy for our clients to compare our results against what they have received in the past

Preparing coding in R

With R, there are many ways to code for logistic regression.

In the previous chapters, we used the R function `glm` with the following code:

```
Model1 <-glm(good_bad ~.,data=train,family=binomial())
```

For consistency, we will continue to use the `glm` function here.

Random forest and decision trees

Random forest is an ensemble learning method for classification and regression that builds hundreds or more decision trees at the training stage, and then combines their output for the final prediction.

Random forest is quite a popular machine learning method, because its interpretation is very intuitive and it usually leads to good results with less effort than that needed for logistic regression. There are many algorithms developed in R, Java, and others for implementing Random forest, so preparation is relatively easy.

As our focus for this project is on logistic regression, Random forest comes in to assist our logistic regression for feature selection and for calculating the importance of features.

As mentioned before, decision trees, in combination with logistic regression, often provide good results. So we bring in decision tree modeling here, and also use the decision tree model for our client to test rule-based solutions, and compare them to our score-based solutions.

Preparing coding

In R, we need to use the R package `randomForest`, as originally developed by Leo Breiman and Adele Cutler.

To get a random forest model estimated, we can use the following R code, where we use the training data and `2000` trees.

```
library(randomForest)
Model2 <- randomForest(default ~ ., data=train, importance=TRUE,
ntree=2000)
```

Once the models get estimated, we can use functions `getTree` and `importance` to obtain the results.

For decision trees, there are a few ways of coding in R:

```
Model3 <- rpart(default ~ ., data=train)
```

For a good example of running Random forest on Spark, please go to `https://spark-summit.org/2014/wp-content/uploads/2014/07/Sequoia-Forest-Random-Forest-of-Humongous-Trees-Sung-Chung.pdf`.

Data and feature preparation

In the section *Feature extraction* of *Chapter 2, Data Preparation for Spark ML*, we have reviewed a few methods for feature extraction, and discussed their implementation in Apache Spark. All the techniques discussed there can be applied to the risk scoring project here.

For this project, as mentioned earlier, the main concern is to get everything organized as workflows for repeatability, and possibly automation. So we will adopt OpenRefine for data and feature preparation. We will use OpenRefine within the DataScientistWorkbench environment where it has been integrated.

OpenRefine

OpenRefine, formerly *Google Refine*, is an open source application for data cleaning.

To use OpenRefine, please go to: `https://datascientistworkbench.com/`

After logging in, you will see the following screen:

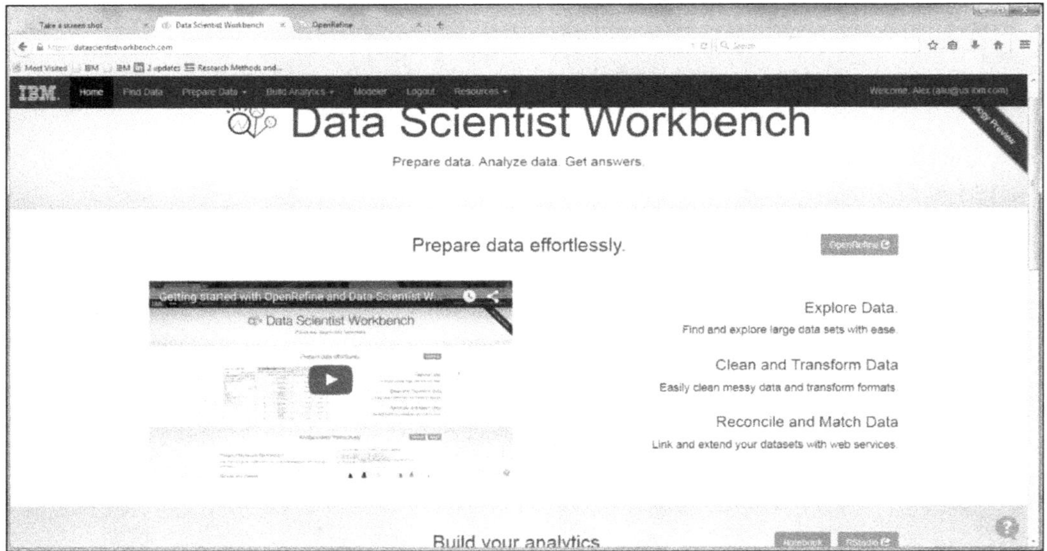

Then, please click on the **OpenRefine** button on the upper-right corner of the screen:

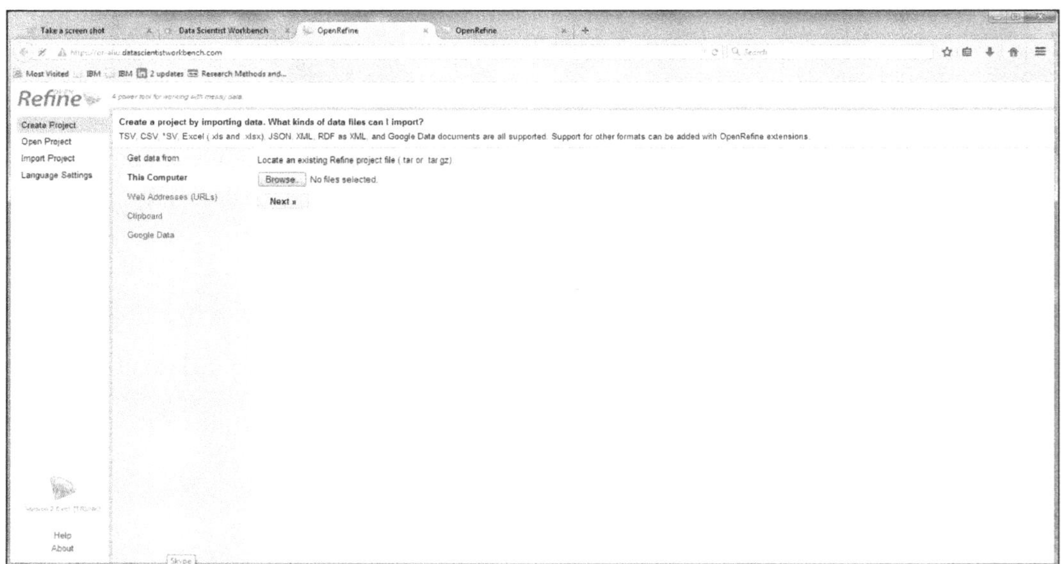

Here, you can import datasets from your computer or from a URL address.

Then you can create an OpenRefine project for data cleaning and preparation. After that, you can export the prepared data, or send the data to a notebook by drag and drop.

For this project, we specially used OpenRefine for identity matching (reconciliation), deleting duplicates, and merging datasets.

Model estimation

In this section, we will describe the methods and procedures for utilizing R notebooks within the DataScientistWorkbench to complete our model estimation.

The DataScientistWorkbench for R notebooks

As soon as we get our data ready by using OpenRefine, we should develop an R notebook within the which applies the codes prepared in section, *Methods for risk scoring* and the features prepared in section, *Data and feature preparation* to the data.

As seen in the following screenshot, the DataScientistWorkbench allows us to create an interactive R notebook, run it, and share it as well.

R studio, a favorite with R users, is also integrated with the DataScientistWorkbench:

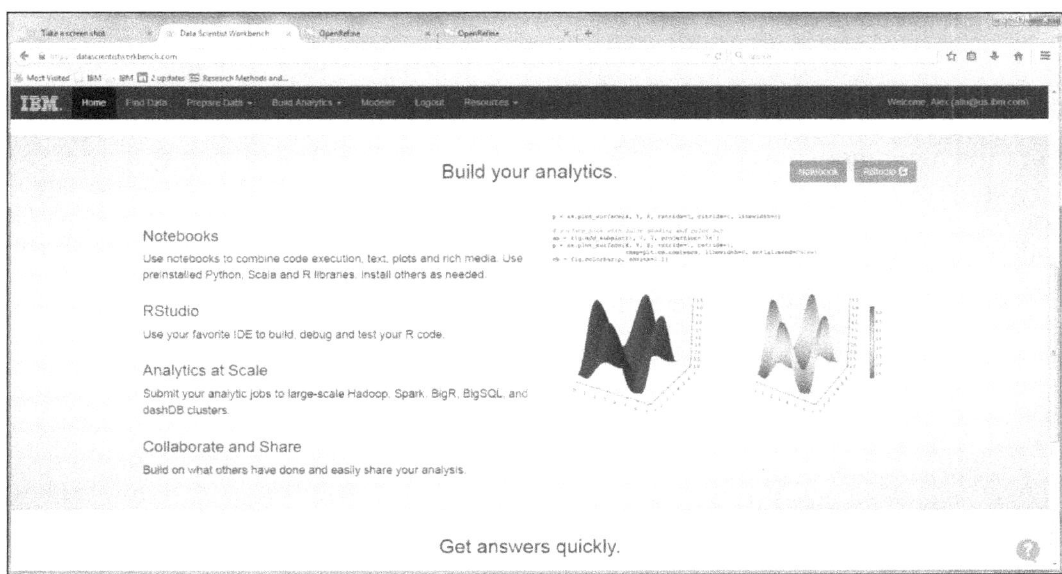

To start a notebook, you can click on **Build Analytics**, and then on **Notebook,** or you can directly click on the **Notebook** blue button as seen in the following screenshot:

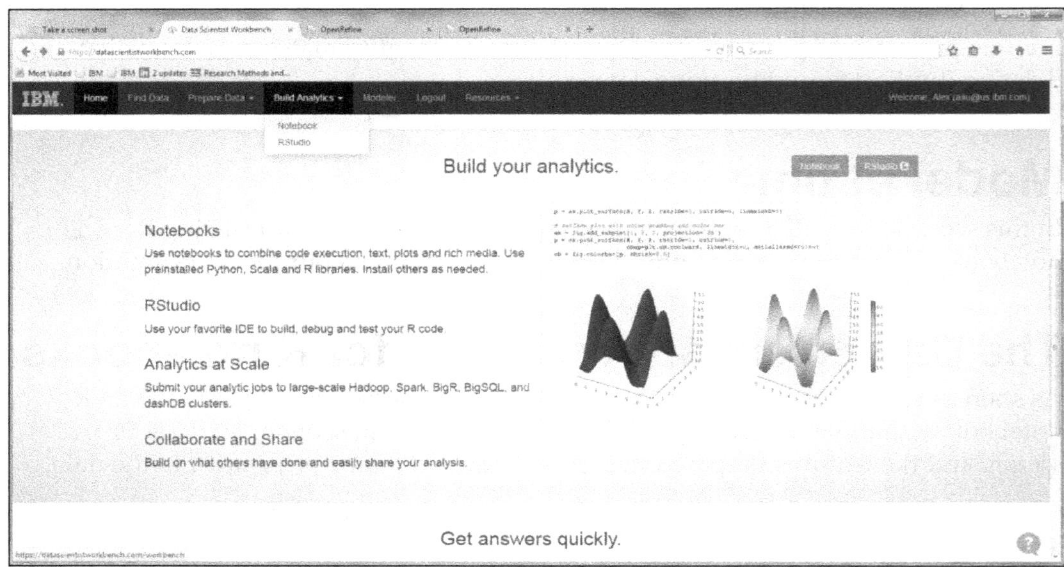

Once an R notebook is developed, it can be seen under **Recent Notebooks**, and you can run it to obtain results as in other environments.

R notebooks implementation

For estimating models, the main task is to schedule the implementation of R notebooks within the Data Scientist Workbench environment. To do so, we need to use R notebooks started in the previous section, for which we need to insert all the following R code:

- **Logistic regression**: The following code is needed for the R notebook:

```
Model1 <-glm(good_bad ~.,data=train,family=binomial())
```

- **Random Forest**: The following code is needed for the R notebook:

```
library(randomForest)
randomForest(default~ ., data=train, na.action=na.fail,
importance=TRUE, ntree=2000)
```

- **Decision tree**: The following codes is needed for the R notebook to estimate decision trees:

```
f.est1 <- rpart(default~ r1 + … + r21, data=train, method="class")
```

Model evaluation

After completing our model estimation as described in the preceding section, we need to evaluate these estimated models to see if they fit our client's criterion so that we can either move to the explanation of results or go back to some previous stage to refine our predictive models.

To perform our model evaluation, in this section, we will utilize confusion matrix numbers to assess the quality of fit for our models, and then expand to other statistics.

As always, to calculate them, we need to use our test data rather than the training data.

Confusion matrix

In R, we can produce the model's performance indices with the following code:

```
model$confusion
```

Once a cutting point is determined, the following confusion matrix is produced, which shows a good result:

Model's Performance	Predicted as Default	Predicted as NOT (Good)
Actual Default	89%	11%
Actual Not (Good)	12%	88%

For this project, the preceding table is the most important evaluation, as the company wants to increase the ratio in the top-left cell, which is to disapprove risky applicants as much as possible. But, they also need to reduce the ratio in the bottom-left cell, which is to reduce the false positive ratio as much as possible, that is, not to reject any good customers.

However, the preceding results depend on how to choose a cutting point, so it is not the best table for comparing scores. For this reason, we need to use ROCs and KS, as they are summary statistics, rather than statistics relying on a single point.

ROC

A **Receiver Operating Characteristic Curve** (**ROC**) is a standard technique for summarizing classifier performance over a range of trade-offs between **True Positive** (**TP**) and **False Positive** (**FP**) error rates. The ROC curve is a plot of sensitivity (the ability of the model to predict an event correctly) versus 1-specificity for the possible cut-off classification probability values, п0.

Here, *sensitivity=P(y^=1 | y=1)* and *specificity=P(y^=0 | y=0)*.

The ROC curve is more informative than the confusion matrix, since it summarizes the predictive power of all possible cutting-off points.

As shown in the following graph, the area under the ROC curve as 1 implies a perfect model, while the area under the ROC curve as 0.5 implies a worthless model.

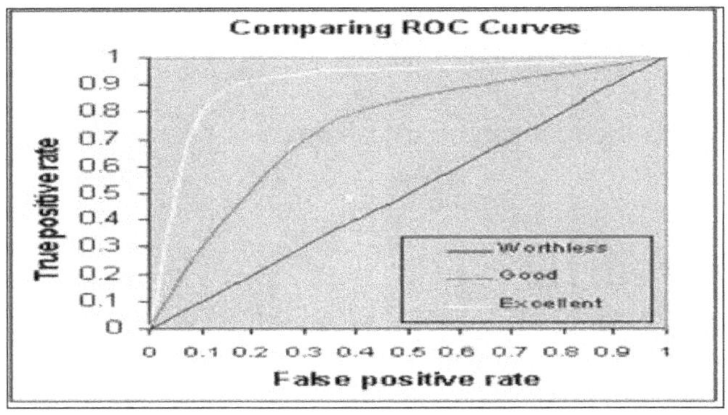


```
#load library
library(ROCR)
#score test data set
test$score<-predict(m,type='response',test)
pred<-prediction(test$score,test$good_bad)
perf <- performance(pred,"tpr","fpr")
plot(perf)
```

Kolmogorov-Smirnov

The Kolmogorov-Smirnov (**KS**) value is the maximum difference between the cumulative true positive and cumulative false positive rate, which is heavily used in the industry to assess models.

This code builds on the ROCR library by taking the *max delt* between the cumulative bad and good rates being plotted by ROCR:

```
max(attr(perf,'y.values')[[1]]-attr(perf,'x.values')[[1]])
```

With the R codes in this section combined with the R codes from the previous sections, we have a complete process for estimating our logistic regression models, and for obtaining ROC values and the KS value for the estimated models.

For various financial services' products and for various customer segments along with various feature combinations, we've got a lot of models to run, but we can complete them quickly with our notebook approach towards DataScientistWorkbench on Apache Spark.

For all the models estimated, our clients first select the ones with the KS values greater than 0.40 and ROC values greater than 0.67. After that, they use subject knowledge to finalize the selections.

Results explanation

As before, once we pass the model evaluation stage and select the estimated model as our final model, the next task is to interpret the results for the company executives and technicians.

In the next section, we will work on results explanation focusing on some big influencing variables. With the big influencing variables identified, the company could use them to improve their marketing effort to recruit the right customers.

Big influencers and their impacts

With logistic regression results, we can explain the impact of each feature by using regression coefficients, and identify big influencers by comparing those coefficients.

With the same logic, we can also rank each feature by its effects as calculated by the logistic regression coefficients.

Another way is to use the R package of effect, which was created by John Fox and others especially for the display of the effects of linear and generalized linear models. By using this package, we can obtain a list and some graphical displays with the function of plot (effect) .

To take this to a higher level, users may consider using the R package `relaimpo`, specially created to assess the relative importance of predictors, for which the following code should be used:

```
library(relaimpo)
calc.relimp(model1, type = c("lmg"), rela = TRUE)
```

Here, `"lmg"` refers to the authors Lindeman, Merenda, and Gold for their special methods.

As used in the previous chapters, with the `randomForest` package in R, a simple code of `estimatedModel$importance` will return a ranking of variables by order of their importance in determining the default risk.

However, to obtain the importance of variables through `randomForest` functions, we need a full model estimated, with all data complete. So it does not really solve our problems.

For this project, we will rely on results obtained from logistic regression.

As for our client, we find a few very interesting insights, among which are a few features with big impacts, which include the length of stay at the current address and social media influence.

Deployment

As demonstrated in the previous chapters, turning estimated models into scores is not very challenging, and could be done under non-Spark platforms. However, Apache Spark makes things easy and fast as demonstrated.

With the notebook approach adopted in this chapter, we will fully achieve the advantage to quickly produce new scores when data and customer requirements get changed.

Users will find some similarity to the deployment work in the last chapter—the deployment of scoring for fraud detection.

Scoring

From coefficients of our predictive models, we can derive a risk score for possible default, which takes some work. But it gives the client the flexibility of changing it whenever needed.

With logistic regression, the process of producing scores is relatively easy—it uses the following formulae for logistic regression:

$$\ln(\frac{P}{1-P}) = a + bX$$

$$\frac{P}{1-P} = e^{a+bX}$$

$$P = \frac{e^{a+bX}}{1+e^{a+bX}}$$

Specifically, `Prob(Yi=1) = exp(BXi)/(1+exp(BXi))` produces the default probability, with `Y=1` as the default, and X is a sum of all the features. In R, `exp(coef(logit_model))` returns the needed odd ratios.

In R, the quick way is to use the function of predict as follows:

```
prob=predict(model,x,type="prob")
```

Specifically, this function will produce a probability value for default, which can be used directly as a score for this project.

However, in order to use the score, we still need to select a cutting out score. For example, we can choose to take action only when the risk score is over 90.

Different score cutting points will produce different false positive ratios, and also the ratios of excluding bad applicants, for which the users need to make a decision about how to balance the results.

By taking advantage of Spark's fast computing, results can be calculated fast, which allows the company to select a cutting point instantly and to make changes when needed.

As similar to other applications, another way to deal with this issue is to use the R package, `OptimalCutpoints`.

Summary

In this chapter, we have turned our focus to a notebook approach to Apache Spark, and specifically developed R notebooks for estimating and assessing models, with which we developed risk scores to help the company XST to improve their risk management.

We first selected a few machine learning methods with our focus on the logistic regression method, along with random forest and decision trees. We then worked on data cleaning and feature development by using a special tool called OpenRefine. Next, we estimated the model coefficients. We then evaluated these estimated models by using a confusion matrix, ROC, and KS. Then we interpreted our machine learning results. And finally, we deployed our machine learning results with a scoring approach.

With a notebook approach, all the preceding machine learning steps are implemented in R, with all the R codes stored in notebooks so that the process is repeatable and can be partially automated. To get everything organized well and integrated with Apache Spark, we used the DataScientistWorkbench here.

After this chapter, readers will have gained a full understanding of the notebook approach to Apache Spark as well as some machine learning techniques for risk scoring and the DataScientistWorkbench. To sum up, readers will gain good knowledge about R, notebook, DataScientistWorkbench, and Spark. For more information on Apache Spark and DataScientistWorkbench, you can go to `http://www.db2dean.com/Previous/Spark1.html`.

6
Churn Prediction on Spark

In this chapter, we will focus on the utilization of some Apache Spark machine learning libraries, especially MLlib, as applied to a churn predictive modeling project.

Specifically, in this chapter, we will first review machine learning methods and the related computing for a churn prediction project, and will then discuss how Apache Spark MLlib makes things easy and fast. At the same time, with a real life churn prediction example, we will illustrate the step-by-step process of predicting churns with Big Data. The following topics will be covered in this chapter:

- Spark for churn prediction
- Methods for churn prediction
- Feature preparation
- Model estimation
- Model evaluation
- Results explanation
- Model deployment

Spark for churn prediction

In this section, we will start with a real-life business case description, and then review the steps for preparing the Apache Spark computing for our churn prediction project.

The use case

The YST Corporation is a big auto corporation selling and leasing vehicles to millions of customers. The company wishes to improve customer retention by using machine learning with Big Data, as they understand that consumers today go through a complex decision making process before purchasing or leasing a car, that it is becoming increasingly important to proactively identify customers that have a tendency to leave, and take preventive interventions to retain such customers.

The company has collected a lot of customer satisfaction data through their dealers and service centers as well as through their frequently conducted customer surveys. At the same time, the company has collected data for customers' online behavior from their web sites along with some social media data. Of course, the company has its transaction data for each purchase and car lease, and also a lot of data about their products and their services besides the various promotions and interventions they implemented in the past. The goal of this machine learning project is to build a predictive model for the company to understand how their product features and service improvements, together with promotion interventions, affect customer satisfaction, and then customer churns.

To sum up, for this project, we have a target variable, customer defection, and a lot of data about customer behavior, products, and services as well as company interventions such as promotions to form features as predictors.

Through some preliminary analysis, the company understands some of their data challenges as follows:

- Data is not ready to use; the web log data, especially, needs to be extracted into features ready for machine learning
- There are many kinds of cars with various leasing and purchasing options for various kinds of customers, for which the customer churn patterns are very different from each other
- Data exists in different silos, which needs to be merged together

To deal with the aforementioned challenges, in the actual process of delivering good machine learning results for this real-life project, we utilized some techniques presented in *Chapter 3, A Holistic View on Spark* to merge all the datasets together, and also some feature extraction techniques along with some distributed computing techniques discussed in the previous chapters. In this chapter, we will focus our efforts on utilizing machine learning libraries to attack problems, and to complete good machine learning.

Spark computing

As seen in the preceding chapter, for this machine learning project of customer churn prediction, parallel computing is needed due to the many kinds of cars for various customer segments. For this, we need to set up clusters and worker nodes as before, while completing our Apache Spark installation.

As discussed in section, *Spark overview* of *Chapter 1*, *Spark for Machine Learning*, Apache Spark has a unified platform which consists of the Spark core engine and four libraries that include Spark SQL, Spark Streaming, MLlib, and GraphX. All four libraries have Python, Java, and Scala programming APIs.

Among the four libraries, MLlib is the one that is most needed for this chapter. Besides the aforementioned built-in library MLlib, there are also many machine learning packages available for Apache Spark, as provided by third parties. One example is IBM's SystemML, which contains a lot more algorithms than those offered by MLlib. SystemML is being integrated with Apache Spark.

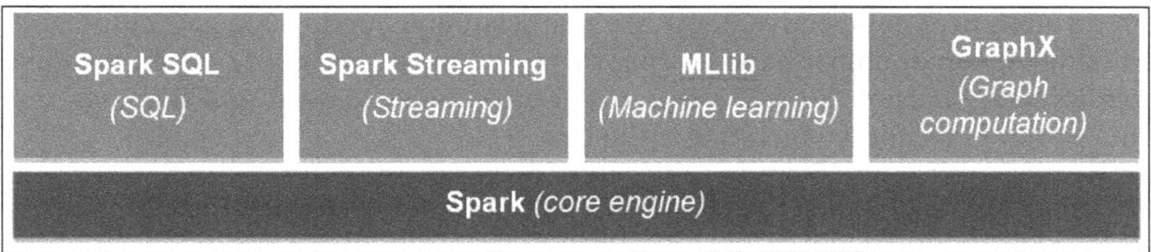

Because MLlib is Apache Spark's built-in machine learning library, there is not much work needed to prepare it, which is a great advantage over other machine learning libraries. Another advantage is that it is scalable, and consists of many commonly used machine learning algorithms such as algorithms for:

- Performing classification and regression modeling
- Collaborative filtering
- Performing dimensionality reduction
- Conducting feature extraction and transformation
- Exporting PMML models

We will need all the preceding algorithms for this project. Spark MLlib is still under active development, with new algorithms expected to be added with every new release.

To download Apache Spark, readers can go to `http://spark.apache.org/downloads.html`.

To install Apache Spark and start running it, readers can consult its latest documentation at `http://spark.apache.org/docs/latest/`.

Methods for churn prediction

In the previous section, we have completed our task of describing the business use case, and that of preparing our Spark computing platform and our datasets. In this section, we need to select our analytical methods or predictive models (equations) for this churn prediction project, that is, to map our business use case to machine learning methods.

As per the research done over a period of many years, customer satisfaction professionals believe that product and services features affect the quality of services, which affects customer satisfaction, finally affecting customer churns. Therefore, we should somehow incorporate this piece of knowledge into our model design or equation specification.

From an analytical perspective, there are many suitable models for modelling and predicting customer churns, and among them, the most commonly used are logistic regression and decision trees. For this exercise, we will use both, and then use evaluation to determine which one is the best.

As always, once we finalize our decision for analytical methods or models, we will need to prepare the related target variable and also prepare for coding, in this case with the Spark machine learning libraries.

Regression models

Regression is one of the most commonly used methods for prediction, and has been used to model customer churns by many machine learning professionals.

- **Types of regression models**: There are two main kinds of regression models that are suitable for churn prediction. One is *linear regression,* and the other is *logistic regression*. For this project, logistic regression is more suitable, as we have a target variable about whether the customer departed, with discrete values. But, for the real-life project, we have also used linear regression to model customer satisfaction, as many predictors impact customer satisfaction and, thus, customer churns. But in this case, as an example, our focus will be on logistic regression. To further improve our model performance, we may try *LassoModel* and *RidgeRegressionModel*, which are available in MLlib.

- **Preparing coding**: In MLlib, for linear regression, we will use the same code used earlier as follows:

  ```
  val numIterations = 95
  val model = LinearRegressionWithSGD.train(TrainingData,
  numIterations)
  ```

  Also for logistic regression, we will the code used earlier as follows:

  ```
  val model = new LogisticRegressionWithSGD()
    .setNumClasses(2)
    .run(training)
  ```

Decision trees and Random forest

Both decision trees and random forest aim to model classifying cases, which is about classifying into departed or not departed for our use case, in sequence with results to be illustrated by trees.

- Introduction to Decision trees and Random forest.

  Specifically, decision tree modeling uses tree branching based on value comparisons to illustrate the impacts of predictive features, which in comparison to logistic regression, is easy to use and also robust with missing data. Robustness with missing data has a big advantage for this use case, as we do have a significant amount of data incompleteness here.

  Random Forest comes from a set of trees, and often hundreds of trees, with ready-to-use functions for producing risk scores (churn probabilities), and for ranking predictive variables by their impact on the target variable, which is very useful for us to help identify bigger interventions for reducing customer churns.

  However, the mean results of hundreds and hundreds of trees somehow obscures the details, so a decision tree explanation can still be very intuitive and valuable.

- Prepare coding.

  As done earlier, within MLlib, we can use the following code:

  ```
  val numClasses = 2
  val categoricalFeaturesInfo = Map[Int, Int]()
  val impurity = "gini"
  val maxDepth = 6
  val maxBins = 32

  val model = DecisionTree.trainClassifier(trainingData, numClasses,
  categoricalFeaturesInfo,
    impurity, maxDepth, maxBins)
  ```

We may also expand our work to Random Forest and, in MLlib, we can use the following code for random forest:

```
// To train a RandomForest model.
val treeStrategy = Strategy.defaultStrategy("Classification")
val numTrees = 300
val featureSubsetStrategy = "auto" // Let the algorithm choose.
val model = RandomForest.trainClassifier(trainingData,
  treeStrategy, numTrees, featureSubsetStrategy, seed = 12345)
```

More guidance about coding for decisions can be found at:

`http://spark.apache.org/docs/latest/mllib-decision-tree.html`

and for Random Forest at:

`http://spark.apache.org/docs/latest/mllib-ensembles.html`

Feature preparation

In section, *Feature extraction* of *Chapter 2, Data Preparation for Spark ML,* we have reviewed a few methods for feature extraction and discussed their implementation in Apache Spark. All the techniques discussed there can be applied to our data here, especially the ones for utilizing time series and feature comparison to create new features. For example, the customer satisfaction response change over time is considered as possibly an excellent predictor.

For this project, we will need to conduct both feature extraction and feature selection, which will allow us to utilize all the techniques discussed in *Chapter 2, Data Preparation for Spark ML* and also *Chapter 3, A Holistic View on Spark.*

The data merging part is also necessary, but its implementation is similar to what was described in the previous chapters, to be completed at ease.

Feature extraction

In the previous chapters, we used Spark SQL and R for feature extraction and, for this real-life project, we will try to use MLlib for feature extraction; even in reality, users may use all the tools available.

A complete guide for MLlib feature extraction can be found at `http://spark.apache.org/docs/latest/mllib-feature-extraction.html`.

Here, we will use the `Word2Vec` method for extracting features from the social media data. The following code can be used to load a text file, parse it as an RDD of `Seq[String]`, construct a `Word2Vec` instance, and then fit a `Word2VecModel` with the input data. Finally, we display the top 40 synonyms of some specific words such as leave or bad service.

```
import org.apache.spark._
import org.apache.spark.rdd._
import org.apache.spark.SparkContext._
import org.apache.spark.mllib.feature.{Word2Vec, Word2VecModel}

val input = sc.textFile("text8").map(line => line.split(" ").toSeq)

val word2vec = new Word2Vec()

val model = word2vec.fit(input)

val synonyms = model.findSynonyms("china", 40)

for((synonym, cosineSimilarity) <- synonyms) {
  println(s"$synonym $cosineSimilarity")
}

// Save and load model
model.save(sc, "myModelPath")
val sameModel = Word2VecModel.load(sc, "myModelPath")
```

Feature selection

MLlib also has a few functions to be used for feature selection, which are similar to what you learned in the previous chapters, so we are not going to repeat them here.

An online guide on feature selection with MLlib can be found at `http://spark.apache.org/docs/latest/mllib-feature-extraction.html#feature-selection`.

Model estimation

Once the feature sets get finalized in our last section, what follows is the estimation of parameters of the selected models, for which we will use MLlib. As earlier, we need to arrange distributed computing, especially for this case with various cars for various customer segments.

As MLlib is a built-in package for Apache Spark, the computation is a straightforward process for which the readers may consult *Chapter 1, Spark for Machine Learning*.

One of the main reasons for our client utilizing Apache Spark is to take advantage of its computation speed and the ease of implementing parallel computing. For this project, as we need to build models for more than 40 products and many customer segments, we will perform machine learning only against segments by age.

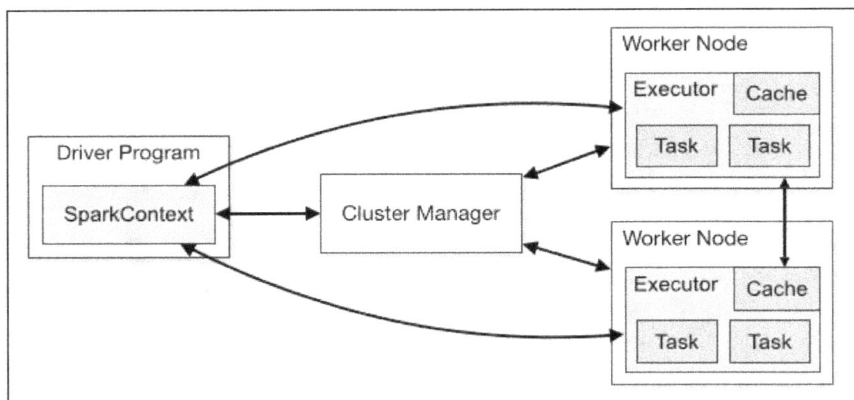

For updated information about implementing parallel computing with Spark and especially about submitting and monitoring application jobs, users should always consult Apache Spark's updated and detailed guidelines at `http://spark.apache.org/docs/latest/cluster-overview.html`.

Spark implementation with MLlib

With MLlib for random forest, we use the following code:

```
// Train a RandomForest model.
val treeStrategy = Strategy.defaultStrategy("Classification")
val numTrees = 300
val featureSubsetStrategy = "auto" // Let the algorithm choose.
val model = RandomForest.trainClassifier(trainingData,
  treeStrategy, numTrees, featureSubsetStrategy, seed = 12345)
```

For decision tree, we use the following code:

```
val categoricalFeaturesInfo = Map[Int, Int]()
val impurity = "variance"
val maxDepth = 5
```

```
val maxBins = 64 # larger = higher accuracy

val model = DecisionTree.trainClassifier(trainingData, numClasses,
categoricalFeaturesInfo,
  impurity, maxDepth, maxBins)
```

In MLlib for linear regression, we will use:

```
val numIterations = 90
val model = LinearRegressionWithSGD.train(TrainingData, numIterations)
```

For logistic regression, we will use:

```
val model = new LogisticRegressionWithSGD()
  .setNumClasses(2)
```

Model evaluation

Once our model gets estimated as in the preceding section, it is time for us to evaluate these estimated models to see if they fit our client's criteria so that we can either move to the results explanation stage or go back to some previous stage to refine our predictive models.

From the client's perspective, there are two common error types in machine learning for churn prediction.

The first one is False Negative (Type I Error), which is about failing to identify a customer who has a high propensity to depart.

From a business perspective, this is the least desirable error as the customer is very likely to leave, and the company does not know that it lost the chance to act to keep the customers, thus adversely affecting the the company's revenue.

The second one is False Positive (Type II Error), which is about classifying a good, satisfied customer as one who is one likely to churn.

From a business perspective, this may be acceptable as it does not impact revenue, but will create confusion leading to some negative consequences, and may waste some of the company's expenses, as the company will act or even offer some discounts to save these customers.

To sum up, in order to perform our model evaluation, in this section we will use the aforementioned error numbers that are parts of a confusion matrix, and also RMSE to assess our regression models.

To calculate them, we need to use our test data rather than training data.

As discussed earlier, MLlib has algorithms to return RMSE values, confusion matrices, and even false positive numbers directly.

In MLlib, we can use the following code to calculate RMSE:

```
val valuesAndPreds = test.map { point =>
    val prediction = new_model.predict(point.features)
    val r = (point.label, prediction)
    r
    }
val residuals = valuesAndPreds.map {case (v, p) => math.pow((v - p),
2)}
val MSE = residuals.mean();
val RMSE = math.pow(MSE, 0.5)
```

Besides this, MLlib also has some functions in the `RegressionMetrics` and `RankingMetrics` classes for us to use for RMSE calculation apart from `confusionMatrix` and `numFalseNegatives()`

The following code calculates error ratios:

```
// Evaluate model on test instances and compute test error
val testErr = testData.map { point =>
  val prediction = model.predict(point.features)
  if (point.label == prediction) 1.0 else 0.0
}.mean()
println("Test Error = " + testErr)
println("Learned Random Forest:n" + model.toDebugString)
```

The following code may be used to obtain evaluation metrics for the estimated models:

```
// Get evaluation metrics.
val metrics = new MulticlassMetrics(predictionAndLabels)
val precision = metrics.precision
println("Precision = " + precision)
```

In our case, we used multiple algorithms on test datasets to obtain RMSEs, a confusion matrix, and error numbers. The following tables shows some example results for two of the models:

Model 1: Decision Tree:

CONFUSION MATRIX Departed		Predicted Stay	
Actual	Departed (10.5%)	10%	0.5% Type I Error
	Stay (89.5%)	7% Type II Error	82.5%

Model 2: Random Forest:

CONFUSION MATRIX Churn=1		Predicted NOT	
Actual	Churn=1 (10.5%)	10%	0.5% Type I Error
	NOT (89.5%)	6% Type II Error	83.5%

For this project, as we need to evaluate tens of models, the best thing is to calculate error numbers with `numFalseNegatives()` so that we can easily sort all the models and then compare to select the good ones.

With the preceding two tables as our example, our program will look for Type I Errors first, for which the two models perform the same. In this case, the program will look at Type II Error for which the second model is better than the first one.

In practice, we should use RMSEs to evaluate models, but for this project, the client prefers using error numbers.

Results explanation

After passing our model evaluation stage, and deciding to select the estimated and evaluated model as our final model, our next task is to interpret the results for the company executives and technicians.

In terms of explaining the machine learning results, the company is particularly interested in understanding how their past interventions affected customer churns, and also how their product features and services influence customer churns.

So, we will work on results explanation, focusing on calculating the effects of several interventions or some product and service features for which MLlib does not offer good functions now. Therefore, in reality, we export the estimated models, and use other tools for results explanation and visualization. However, it is expected that the future releases of MLlib will have these easy functions included soon.

Calculating the impact of interventions

With logistic regression, the process of producing scores is relatively easy; it uses the following formulae for logistic regression:

$$\ln(\frac{P}{1-P}) = a + bX$$

$$\frac{P}{1-P} = e^{a+bX}$$

$$P = \frac{e^{a+bX}}{1+e^{a+bX}}$$

Specifically, `Prob(Yi=1) = exp(BXi)/(1+exp(BXi))` produces the default probability, with `Y=1` as default, `X` as a sum of all the features, and `B` as a vector of coefficients.

So, we will need to write some code with coefficients obtained from the previous sections to directly produce the impact assessments.

On the other hand, we can use the following code to produce the needed impact assessments for which we can load new data, calculate the predicted values, and then export them.

```
// Compute raw scores on the test set.

val predictionAndLabels = test.map { case LabeledPoint(label,
features) =>
  val prediction = model.predict(features)
  (prediction, label)
}
```

According to the model evaluation work described in the previous section, `randomForest` models perform the best. With `randomForest`, we can list out all the features by their importance, which gives another insight for interpreting the effects of features on customer churn.

Deployment

As discussed earlier, MLlib supports model export to **Predictive Model Markup Language (PMML)**. Therefore, we do export some developed models to PMML for this project. However, in practice, the users for this project are more interested in rule-based decision making to use some of our insights besides score-based decision making to prevent frauds.

As for this project, the client is interested in applying our results for the following:

- Deciding what interventions to use for a combination of car products or services with a special customer segment
- When the company needs to start some interventions depending on the customer churn score

Therefore, we need to produce a customer churn risk score for the client with which the client will start some intervention when the score is above a cutting value. At the same time, we need to use the results from our logistic regression to recommend interventions.

For more on exporting results from MLlib to PMML, please go to `https://spark.apache.org/docs/1.5.2/mllib-pmml-model-export.html`.

Scoring

Similar to the deployment used in *Chapter 5, Risk Scoring on Spark*, here we can use the churn probabilities as our scores, and employ the same methods to obtain them:

```
// Compute raw scores on the test set.
val predictionAndLabels = test.map { case LabeledPoint(label,
features) =>
  val prediction = model.predict(features)
  (prediction, label)
}
```

Intervention recommendations

From last section's work on results explanation, we also gain an understanding about which interventions as well as product or service features have bigger effects than the others. Therefore, we can make good recommendations based on them.

As for the client for this project, a good churn probability score and some recommendations satisfies them as this provides real help for them to improve customer loyalty.

Summary

In this chapter, we have refocused our efforts on machine learning libraries, especially the MLlib with which we processed data on Spark, and then built models to predict customer churns and develop scores to help the company YST to improve their customer retention.

Specifically, we first selected regression models and decision tree models as per business needs after we prepared Spark computing and loaded in pre-processed data. We then worked on feature extraction with MLlib. Then we estimated the model coefficients with distributed computing. Further, we evaluated these estimated models by using a confusion matrix and false positive ratios as well as RMSE. Then we interpreted our machine learning results. And finally, we deployed our machine learning results with our focus on scoring along with using insights to design interventions.

After this chapter, readers will have gained a better understanding of how Apache Spark, with its machine learning libraries, can be utilized to make our work easier and faster in conducting supervised machine learning, and developing customer retention systems.

7
Recommendations on Spark

In this chapter, we will switch our focus to SPSS on Apache Spark as SPSS is a widely used tool for machine learning and data science computing.

Specifically, in this chapter, with a process similar to what we used in previous chapters, we will start with discussing setting up our SPSS on a Spark system for a recommendation project, together with a full description of this real-life project. Then, we will select machine learning methods and prepare the data. With SPSS Analytic Server, we will estimate models on Spark and then evaluate models with a focus on using error ratios. Finally, we will deploy the models for our client. Here are the topics that will be covered in this chapter:

- Spark for a recommendation engine
- Methods for recommendation development
- Data treatment
- Model estimation
- Model evaluation
- Recommendation deployment

Apache Spark for a recommendation engine

In this section, we will continue to demonstrate Spark's computation speed and ease of coding for a real-life project of movie recommendation, but to be completed by SPSS on Apache Spark.

SPSS is a widely used software package for statistical analysis. SPSS originally stood for Statistical Package for Social Science, but it is also used by market researchers, health researchers, survey companies, government, education researchers, marketing organizations, data miners, and others. Long produced by SPSS Inc., it was acquired by IBM in 2009. Since then, IBM further developed it and turned it into a popular tool for data scientists and machine learning professionals. To make Spark available to SPSS users, IBM developed technologies making SPSS Spark integration easy, which will be covered in this chapter.

The use case

This project is to help movie rental company ZHO improve its movie recommendations to its customers.

The main data set contains tens of million ratings from more than 20,000 users on more than 10,000 movies.

Using the preceding rich dataset, the client hopes to improve its recommendation engine so that the recommendations are more useful to its customers. At the same time, the company wishes to take advantage of Spark so that it can update models quickly and also take advantage of Spark's parallel computing to develop recommendations for various movie categories as per special customer segmentations.

The company's analytical team learned about using Spark MLlib for movie recommendation cases and is familiar with the related literature, such as the one at `http://ampcamp.berkeley.edu/big-data-mini-course/movie-recommendation-with-mllib.html`.

However, the company's IT teams have utilized SPSS and SPSS Modeler for their analytics for many years, with a lot of analytical assets built on SPSS already, and their teams have used SPSS Modeler to organize analytical workflows for a long time; this is because they are heading toward some analytics automation, so the team prefers the approach of using SPSS on Spark.

Another reason for ZHO to adopt SPSS is to follow Cross-Industry Standard Process for Data Mining, which is an industry-proven standard process for machine learning, as shown in the following graph:

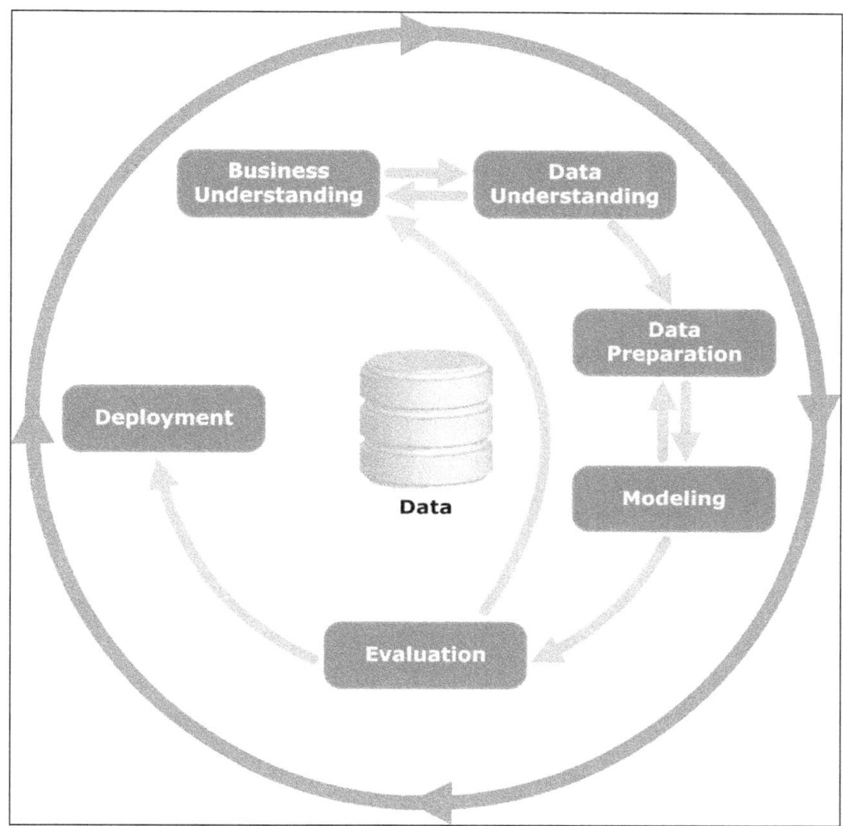

SPSS on Spark

To use SPSS on Spark, we will need to use IBM SPSS Modeler 17.1 and IBM SPSS Analytics Server 2.1, which have good integration with Apache Spark.

Also, to adopt MLlib collaborative filtering on SPSS Modeler, you need to download IBM Predictive Extensions, as described in `https://developer.ibm.com/predictiveanalytics/downloads/#tab2`.

To install IBM Predictive Extensions, perform the following steps:

1. Download the extension at **Download**
2. Close IBM SPSS Modeler. Save the `.cfe` file in the CDB directory, which is located by default on Windows in `C:\ProgramData\IBM\SPSS\Modeler\17.1\CDB` or under your IBM SPSS Modeler installation directory.

3. Restart IBM SPSS Modeler, and the node will now appear in the **Model** palette.

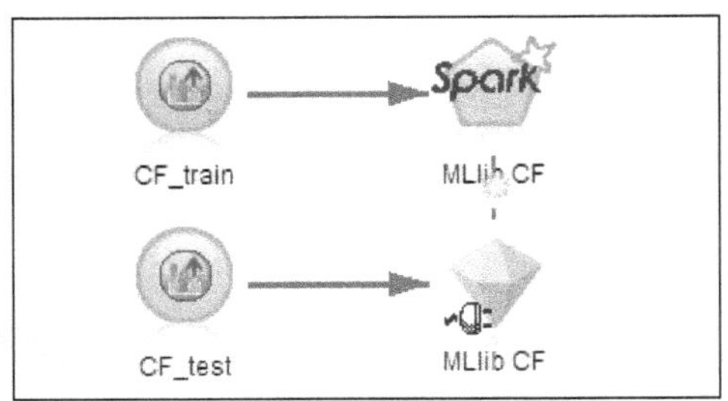

A more complete summary of SPSS on Spark can be founded at `https://developer.ibm.com/predictiveanalytics/2015/11/06/spss-algorithms-optimized-for-apache-spark-spark-algorithms-extending-spss-modeler/`.

The following is a screenshot of IBM SPSS Modeler, as you can see. SPSS users can move nodes into the central box to build modeling streams and then run them to obtain results:

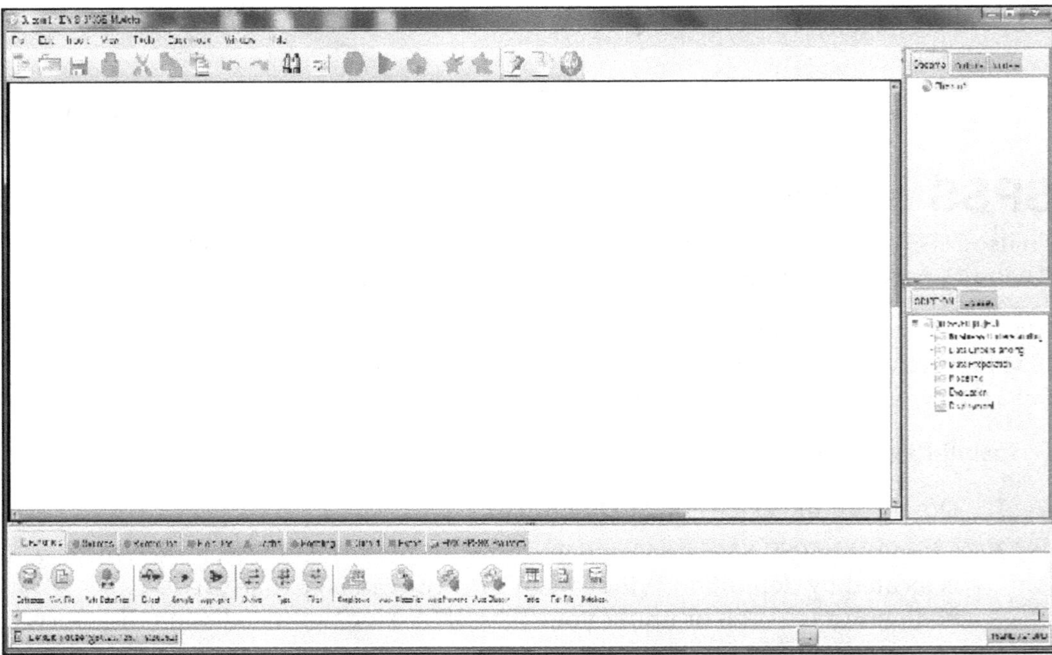

With the SPSS Spark integration as described previously, SPSS Modeler users now gain a lot more advantages. Users can now create new Modeler nodes to exploit MLlib algorithms and share them.

For example, users can also use the custom dialog builder to access Python for Spark. The following screenshot shows the usage of **Custom Dialog Builder** for **Python for Spark**:

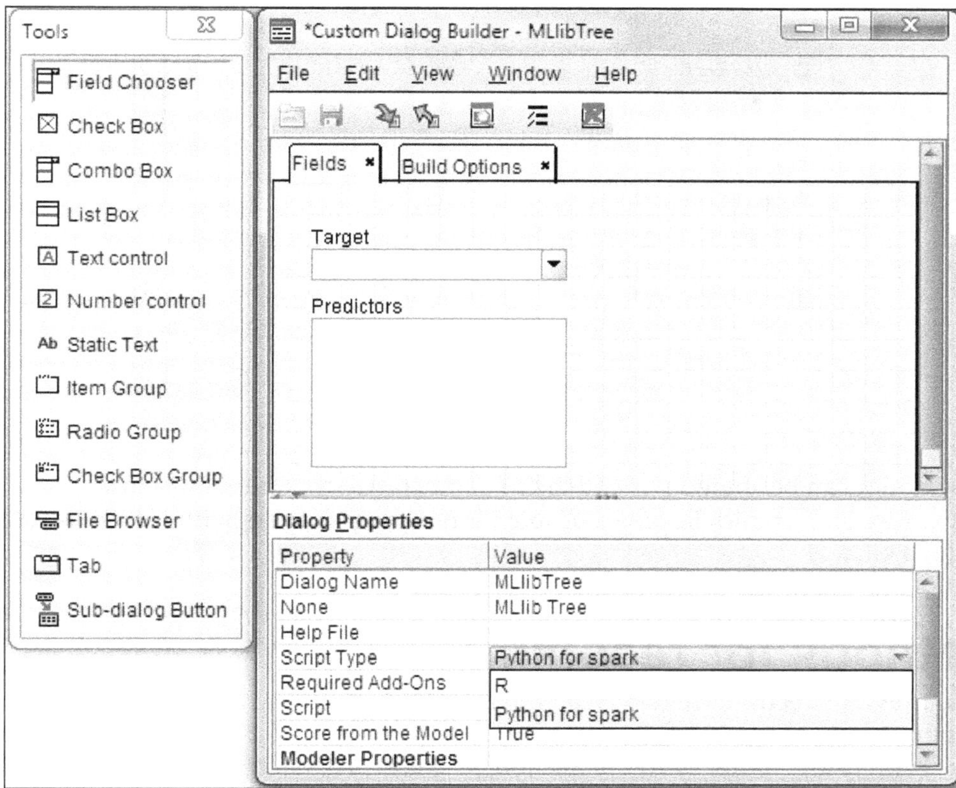

Specifically, **Custom Dialog Builder** adds Python for Spark support, which provides access to:

- Spark and its machine learning library (MLlib)
- The other common Python libraries such as Numpy, Scipy, Scikit-learn, and Pandas

After doing so, users can create new Modeler nodes (extensions) that exploit algorithms from MLlib and other PySpark processes.

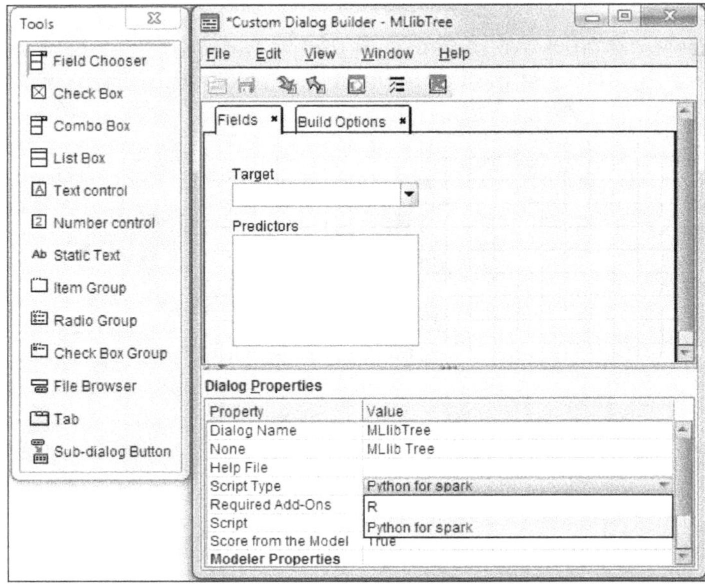

These nodes can be shared with others to democratize the access to Spark capabilities. Here, Spark becomes usable for nonprogrammers with code abstracted behind a GUI.

Methods for recommendation

In the previous section, we described the use case of building a movie recommendation engine for the company ZHO and also prepared SPSS on the Spark computing platform. In this section, as before, we need to select our analytical methods (equations) for this movie recommendation project, which again means mapping our use case to machine learning methods.

For this exercise, we will use collaborative filtering because this analytical method is well developed and tested on many recommendation projects. At the same time, analytical processes and related algorithms are also well-developed for this method, which are available in R as well as MLlib.

By following the same methodology, once we finalize our decision for analytical methods or models, we will then need to prepare the coding.

Collaborative filtering

Collaborative filtering is a method used very commonly to build recommender systems. Simply speaking, collaborative filtering is an analytical method of producing predictions (filtering) about the interests of a user with preferences of many other users (collaborating). The underlying assumption of this analytical approach is as follows:

If user A has the same opinion as user B on a movie, user A is more likely to have user B's opinion on a different movie x than to have the opinion on x of another user chosen randomly.

Specifically, the techniques of collaborative filtering here aim to fill in the missing entries of a user-movie association matrix. MLlib currently supports model-based collaborative filtering, in which users and movies are modeled by a set of latent factors that can be used to predict missing entries.

MLlib uses the **Alternating Least Squares** (**ALS**) algorithm to learn these latent factors. Its implementation in MLlib has the following parameters:

- *numBlocks* is the number of blocks used to parallelize computation (set to -1 to autoconfigure)
- *rank* is the number of latent factors in the model
- *iterations* is the number of iterations to run
- *lambda* specifies the regularization parameter in ALS
- *implicitPrefs* specifies whether to use the explicit feedback ALS variant or one adapted for an implicit feedback data
- *alpha* is a parameter applicable to the implicit feedback variant of ALS that governs the baseline confidence in preference observations

The standard approach to matrix factorization-based collaborative filtering treats the entries in the user-item matrix as explicit preferences given by the user to the item. However, it is common in many real-world use cases to only have access to implicit feedback (for example, views, clicks, purchases, likes, shares, and so on). Essentially, instead of trying to model the matrix of ratings directly, this approach treats the data as a combination of binary preferences and confidence values. The ratings are then related to the level of confidence in observed user preferences rather than the explicit ratings given to the items.

A detailed MLlib guide to collaborating filtering can be founded at `http://spark.apache.org/docs/latest/mllib-collaborative-filtering.html`.

Preparing coding

In our data, each row consists of a user, a movie, and a rating. Here, we will use the default `ALS.train()` method with the ratings assumed as explicit. The recommendations are evaluated by measuring the Mean Squared Error of rating prediction. Take a look at the following code:

```
# Build the recommendation model using Alternating Least Squares
rank = 10
numIterations = 10
model = ALS.train(ratings, rank, numIterations)

# Evaluate the model on training data
testdata = ratings.map(lambda p: (p[0], p[1]))
predictions = model.predictAll(testdata).map(lambda r: ((r[0], r[1]),
r[2]))
ratesAndPreds = ratings.map(lambda r: ((r[0], r[1]), r[2])).
join(predictions)
MSE = ratesAndPreds.map(lambda r: (r[1][0] - r[1][1])**2).mean()
print("Mean Squared Error = " + str(MSE))
```

If the rating matrix is derived from another source of information, you can use the `trainImplicit` method to get better results, as follows:

```
# Build the recommendation model using Alternating Least Squares based
on implicit ratings
model = ALS.trainImplicit(ratings, rank, numIterations, alpha=0.01)
```

Data treatment with SPSS

There are always many common data and feature issues to work with for any machine learning project, including this movie recommendation project for which we can use SPSS Modeler.

In comparison with other projects in this book, the data structure here is relatively simple; however, one special issue for the data to be used for this project is about missing values because some users do not rate some movies. To deal with this, SPSS Modeler has a few super nodes to deal with the issue. In other words, we need to develop a special SPSS Modeler Stream, which include nodes for missing value treatments. After this job, we need to separate the data into parts to train and test.

Missing data nodes on SPSS modeler

To deal with missing values and build a special data stream, we need to start with a Type Node with some Super Nodes to handle missing values to be filled with imputed values.

Specifically, you can do this from the Data Audit report, which allows you to specify options for specific fields as appropriate and then generate a Super Node that imputes values using a number of methods. This is the most flexible method and it also allows you to specify the handling for a large number of fields in a single node.

The following is a screenshot of SPSS Modeler Stream for missing data treatment:

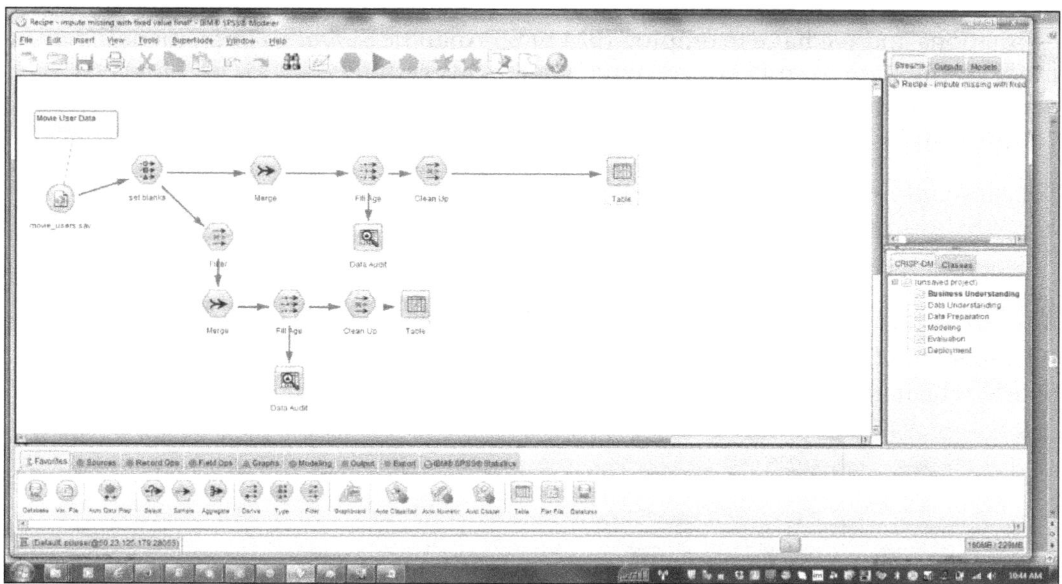

For more details about handling missing values with SPSS Modeler 17.0, refer to *Chapter 7* of the Modeler 17.0 guide at `ftp://public.dhe.ibm.com/software/analytics/spss/documentation/modeler/17.0/en/ModelerUsersGuide.pdf`.

Model estimation

For this project, our strategy for model estimation is to employ a complete SPSS Modeler stream developed from previous sections and then use SPSS Analytics Server for Spark Implementation. Our stream consists of SPSS Modeler Nodes for data treatment, as described in section, *Data treatment* and also model training Nodes with MLlib codes described in section, *Methods for recommendation development* as we prepared our SPSS Modeler to be ready to use MLlib in section, *Spark for a recommendation engine.*

As noted before, our IBM SPSS Modeler nodes created from **Custom Dialog Builder** depend on the Spark environment and will only run against IBM SPSS Analytic Server. SPSS Analytics Server is a tool to manage all the computing for model estimations and we have to employ IBM SPSS Analytic Server to implement the model estimation for this project, which makes everything easy for us. However, we also need to arrange for SPSS on the Spark system to run models for each movie category and also for each customer segment for us.

For more information about IBM SPSS Analytic Server, take a look at IBM Knowledge Center.

SPSS on Spark – the SPSS Analytics server

IBM SPSS Modeler 17.1 and Analytic Server 2.1 offer easy integration with Apache Spark, which allows us to implement the data and modeling streams built so far.

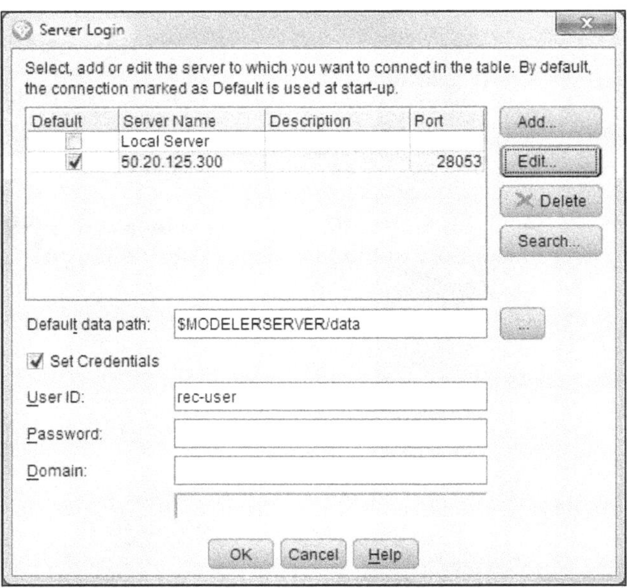

For more information about SPSS Analytic Server V 2.1, refer to its administrative guide at:

- `ftp://public.dhe.ibm.com/software/analytics/spss/documentation/analyticserver/2.1/English/IBM_SPSS_Analytic_Server_2.1_Administrators_Guide.pdf`
- `http://www-01.ibm.com/support/knowledgecenter/SSWLVY_2.1.0/analytic_server/knowledge_center/product_landing.dita`

Model evaluation

In the last section, we completed our model estimation. Now it is the time for us to evaluate these estimated models to see whether they fit our client's criteria so that we can either move to results explanation or go back to some previous stage to refine our predictive models.

As mentioned earlier for this project, using MLlib codes, our recommendations are evaluated by measuring the Mean Squared Error of rating predictions. However, most users may want to perform more evaluations with their favored measurements.

In practise, the model estimation results from SPSS Modeler may be exported for evaluation with other tools, such as R, as some users may wish. Within SPSS Modeler, we can create a Modeler Node against the test data to evaluate our results.

One of the most commonly used ways to evaluate is to measure the correlation between the predicted and actual ratings for our test dataset of movie users.

Another commonly used error index with *Memory-Based algorithms* can be calculated through the following steps:

1. For each user *a* in the test set:
    1. Split *a*'s votes into observed (I) and predict (P).
    2. Measure the average absolute deviation between predicted and actual votes in P.
    3. Predict the votes in P and form a ranked list.
    4. Score the list by its expected utility (Ra) by assuming (a) the utility of the kth item in the list is `max(va,j-d,0)`, where d is the *default vote* (b), the probability of reaching the *k* rank drops exponentially in *k*.
2. Average *Ra* over all test users.

On SPSS Modeler, once the model gets built, you can:

1. Attach a **Table** node to explore your results.
2. Use the **Analysis** node to create a coincidence matrix showing the pattern of matches between each predicted field and its target field. Run the **Analysis** node to see the results.

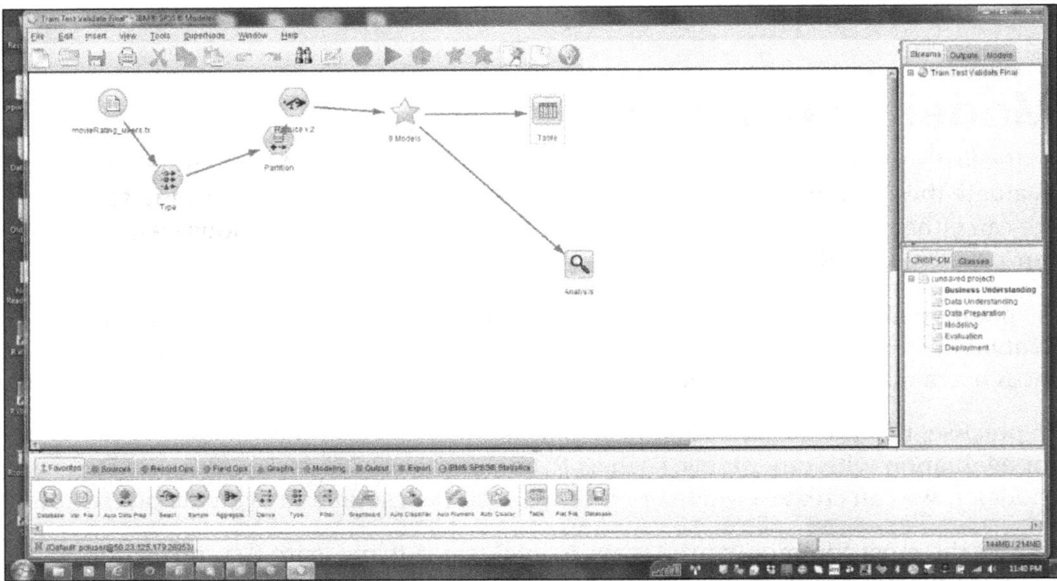

Recommendation deployment

The way of implementing the machine learning results for this project as required by the customer is to use them to make new movie recommendations when new movies come in or new users come in. One example of this typical use is to make movie recommendations for new users, which is what we will discuss in this section.

To make recommendations for a new user, we need to learn this new user's taste by asking the user to rate a few movies, for which we need to select a small set of movies that received the most ratings from users in our movie dataset.

Once we have the data of new users, then we can apply the trained model for new predictions, which can be obtained via the following code:

```
class MatrixFactorizationModel(object):
    def predictAll(self, usersProducts):
        # ...
        return RDD(self._java_model.predict(usersProductsJRDD._jrdd),
                   self._context, RatingDeserializer())
```

After we get all the predictions, we can list the top recommendations, and we will see an output that will be similar to the following:

```
Movies recommended for you:

 1: Saving Private Ryan (1998)
 2: Star Wars: Episode IV - A New Hope (1977)
 3: Braveheart (1995)
   ......
```

If we are working within IBM SPSS Modeler, we can just add a new Node with the data imported to complete the prediction.

Also, IBM® SPSS® Modeler provides a number of mechanisms to export the entire machine learning workflow to external applications so that the work completed here can be used to your advantage outside of IBM SPSS Modeler as well.

The IBM SPSS Modeler streams can also be used in conjunction with:

- IBM SPSS Modeler Advantage
- Applications that can import and export files in the PMML format

IBM SPSS Modeler can import and export PMML, making it possible to share models with other applications that support this format, such as IBM SPSS Statistics. To do so, you need to:

1. Right-click on a model nugget on the models palette. (Alternatively, double-click on a model nugget on the canvas and select the **File** menu).
2. On the menu, click on **Export PMML**.
3. In the **Export** (or **Save**) dialog box, specify a target directory and a unique name for the model.

> For more details about handling missing values with SPSS Modeler 17.0, refer to *Chapter 7* of the Modeler 17.0 guide at `ftp://public.dhe.ibm.com/software/analytics/spss/documentation/modeler/17.0/en/ModelerUsersGuide.pdf`.

To use it, we can:

- Deliver analytical results as customer interactions occur through integration with business user systems—combining the information gathered during the interaction with historical data to determine the next best action
- Deploy streams created in SPSS Modeler to be executed in an operational environment
- Incorporate features that ensure scalability, reliability, and security
- Integrate with the existing authentication systems for authentication and single sign-on capabilities
- Support application server clustering and virtualization for a more effective use of resources

- Create a unified platform that can increase the impact of your analytics investment with IBM SPSS Collaboration and Deployment Services for System z. This version combines the predictive analytics power of IBM SPSS Modeler and IBM SPSS Analytical Decision Management with the security, high availability, and reliability of the System z platform.

For more information on utilizing IBM SPSS Collaboration and Deployment Services, go to `http://www-01.ibm.com/support/docview.wss?uid=swg27043649`.

Summary

In this chapter, we switched our focus to SPSS on Spark with which we processed data on Spark and then built a model for movie recommendations; using this, we produced movie recommendations for individual users.

Specifically, we first selected collaborative filtering as our method as per business needs after we prepared Spark computing with SPSS and loaded in preprocessed data. Second, we worked on data preparation with SPSS Modeler. Third, we implemented model estimation using SPSS Analytic Server. Fourth, we evaluated these estimated models by assessing error ratios. And finally, we deployed our machine learning results with some examples of recommending movies for individual users.

After this chapter, you will have gained a full understanding of how Apache Spark can be utilized to make your work easier and faster in conducting supervised machine learning and also gained a deeper understanding of developing recommendation engines. At the same time, you will have learned how SPSS and Spark can work well together.

8
Learning Analytics on Spark

To continue our machine learning on Spark, we will further extend our application to serve the educational sector in this chapter and the government sector in next chapter. Specifically, in this chapter, we will extend our application to serve learning organizations, such as universities and training institutions, for which we will apply machine learning to improve the learning analytics for a real case of predicting student attrition. In the next chapter, we will utilize our Apache Spark machine learning to serve city governments, for which we will demonstrate our application with a real use case of predicting service requests.

By following the structures and processes established in previous chapters, in this chapter, we will first review machine learning methods and related computing for the real case of predicting student attrition, and we will then discuss how Apache Spark comes in to make them easy. At the same time, by working on this real-life student attrition prediction example, we will illustrate our machine learning process of predicting attritions step by step with Big Data in the following sections:

- Spark for attrition prediction
  - Processing Big Data fast and easy with Spark
- Methods for attrition prediction
  - Regression and decision trees
- Feature preparation
  - Feature extraction and data merging
- Model estimation
  - Distributed model estimation
- Model evaluation
  - Confusion matrix and false positive ratio

- Results explanation
    - Significant features and impacts
- Model deployment
    - Rules and scoring

Spark for attrition prediction

In this section, we will start with a real use case and then describe how to prepare Apache Spark for this attrition prediction project.

The use case

NIY University is a private university and wants to improve its student retention using predictive modeling with Big Data. According to ACT's research (refer to `http://www.act.org/research/policymakers/pdf/retain_2015.pdf`), the average retention rate for American colleges was only about 68% in 2015, and it is even lower for two-year public colleges at 54.7% and for private two-year colleges at 63.4%. That is, about 32% of students left school before graduation, and the attrition is even at greater for two-year public colleges at 45.3% and for two-year private colleges at 36.6%. As student attrition costs both colleges and students a lot, using Big Data to predict students' attrition and designing interventions to prevent them has a lot of value.

The university has a lot of information about student demographics and the past test scores of its students. At the same time, the university also collected its students' online behavior data on university websites as well as some social media data along with some data of campus social activity. The university especially collected a lot of data on their learning management systems as it uses MOODLE as the main learning platform. The goal of this project is to build a model for the university to identity students at risk, understand how some of their interventions affect students' academic performance, and then work on student retention.

To sum up, for this project, we have a target variable of student performance measured by test scores as well as a categorical variable of attrition along with a lot of data on demographics, behavior, performance, and interventions.

Through some preliminary analysis, the university understands some of their data challenges as follows:

- The data is not ready to use, especially the web log data, and some of the learning management system data needs to be developed into useful features ready for machine learning

- Students with various backgrounds major in various subjects with various career goals, for which attrition patterns are very different from each other

To deal with the challenges mentioned here, for this real project, we will utilize some feature development techniques plus some distributed computing techniques discussed in the previous chapter, for which we will specially focus our effort on organizing our computations with some notebooks and then implementing them in an integrated environment to distribute computing.

Spark computing

After learning about Spark computing in the previous seven chapters, you must be very familiar with setting up Spark computing projects by now, for which there are a few options that include the Databricks platform, IBM DataScientistWorkbench, SPSS on Spark, and Apache Spark with MLlib alone.

Either one of the preceding mentioned approaches should work well for this learning analytics project. Therefore, in the following section, we will touch on using one of the four approaches but will focus our efforts more on utilizing the Zeppelin notebook as this approach of using the Zeppelin notebook was only briefly discussed in *Chapter 5, Risk Scoring on Spark*. The Zeppelin notebook is widely utilized, and it is similar to the Jupyter notebook used in IBM DataScientistWorkbench. Both Zeppelin and Jupyter have a similar coding style, embed images, and run different programming languages.

The Jupyter notebook is more mature in terms of abilities and utility, but its Scala version is weak. With Zeppelin, it's easier to mix languages in the same notebook. You can do some SQL and Scala, then mark down to document it all together. You can also easily convert your notebook into a presentation style to maybe present it to the management or use it in dashboards.

Also, for practical use, you may take the code developed here in this chapter, put them on a different notebook, and then implement the notebook with any other approaches, as mentioned in the preceding paragraph, so that you will not be limited by our Zeppelin with Spark approach.

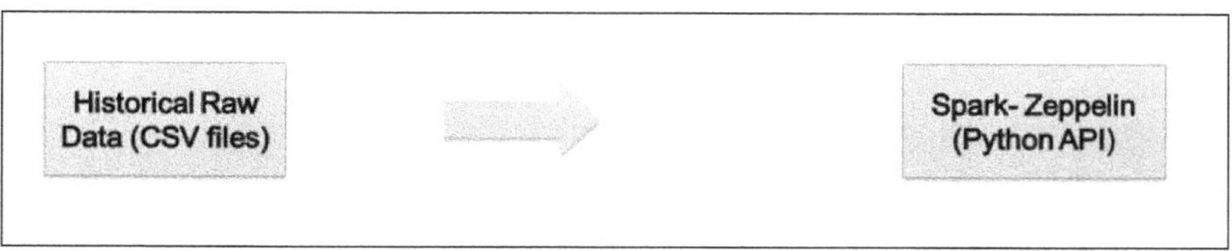

Data uploading

> For more information about setting up the Zeppelin notebook, visit `http://sparktutorials.net/setup-your-zeppelin-notebook-for-data-science-in-apache-spark` or `http://hortonworks.com/blog/introduction-to-data-science-with-apache-spark/`.

The following screenshot shows how the Zeppelin starting page looks:

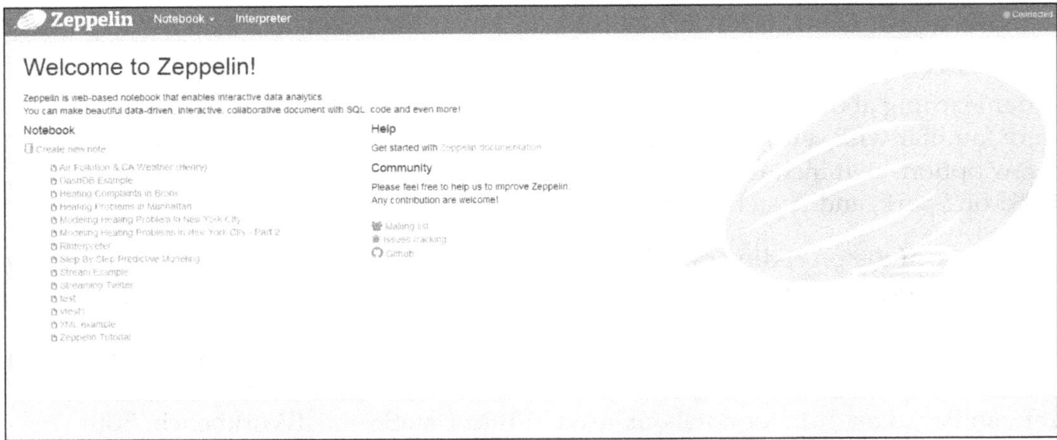

Users can click on **Create new note**, the first line under **Notebook** in the left-hand side column, to start. Then a box will open to allow users to type in the notebook's name and then click on **Create Note** to create a new notebook:

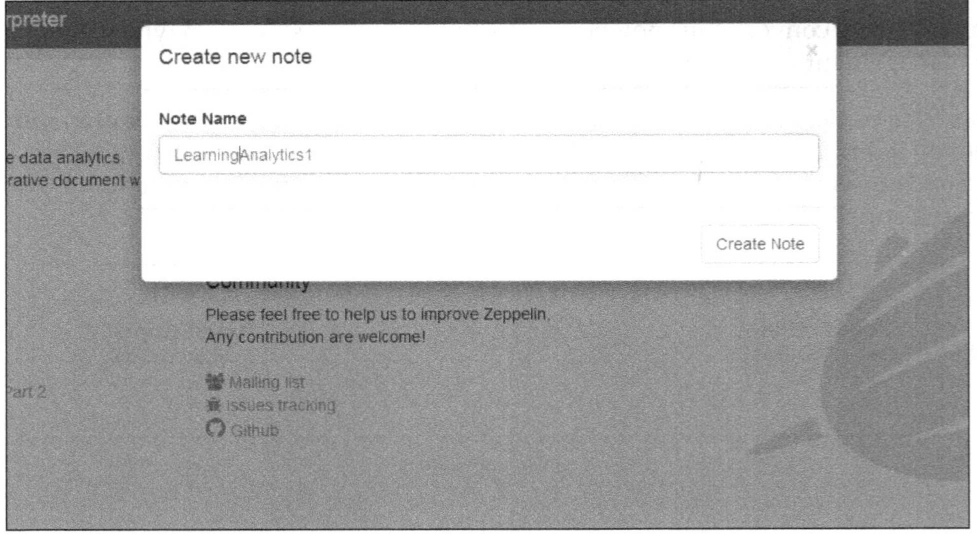

Methods of attrition prediction

In the previous section, we described our use case of predicting student attrition and also prepared our Spark computing platform. In this section, we need to perform the task of mapping our use case to machine learning methods, which is to select our analytical methods or predictive models (equations) for this attrition prediction project.

To model and predict student attrition, the most suitable models include logistic regression and decision tree, as both of them yield good results. Some researchers use neural network and SVM models, but the results are no better than logistic regression. Therefore, for this exercise, we will focus our efforts on logistic regression and decision trees, as well as random forest as an extension of decision tree, and then use model evaluation to determine which one is the best.

As always, once we finalize our decision regarding analytical methods or models, we need to prepare for coding.

Regression models

Regression was used in the previous chapters; especially in *Chapter 6, Churn Prediction on Spark*, we used logistic regression with good results. As predicting student attrition has a lot in common with the work of predicting customer churn, we will reuse a lot of the work presented in *Chapter 6, Churn Prediction on Spark*.

About regression

There are two kinds of regression modeling that are suitable for attrition prediction, similar to churn prediction. One is linear regression, and another is logistic regression. For this project, logistic regression is more suitable as we have a target variable about whether the student left; we even have the target variable of student performance. Logistic regression is an alternative method to modeling discrete choice using maximum likelihood estimation based on the logistic function as opposed to ordinary least squares (linear probability models). A major advantage of logistic regression for dichotomous dependent variables is that it overcomes the inherent heteroskedasticity (that is, nonconstant variance) associated with linear probability models, which is often a special concern for our student data.

Preparing for coding

As before, in MLlib, for logistic regression, we will use the following:

```
val model = new LogisticRegressionWithSGD()
.setNumClasses(2)
```

Decision trees

As discussed briefly in *Chapter 6, Churn Prediction on Spark,* in comparison to regression, decision tree is easy to use, robust with missing data, and easy to interpret. Here, our reason to use decision tree is mainly due to its robustness with missing data, as missing data is a big issue with this real use case. Also, decision tree models produce good charts that clearly express the impact of various features on leading a student to leave, so it is very useful for result interpretation and intervention design.

Random forest comes from a set of trees, often hundreds of trees, with good functions to produce scores and rank independent variables by their impact on the target variable. For these two reasons, we will also use random forest for this case.

Preparing for coding

As before, within MLlib, we can use the following code:

```
val numClasses = 2
val categoricalFeaturesInfo = Map[Int, Int]()
val impurity = "gini"
val maxDepth = 6
val maxBins = 32
val model = DecisionTree.trainClassifier(trainingData, numClasses,
  categoricalFeaturesInfo, impurity, maxDepth, maxBins)
```

We need to expand our work to random forest, so with MLlib, we will use the following code for this:

```
// To train a RandomForest model.
val treeStrategy = Strategy.defaultStrategy("Classification")
val numTrees = 300
val featureSubsetStrategy = "auto" // Let the algorithm choose.
val model = RandomForest.trainClassifier(trainingData,
  treeStrategy, numTrees, featureSubsetStrategy, seed = 12345)
```

Feature preparation

In the *Feature extraction* section of *Chapter 2, Data Preparation for Spark ML*, we reviewed a few methods for feature extraction as well as their implementation on Apache Spark. All the techniques discussed there can be applied to our datasets here, especially the ones of utilizing time series to create new features.

As mentioned earlier, for this project, we have a target categorical variable of student attrition and a lot of data on demographics, behavior, performance, as well as interventions. The demographic data is almost ready to be used but needs to be merged with the following table for a partial list of the features:

FEATURE NAME	Description
`ACT`	These are the average ACT scores
`AGE`	This is the age
`UNEMPLOYMENT`	This is the student's county unemployment rate
`FIRST_GENERATION`	This is a first-generation student indicator using the "Y/N" options
`HS_GPA`	This is the high school GPA
`PUBLIC_CODE`	This is an indicator of the type of high school
`REP_RACE`	This is the student's reported race/ethnicity
`DISTANCE`	This is the distance of the student's home from campus
`SEX`	This is the student's gender
`STARBUCKS`	This is the number of Starbucks located in the student's county

Many log files about students' web behavior are also available for this project, for which we will use techniques similar to what discussed in the *Feature preparation* section of *Chapter 4, Fraud Detection on Spark*.

For this project, our focus on feature preparation is to extract more features from the MOODLE learning management system as this is the main and unique data source for learning analytics, which cover many rich characteristics of the students' learning. They often include students' clicks, timing, and total hours spent on each learning activity along with statistics on access to reading materials, syllabus, assignments, submission timing, and so on.

All the methods and procedures discussed here for Moodle can also be applied to other learning management systems, such as Sakai and Blackboard. However, for data about student behavior, especially for these behavior characteristics that need to be measured with the data points from Moodle, a lot of work is needed to get them organized, make them meaningful, and then merge them into the main dataset; all this will covered in this chapter.

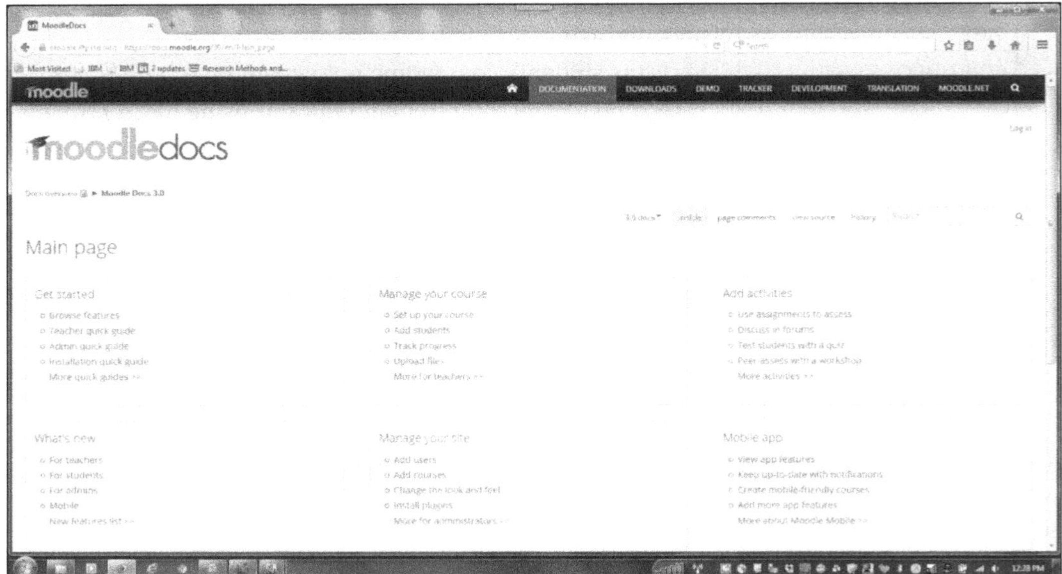

Feature development

In the previous chapters, we used SparkSQL, MLlib, and R for feature extraction. Here, for this project, we can use all of them with SparkSQL and MLlib as the most effective tools.

For your convenience, a complete guide to MLlib feature extraction can be found at `http://spark.apache.org/docs/latest/mllib-feature-extraction.html`.

For this project, extracting useful features from web log files adds a lot of value. However, the main challenge actually stays with organizing existing datasets and then developing new features from them. Especially for data exported from Moodle, some of it is easily organized, such as that of student performance and classroom participation. However, even with performance features, if we introduce the time dimension into our feature development, the performance changes over time to become something useful. Along with this logic, many new features can be developed.

Besides the preceding features, there are also some important time-related items, such as the specific time when the students submitted their homework, whether it was the middle of the night or afternoon time or days or hours before the due time, for which some categorical features can be created. Time intervals between periods of participation are also of significance to form some new features.

Some social network analysis tools are available to extract features from the learning data to measure student interaction with teachers as well as with classmates to form new features.

With all the preceding points taken into consideration, for this use case, we can develop more than 200 features that are of potentially high value to our modeling.

Feature selection

Hundreds of features in hand to use will enable us to obtain good prediction models. However, feature selection is definitely needed, as discussed in *Chapter 3, A Holistic View on Spark*, partially for a good explanation and also to avoid overfitting.

For feature selection, we will adopt a good strategy that we tested in *Chapter 3, A Holistic View on Spark*, which is to take three steps to complete our feature selection. First, we will perform **principal components analysis** (**PCA**). Second, we will use our subject knowledge to aid the grouping of features. Then, finally, we will apply machine learning feature selection to filter out redundant or irrelevant features.

Principal components analysis

If you are using MLlib for PCA, visit `http://spark.apache.org/docs/latest/mllib-dimensionality-reduction.html#principal-component-analysis-pca`. This link has a few example codes that users may adopt and modify to run PCA on Spark. For more information on MLlib, visit `https://spark.apache.org/docs/1.2.1/mllib-dimensionality-reduction.html`.

To use R, there are at least five functions to perform PCA, which are as follows:

- `prcomp() (stats)`
- `princomp() (stats)`
- `PCA() (FactoMineR)`
- `dudi.pca() (ade4)`
- `acp() (amap)`

The `prcomp` and `princomp` functions from the basic package stats are commonly used, for which we also have good functions for the result summary and plots. Therefore, we will use these two functions.

Subject knowledge aid

As is always the case, if some subject knowledge can be used, feature reduction results can be improved greatly.

For our example, some concepts used by previous student attrition research are good to start with. They include the following:

- Academic performance
- Financial status
- Emotional encouragement from personal social networks
- Emotional encouragement in school
- Personal adjustment
- Study patterns

As an exercise, we will group all the developed features into six groups according to whether they are indicators measuring one of the preceding six concepts. Then, we will perform PCA six times, one for each data category. For example, for academic performance, we need to perform PCA on 53 features or variables to identify factors or dimensions that can fully represent the information we have about academic performance.

At the end of this PCA exercise, we obtained two to four features for each category, as summarized in the following table:

Category	Number of Factors	Factor Names
Academic Performance	4	AF1, AF2, AF3, AF4
Financial Status	2	F1, F2
Emotional Encouragement 1	2	EE1_1, EE!_2

Category	Number of Factors	Factor Names
Emotional Encouragement 2	2	EE2_1, EE2_2
Personal Adjustment	3	PA1, PA2, PA3
Study Patterns	3	SP1, SP2, SP3
Total	16	

ML feature selection

In MLlib, we can use the `ChiSqSelector` algorithm as follows:

```
// Create ChiSqSelector that will select top 25 of 240 features
val selector = new ChiSqSelector(25)
// Create ChiSqSelector model (selecting features)
val transformer = selector.fit(TrainingData)
```

In R, we can use some R packages to make the computation easy. Among the available packages, CARET is one of the commonly used packages.

Model estimation

Once the feature sets get finalized, in our last section, what follows is the estimating of parameters of the selected models, for which we can use MLlib on the Zeppelin notebook.

Similar to what we did before, for the best modeling, we need to arrange distributed computing, especially for this case, with various student segments for various study subjects. For this distributed computing part, readers may refer to previous chapters as we will not repeat them here.

Spark implementation with the Zeppelin notebook

With MLlib for SCALA code for random forest, we will use the following code:

```
// Train a RandomForest model.
val treeStrategy = Strategy.defaultStrategy("Classification")
val numTrees = 300
val featureSubsetStrategy = "auto" // Let the algorithm choose.
val model = RandomForest.trainClassifier(trainingData,
  treeStrategy, numTrees, featureSubsetStrategy, seed = 12345)
```

For decision tree, we will execute the following code:

```
val model = DecisionTree.trainClassifier(trainingData, numClasses,
  categoricalFeaturesInfo, impurity, maxDepth, maxBins)
```

In MLlib, for linear regression, we will run the following code:

```
val numIterations = 90
val model = LinearRegressionWithSGD.train(TrainingData,
numIterations)
```

For logistic regression, we will use the following code:

```
val model = new LogisticRegressionWithSGD()
.setNumClasses(2)
```

To get all them implemented, we need to first input all the preceding codes into our Zeppelin notebook and then complete their computing over there.

In other words, we need to input the codes described before into the Zeppelin notebook, as follows:

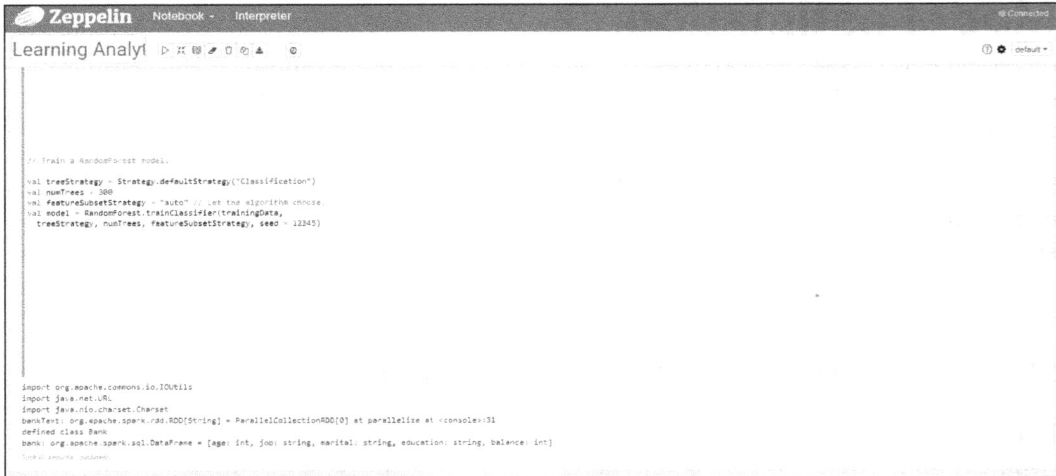

Then we can press *Shift* + *Enter* to run these commands and then obtain results similar to the following screenshot:

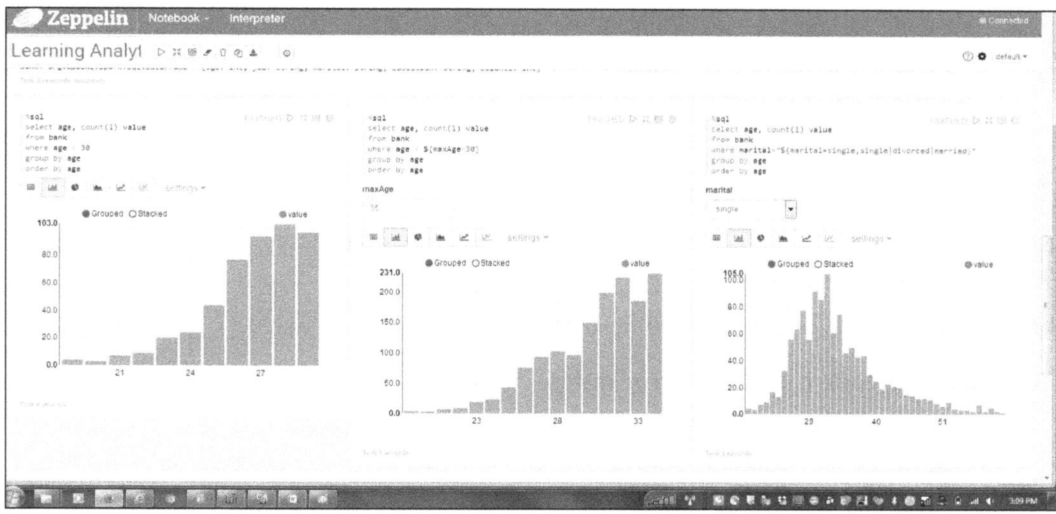

Model evaluation

In the previous section, we completed our model estimation. Now it is the time for us to evaluate these estimated models to check whether they fit our client's criteria so that we can either move to the explanation of results or go back to some previous stages to refine our predictive models.

To perform our model evaluation, in this section, we will use a confusion matrix and error ratio numbers. To calculate them, we need to use our test data rather than training data.

Here are the two common error types in student attrition prediction:

- **False negative (Type I error)**: This involves failing to identify a student who has a high propensity to leave.

  From a practical perspective, this is the least desirable error as the student is very likely to leave and the university lost its chance to act to keep the students, thus adversely affecting its income and also the students' future career.

- **False positive (Type II error)**: This involves classifying a good, satisfied student as one likely to leave.

  From a practical perspective, this may be acceptable as it does not impact the income or students' future career, but it will create confusion and may waste some of the university's resources as the university will act or even offer some special assistance to save these students.

A quick evaluation

As discussed before, MLlib has algorithms to return a confusion matrix and even false positive numbers.

MLlib has `confusionMatrix` and `numFalseNegatives()` to use.

The following code calculates error ratios:

```
// Evaluate model on test instances and compute test error
val testErr = testData.map { point =>
  val prediction = model.predict(point.features)
  if (point.label == prediction) 1.0 else 0.0
}.mean()
println("Test Error = " + testErr)
println("Learned Random Forest:n" + model.toDebugString)
```

The following code may be used to obtain evaluation metrics for the estimated models:

```
// Get evaluation metrics.
val metrics = new MulticlassMetrics(predictionAndLabels)
val precision = metrics.precision
println("Precision = " + precision)
```

To visualize the performance of our classifiers, we can use the ROCR R package. For more info about using ROCR, readers may visit `https://rocr.bioinf.mpi-sb.mpg.de/`.

The confusion matrix and error ratios

Any predictive algorithm going into production will have to be the one with the least Type I error.

In our case, we used multiple algorithms on a `Test` dataset to predict student attrition. Shown in the following screenshot are the results from the top two performing algorithms:

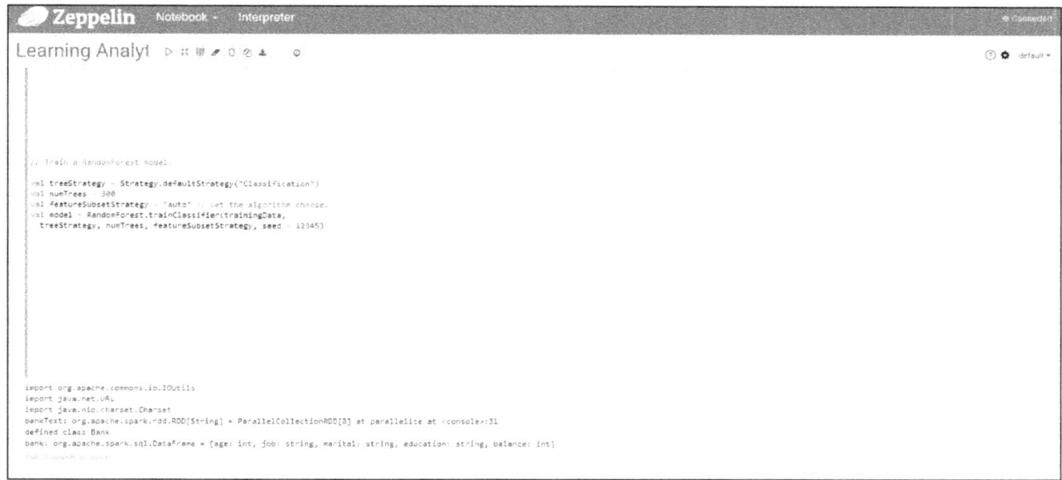

To implement the model evaluation, we need to adopt the same method used in the *Model estimation* section; that is, we need to input all the codes into our Zeppelin notebook and then run the model evaluation part of the code to obtain tables similar to the following one:

		Predicted	
		0	1-attrition
Real	0	4527	733
	1-attrition	57	342

399 students at risk

85.34 % accuracy (4257+342)/(4257+342+57+733)

With the preceding evaluation, we can compare models and select the acceptable ones.

Results explanation

After we have passed our model evaluation stage and decided to select the estimated and evaluated model as our final model, our next task is to interpret results to the university leaders and technicians.

In terms of explaining the machine learning results, the university is particularly interested in, firstly, understanding how their designed interventions affect student attrition, and, secondly, among the common reasons of finances, academic performance, social/emotional encouragement, and personal adjustment, which has the biggest impact.

We will work on results explanation with our focus on big influencing variables in the following sections.

Calculating the impact of interventions

The following summarizes some of the result samples briefly, for which we can use some functions from `randomForest` and decision tree to produce.

With Spark 1.5, you can use the following code to obtain a vector of feature importance:

```
val importances: Vector = model.featureImportances
```

With the `randomForest` package in R, a simple code of `estimatedModel$importance` will return a ranking of variables by their importance in determining attrition.

The table for impact assessment for interventions is as follows:

Feature	Impacts
Teacher interaction	1
Financial aid	2
Study grouping	3
...	

Here, to obtain variable importance through the `randomForest` functions, we need a full model estimated with all the data complete. So, it does not really solve our problems.

What learning organizations really need is to actually use a partial set of available features to estimate a model with limited variables and then assess how good this partial model is, which is to say how good the attrition catching and false positive ratios are. To complete this task, Apache Spark's advantage of fast computing is utilized, which helps us get results.

Calculating the impact of main causes

As we briefly discussed in the *Feature preparation* section, the main predictors selected can be summarized with the following table:

Category	Number of factors	Factor names
Academic performance	4	AF1, AF2, AF3, AF4
Financial status	2	F1, F2
Emotional encouragement 1	2	EE1_1, EE!_2
Emotional encouragement 2	2	EE2_1, EE2_2
Personal adjustment	3	PA1, PA2, PA3
Study patterns	3	SP1, SP2, SP3
Total	16	

The university leaders are interested in learning how these features cause attrition, for which we can perform what was described in the previous section. That is, we need to apply the code used to obtain feature importance to the preceding features to rank their importance.

As for logistic regression results, we can also apply the $Prob(Yi=1) = exp(BXi)/(1+exp(BXi))$ equation to obtain the impact of each feature at a certain point.

Deployment

As discussed before, MLlib supports model export to **Predictive Model Markup Language** (**PMML**). Therefore, we export some developed models to PMML for this project as some other departments of the university are interested in our analytical results and use other systems such as SPSS.

However, for practical purposes, the users of this project are more interested in rule-based decision making to use some of our insights and also in score-based decision making to reduce student attrition.

Specifically, as for this project, the client is interested in applying our results to, firstly, decide which interventions to use for a combination of course adjustments or counseling services with a special student segment, and, secondly, when the university needs to start some interventions as per the student attrition score.

Therefore, we need to turn some of our results into rules and also produce a student attrition risk score for this university.

Rules

All the algorithms either in MLlib or R can produce trees directly so that users may use these trees to derive rules directly.

Also, as discussed before, for R results, there are several tools to help extract rules from developed predictive models.

For the decision tree model developed, we should use the `rpart.utils` R package, which can extract rules and export them in various formats, such as RODBC.

The `rpart.rules.table(model1)` returns an unpivoted table of variable values (factor levels) associated with each branch, that is, sub rules to be used.

However, for this project, partially due to the issue of data incompleteness, it is better for us to use some insight into deriving rules directly. That is, we should use the insight discussed in last section. For example, we can do the following:

- If academic performance is decreasing dramatically, we can contact the teacher
- If the student's social network score is below a certain level and academic performance is also changing dramatically (even now at low scores), some actions are needed

From an analytical perspective, one of the main issues here is to minimize the false positive while catching enough attritions.

The university had a high false positive ratio from using their past rules, and as a result of this, too many alerts were sent out, adding a big burden for manual inspection. Therefore, by taking advantage of Spark's fast computing, we carefully produced rules, and for each rule, we supplied false positive ratios that helped the university use these rules as well as provide useful feedback.

Scoring

From coefficients of our predictive models, we can derive a probability score for attrition, but this takes some work.

Using the following MLlib code, we can obtain probability scores quickly:

```
// Compute raw scores on the test set.
val predictionAndLabels = test.map { case LabeledPoint(label,
  features) =>
  val prediction = model.predict(features)
  (prediction, label)
}
```

The preceding code returns labels, but for binary classification, you can use the `LogisticRegressionModel.clearThreshold` method. After it is called, `predict` will return raw scores:

$$f(z) = \frac{1}{1 + e^{-z}}$$

Unlike the labels mentioned before, these are in the [0, 1] range and can be interpreted as probabilities.

Using R, `model$predicted` will return the case class as `ATTRITION` or `NOT`. However, `prob=predict(model,x,type="prob")` will produce a probability value, which can be used directly as a score.

However, in order to use the score, we need to select a cutting out score. For example, we can choose to take action when the attrition probability score is over 80.

Different score cutting points will produce different false positive ratios and also the ratios of catching possible attrition, for which the users need to make a decision about how to balance the results.

By taking advantage of Spark's fast computing, results can be calculated fast, which allows the university to select a cutting point instantly and make changes whenever needed.

Another way to deal with this issue is to use the `OptimalCutpoints` R package.

Summary

In this chapter, we extended our machine learning on Spark to serve learning analytics, for which we completed a step-by-step process of processing Big Data obtained from learning management systems and other sources for a rapid development of student attrition prediction models on Apache Spark. With the machine learning results obtained, we developed rules and scores to be used by NIY University for interventions to reduce student attrition.

Specifically, we first selected a supervised machine learning approach with a focus on logistic regression and decision trees as per the special needs of this university and the nature of the project, and after this, we prepared Spark computing and loaded in the preprocessed data. Secondly, we worked on feature development and selection. Thirdly, we estimated model coefficients with the Zeppeline notebook on Spark. Next, we evaluated these estimated models using a confusion matrix and error ratios. Then, we interpreted our machine learning results to the university leaders and technicians. Finally, we deployed our machine learning results with some special effort on scoring students as per attrition probabilities, but we also used insight to develop rules.

This process is similar to the process used in the previous chapters for commercial applications, such as churn modeling. However, in working for educational applications, we made some special considerations for feature development and result explanation.

After reading this chapter, you should have gained a complete understanding of how Apache Spark can be utilized to make our work easier and faster in conducting supervised machine learning to serve educational institutions and, specially, develop student attrition prediction models. At the same time, you gained a good understanding of how fast computing can be turned into analytical capabilities for educational organizations.

9
City Analytics on Spark

Following the strategy adopted in *Chapter 8, Learning Analytics on Spark*, in this chapter, we will further extend our Spark machine learning application to smart city analytics, for which we will apply machine learning to open data for city analytics. In other words, we will extend the benefit of machine learning on Spark to serving city governments.

Specifically in this chapter, we will first review machine learning methods and related computing for a service request forecasting project and will then discuss how Apache Spark comes in to make them easy. At the same time, with this real-life service forecasting example, we will illustrate step by step our machine learning process of predicting service requests with Big Data.

Here, we will use the service forecasting project for the purpose of illustrating our technologies and processes. That is, what is described in this chapter is not limited to service request forecasting but can be easily applied to other city analytics projects, such as water usage analytics. Actually, they can be applied to various kinds of machine learning on various kinds of open data, including open data provided by universities and federal agencies, such as that from the well-known LIGO project for gravitational wave detection and studies (for more information on this, refer to `http://www.ligo.org/` and `http://www.researchmethods.org/AlexLiu_CalTech_Jan21.pdf`).

In this chapter, we will cover the following topics:

- Spark for service forecasting
    - Easy computing with Spark
- Methods of service forecasting
    - Regression and time series

- Data and feature preparation
  - Data merging and feature selection
- Model estimation
  - Model estimation
- Model evaluation
  - RMSE
- Results explanation
  - Significant features and trends
- Model deployment
  - Rules and scoring

Spark for service forecasting

In this section, we will describe a real use case of predicting service requests in detail and then describe how to prepare Apache Spark computing for this real-life project.

The use case

In the United States, and worldwide, more and more cities have made their collected data open to the public. As a result, city governments and many other organizations have performed machine learning on these open datasets with good insight into improving decision making and a lot of positive impact, for example, in New York and Chicago. Using large amount of open data is becoming a trend now. For example, using Big Data to measure cities is becoming a research trend, as we can note from `http://files.meetup.com/11744342/CITY_RANKING_Oct7.pdf`.

Using data analytics for cities has a wide impact as more than half of us live in urban centers now, and the percentage is still increasing. Therefore, what you will learn in this chapter will enable data scientists to create a huge positive impact.

Among all the open city datasets, 311 datasets are about service requests from citizens to the city government and are all publicly available, as listed on the following websites for the cities of New York, Los Angeles, Houston, and San Francisco:

- `https://nycopendata.socrata.com/Social-Services/311-Service-Requests-from-2010-to-Present/erm2-nwe9`
- `https://data.lacity.org/dataset/Clean-311/6y5f-2byv`

- `http://data.ohouston.org/dataset/city-of-houston-311-service-requests`
- `https://data.sfgov.org/City-Infrastructure/Case-Data-from-San-Francisco-311-SF311-/vw6y-z8j6`

These datasets are so rich in detail that many cities are interested in using them to forecast future requests and measure effectiveness. One of our collaborators is tasked to use this data in combination with others to predict service needs for several cities, including Los Angeles and Houston, so that these cities can better allocate their resources accordingly.

Through some preliminary data analysis, the research group understands some of their data challenges as the following:

- Data quality is not as good as expected; for example, there are a lot of missing cases
- Data accuracy is another issue to deal with
- Data exists in different silos that need to be merged together

To deal with the challenges mentioned earlier, for this real project, we utilized some techniques presented in *Chapter 2*, *Data Preparation for Spark ML*, to merge all the datasets together and also our Apache Spark technology to treat missing cases to create clean datasets for each city.

As a summary, the following table gives a brief description of these preprocessed datasets:

	Time Period	**# Requests**	**% Closed**	**Top Agent**
NYC	Sep 2012 ~ Jan 2014	2,138,736	75.3%	HPD
SFO	July 2008 ~ Jan 2014	910,573	95.3%	DPW
Los Angeles	Jan 2011 ~ June 30 2014	2,713,630	?	LADBS
Houston	2012	296,019	98.2%	PWE

As we can note from the preceding table, we only used a part of the available open data, mainly for the reason of data completeness. In other words, we only used data from the period when we have enough datasets to merge and also the data quality for service requests is reasonable as per our initial preprocessing data.

Spark computing

To set up Apache Spark for this project of service request forecasting, we will adopt a strategy similar to that we used in *Chapter 8, Learning Analytics on Spark*, for the purpose of enforcing our learning. In other words, for the Apache Spark computing part, readers may use this chapter to review what was learned in *Chapter 8, Learning Analytics on Spark*, as well as what was learned in chapters 1 through 7.

As discussed in the Spark computing section of *Chapter 8, Learning Analytics on Spark*, you may choose one of the following approaches for our kind of projects:

- Spark on Databrick's platform
- Spark on IBM DataScientistWorkbench
- SPSS on Spark
- Apache Spark with MLlib alone

You learned all the details of utilizing them in the previous chapters—that is, from *Chapter 3, A Holistic View on Spark* to *Chapter 7, Recommendations on Spark*.

Either one of the four approaches mentioned before should work very well for this city analytics project, as described. Specifically, you may take the codes as developed in this chapter, put them into a separate notebook, and then implement the notebook with an approach mentioned previously.

With the strategy described here, similar to what we did in *Chapter 8, Learning Analytics on Spark*, we will touch on using one of the four approaches in the following section; however, will spend more effort on utilizing a Zeppelin notebook for users to learn more about the Zeppelin approach and to review the technologies described in *Chapter 8, Learning Analytics on Spark*.

To work with a Zeppelin notework approach, similarly to *Chapter 8, Learning Analytics on Spark*, we will start with the following page:

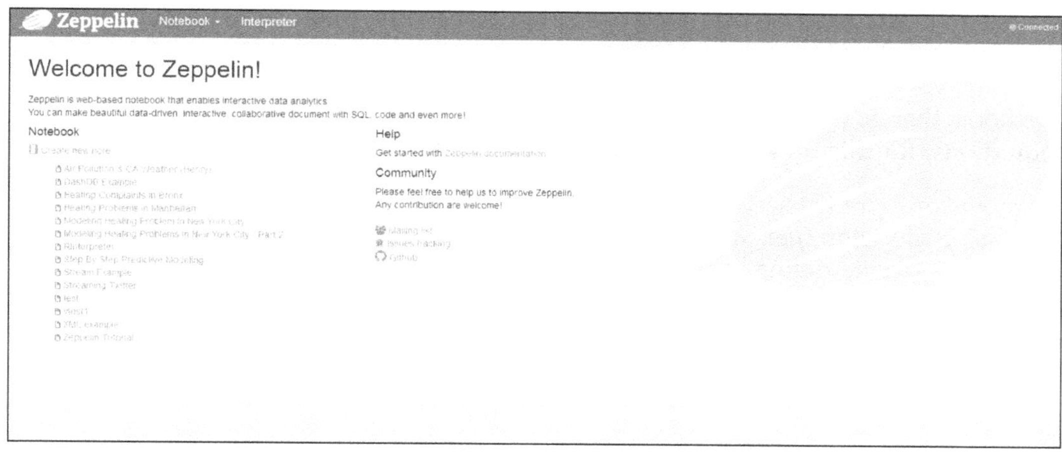

Users can click on **Create new note**, which is the first line under **Notebook** on the left-hand side column, to start organizing code into the notebook.

Then, a box will open to allow users to type in the notebook's name, and after typing in the name, users can click on **Create Note** to create a new notebook:

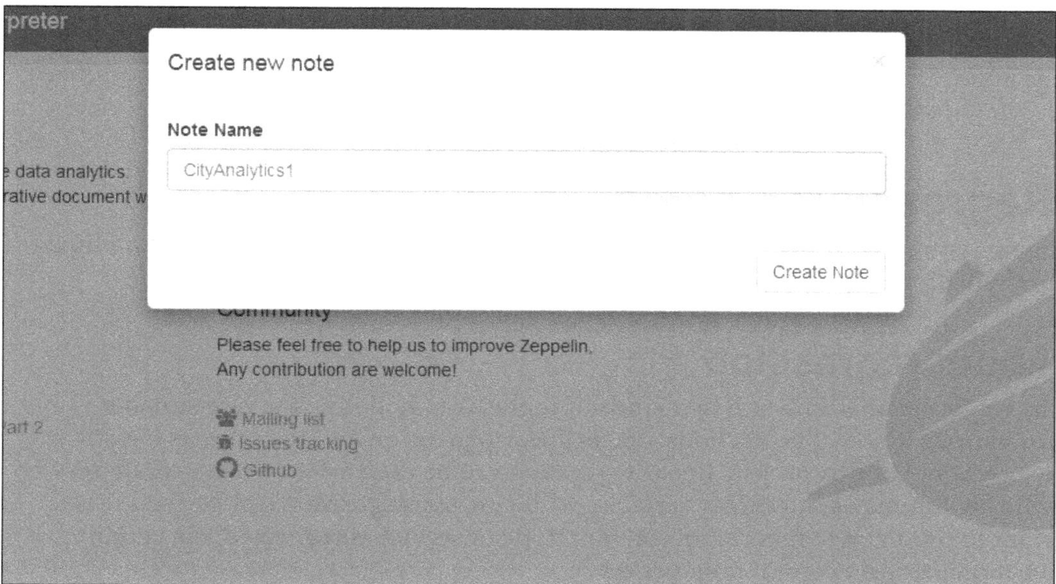

Methods of service forecasting

In the previous section, we described our use case of using open data to forecast service requests and also prepared our Spark computing platform with Zeppelin notebooks as the focus. In our following 4E framework, as the next step in machine learning, we need to complete the task of mapping our use case to machine learning methods; that is, we need to select our analytical methods or predictive models (equations) for this project of predicting service requests with Big Data on Spark.

To model and predict service requests, there are many suitable models, including regression, decision tree, and time series. For this exercise, we will use both regression and time series modeling as time is a significant part of our data, and then, we will use evaluation to determine which one, or whether a combination, of them is the best. However, as regression is already utilized many times in the previous chapters and time series modeling may still be new to some of our readers, we will spend more time on describing and discussing the time series modeling methods.

For our clients of this project—some branches of the city government and civic organizations—the only concerns are whether the service request number will exceed certain levels because problems will follow if so. For this problem, decision tree and random forest are the right methods. However, as an exercise for learning, our focus here will still be on regression and time series modeling because decision tree and random forest are covered many times in our previous chapters. From this method selection discussion, you will understand that we often need to employ a few modeling methods in order to meet clients' needs as well as to achieve best results.

As always, once we finalize our decision for analytical methods or models, we need to prepare the related dependent variable and also prepare for coding.

Regression models

So far, you must know that regression is among the most commonly used methods of prediction and has been utilized for various projects so far.

About regression

As we discussed, there are two kinds of regression modeling that are suitable for various kinds of predictions: one is linear regression and the other is logistic regression. For this project, linear regression can be used when we take daily service request volume as our target variable, while logistic regression can be used if we want to predict whether or not a certain type of service is requested at a certain location during a certain time period.

Preparing for coding

For your convenience in MLlib, we have the following code to be used for linear regression:

```
val numIterations = 90
val model = LinearRegressionWithSGD.train(TrainingData, numIterations)
```

For logistic regression, we can use the following code:

```
val model = new LogisticRegressionWithSGD()
  .setNumClasses(2)
```

Time series modeling

Our data for this project is of a time series nature. Generally speaking, a time series is a sequence of data points that consists of the following:

- Successive measurements made over a time interval
- A continuous time interval

The distance in this time interval between any two consecutive data point is the same. For example, we have parking service requests made on a daily basis so that we have data with the following pattern:

Day 1	Day 2	Day 3	Day 4	Day 5	Day 6	Day 7	Day 8	……
20 requests	31 requests	19 requests	35 requests	22 requests	39 requests	13 requests	28 requests	……

About time series

There are many models specially created to model time series data, such as the ARIMA model, for which algorithms are readily available in R or SPSS.

There are also many introductory materials available to discuss using R to complete time series modeling; some of them are at `http://www.stats.uwo.ca/faculty/aim/tsar/tsar.pdf` or `http://www.statoek.wiso.uni-goettingen.de/veranstaltungen/zeitreihen/sommer03/ts_r_intro.pdf`.

For our time series data of daily service requests, such as SFO data from 2008 to 2014, we plan to use two models: the **autoregressive moving average** (**ARMA**) and **autoregressive integrated moving average** (**ARIMA**) models. Here, the ARMA model provides a parsimonious description of a (weekly) stationary stochastic process in terms of two polynomials: one for the autoregression and the second for the moving average. The ARIMA model is a generalization of the ARMA model.

Both the ARMA and ARIMA models can provide a good forecast of future service requests. Whether the ARMA or ARIMA model is better will depend on our model evaluation using RMSE.

Preparing for coding

R has many packages for time series modeling, such as the timeSeries or ts package.

When estimating the ARIMA model, we need to use the arima function with a code such as the following:

```
fit1<-arima(data1,order=c(1,0,1))
```

Here, we used `c(1,0,1)` to specify orders for the ARIMA model.

As for MLlib, the algorithms for time series modeling are still in development. However, some libraries are being developed to facilitate time series modeling on Spark, such as the `spark-ts` library developed by Cloudera.

This library allows users to preprocess data and then build some simple models as well as evaluate them. The code can be developed in Scala. However, as it is still in development, it is far behind what R can provide.

For an example of using the `spark-ts` library for time series data modeling, go to `http://blog.cloudera.com/blog/2015/12/spark-ts-a-new-library-for-analyzing-time-series-data-with-apache-spark/`.

Data and feature preparation

In the *Feature extraction* section of *Chapter 2, Data Preparation for Spark ML*, we reviewed a few methods of feature extraction and discussed their implementation in Apache Spark. All the techniques discussed there can be applied to our data here.

Besides feature development, for this project, we will also need to spend a lot of effort in merging various datasets together to obtain more features.

Therefore, for this project, we actually need to conduct feature development, then data merging, and then feature selection, which is to utilize all the techniques discussed in *Chapter 2, Data Preparation for Spark ML* and *Chapter 3, A Holistic View on Spark.*

Data merging

To obtain features for predicting, we need to add some external datasets, including weather data from National Weather Service Forecast Office, events as well as calendar data from the Open Data portal, and socio-economic data for each zip code block from census data source.

In the, *Joining data* section of *Chapter 2, Data Preparation for Spark ML*, we described methods to join data together with Spark SQL and other tools. All the techniques described there as well as the ones about identity matching and data cleaning techniques described in *Chapter 2, Data Preparation for Spark ML*, can be used in this chapter.

As for this data merging task, the main focus includes, firstly, merging data on date per day, and, secondly, merging data on location per zip code. That is, first we will reorganize all the 311 requests' data into one dataset with features per day, which is to obtain the number of requests per day and other daily features. Then, the second task is similar; we will reorganize all the 311 requests' data into another dataset with features per location (here, per zip code), to obtain features such as the number of service requests per zip code. To learn how to reorganize datasets, readers may refer to the *Data reorganizing* section in *Chapter 2, Data Preparation for Spark ML.*

After we have created the two datasets mentioned previously, we will merge the first dataset with weather and calendar data and the second dataset with census data.

After merging with events data and calendar data, we will obtain new features for "whether holiday", special events, weekdays versus weekend, and others.

After merging with weather data, we will obtain new features for rainy, snowy, average temperature, temperature range of the day, and other variables.

On the location side, we will work on the zip code level so that after merging with census data, we will obtain some new features about employment, income level, race, and others.

Feature selection

Taking the New York city 311 data as an example, we have more than 50 features in the data, which include information about the time requests that were made, locations for services, government agencies to whom the services request, the types of services requested, and the processing time for requests as well as the results of these requests.

After we merged location-related datasets and time-related datasets as described in the previous section, we will have more than 100 features ready to be used.

As for the feature selection for this project, we could follow what was used in *Chapter 8, Learning Analytics on Spark*, which is to utilize **principal component analysis (PCA)** and subject knowledge to group features and then apply machine learning for final feature selection. However, as an exercise, we will not repeat what was learned but will try something different. That is, we will let the machine learning algorithm pick up the features most useful in prediction.

In MLlib, we can use the `ChiSqSelector` algorithm as follows:

```
// Create ChiSqSelector that will select top 25 of 400 features
val selector = new ChiSqSelector(25)
// Create ChiSqSelector model (selecting features)
val transformer = selector.fit(TrainingData)
```

In R, we can use some R packages to make computation easy. Among the available packages, CARET is one of the commonly used packages.

Model estimation

Once the feature sets get finalized in our last section, what follows is an estimation of all the parameters of the selected models, for which we adopted the approach of using MLlib on the Zeppeline notebook for this project and R notebooks in the Databricks environment because we need to estimate some regression and time series models.

Similarly to before, for the best modeling, we need to arrange distributed computing, especially for this case with various kinds of services. In other words, we will estimate models to predict the daily volume of each kind of service request, which is for heating, construction-related, noise-related, parking-related, and other service requests.

In order to complete this task of estimating models for various service types, we need to group all the services into a set of service types. However, for this exercise, we just selected 50 top service types and then conducted parallel computing for model estimation for all these 50 services.

For this distributed computing part, readers may refer to the model estimation parts in previous chapters, as we will not repeat all the details here. Overall, as we discussed in the *Methods of service forecasting* section of this chapter, we will focus on using two methods: regression and time series modeling. From what we have learned so far, for regression, we can complete the model estimation with Zeppelin notebooks on Spark using MLlib algorithms. As for time series modeling, it is better to use R so that we can implement them in the Databricks or IBM DataScientistWorkbench environment, for which we should refer to *Chapter 3, A Holistic View on Spark* and *Chapter 5, Risk Scoring on Spark*.

Spark implementation with the Zeppelin notebook

As discussed, to utilize regression to predict the daily volume of service requests, we have the following:

- Location-related features, such as employment ratios
- Weather features
- Event-related features

In the *Data and feature preparation* section, we had the data prepared; now, we need to divide them into a training and a test set. So, we can use the training set for model estimation.

In MLlib, for linear regression, we will use the following code:

```
val numIterations = 90
val model = LinearRegressionWithSGD.train(TrainingData, numIterations)
```

For logistic regresssion, we will use the following code:

```
val model = new LogisticRegressionWithSGD()
  .setNumClasses(2)
```

We need to input the preceding code into the Zeppelin notebook as follows:

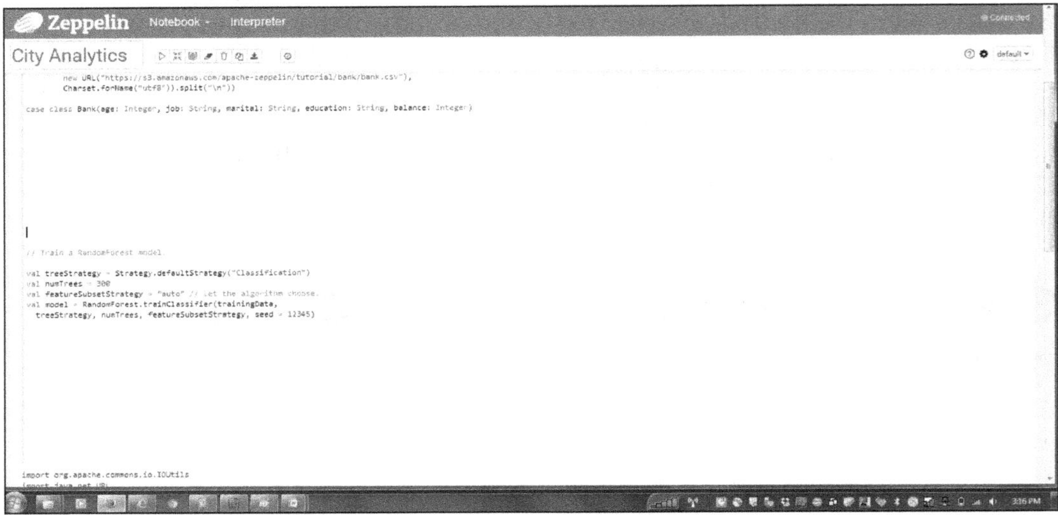

Then we can press *Shift* + *Enter* to run the commands to obtain results, as shown in the following screenshot:

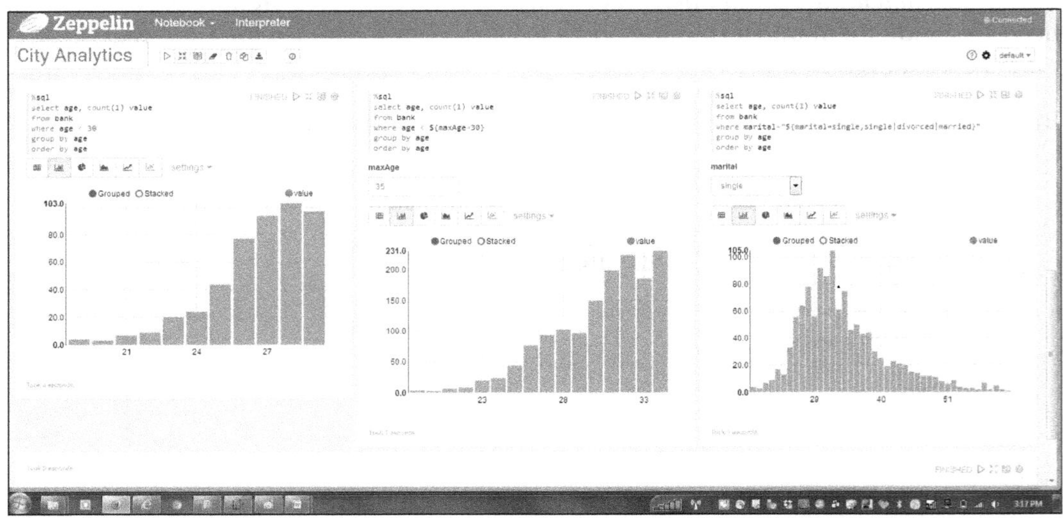

Spark implementation with the R notebook

For time series modeling, as discussed, we will use R notebooks within the Databricks environment similarly to what we did in *Chapter 3, A Holistic View on Spark*.

To do so, we can use the Databricks environment's Job feature. Specifically, within the Databricks environment, we can go to **Jobs** and create jobs, as shown in the following screenshot:

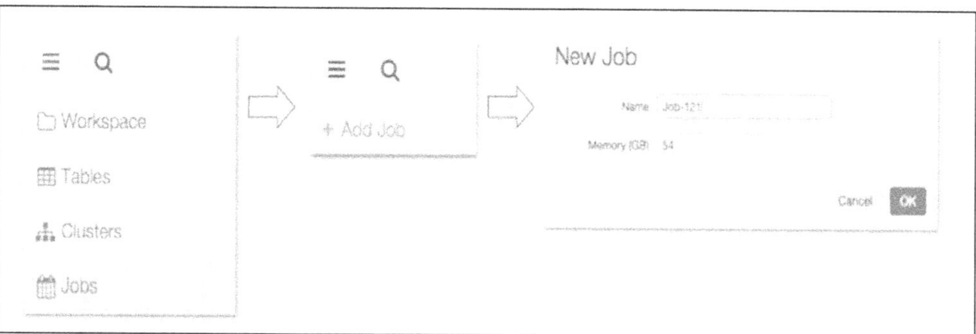

Then users can select notebooks to run, specify clusters, and schedule jobs. Once scheduled, users can also monitor the running and then collect results back.

Model evaluation

In the last section, we completed our model estimation. Now, it is the time for us to evaluate these estimated models to check whether they fit the city's criterions so that we can either move to the results explanation or go back to some previous stages to refine our predictive models.

To perform our model evaluation, in this section, we will mainly use **root mean square error** (**RMSE**) to assess our models for both the regression and time series models. While other measures, such as MSE, can also be used to assess models, as an exercise, we will focus on RMSE as the processes of using other measures are similar.

When working on this real-life project, as mentioned in the *Methods of service forecasting* section of this chapter, we also used decision tree and random forest models, for which we should use a confusion matrix and error ratios to evaluate. Here, we will not discuss these model evaluation methods as they are used a few times in the previous chapters, such as in *Chapter 4, Fraud Detection on Spark*.

Similarly to model estimation, to calculate RMSE, we need to use MLlib for regression modeling to be implemented with Zeppeline notebooks on Spark. For time series modeling, we will use R notebooks to be implemented in the Databricks environment of Spark.

RMSE calculation with MLlib

In MLlib, we can use the following code to calculate RMSE:

```
val valuesAndPreds = test.map { point =>
  val prediction = new_model.predict(point.features)
  val r = (point.label, prediction)
  r
}
val residuals = valuesAndPreds.map {case (v, p) => math.pow((v -
  p), 2)}
val MSE = residuals.mean();
val RMSE = math.pow(MSE, 0.5)
```

Besides the preceding, MLlib also has some functions in the `RegressionMetrics` and `RankingMetrics` classes for us to use for RMSE calculation.

RMSE calculation with R

In R, the `forecast` package has an `accuracy` function that can be used to calculate forecasting accuracy as well as RMSE. Take a look at the following:

```
accuracy(f, x, test=NULL, d=NULL, D=NULL)
```

The measures calculated are:

- **ME (mean error)**
- **RMSE (root mean square error)**
- **MAE (mean absolute error)**
- **MPE (mean percentage error)**
- **MAPE (mean absolute percentage error)**
- **MASE (mean absolute scaled error)**
- **ACF1 (autocorrelation of errors at lag 1)**

To perform a complete evaluation, what we did is to calculate RMSE for all the models we estimated. Then, we compared and picked up the ones with smaller RMSE.

For more information on using the `forecast` R package, refer to the following URL:

`https://cran.r-project.org/web/packages/forecast/forecast.pdf`

Explanations of the results

As before, after we have passed our model evaluation stage and decided to select the estimated and evaluated model as our final model, our next task is to interpret the results for the city management and technicians.

In terms of explaining the machine learning results, the city is particularly interested in understanding what factors influence the service request number and how service requests change over time.

So, to serve the city governments and other interested civic organizations, we need to set our focus on further deriving results about big influencing variables and time series trends with our final models. Then, we need to work on interpretations as well as some visualizations as R provides many good visualization solutions.

Biggest influencers

In terms of finding out the features with the largest impact on the target feature, as you learned from the previous chapters, the random forest method is a good solution. Therefore, once our Zeppelin notebook is up, we should utilize some algorithms for `randomForest`, for which we, of course, need to recode our target feature into a binary one. Then, as we noted in previous chapters, such as in *Chapter 8, Learning Analytics on Spark*, the `randomForest` algorithm can give us a list of all the features as per their impacts on the target variable along with nice visualization graphs.

However, for this project, as we have a nice target feature variable with continuous values, the linear regression results also give us the needed insights directly. In other words, the features with larger coefficients in linear regression have a larger impact on the target feature. Another way of assessing predictors is to use the associated R squared, for which we usually go deep when we conduct feature selection. In other words, this task of finding out the biggest influencers may be performed together with the feature selection work, as described in *Data and feature preparation* section of this chapter.

As per our results, overall, we will find events and holidays as big influencers, followed by weekday versus weekend, and finally followed by weather:

1	Events
2	Holidays
3	Weekend
4	Weather
...	...

Both the linear regression models and ARIMA models confirm similar results.

As discussed before, in *Chapter 5, Risk Scoring on Spark*, R has many special packages for us to assess the predictive features and also visualize them, for which readers are encouraged to explore more.

Visualizing trends

Users of our results, both from city governments and public user communities, are very interested in future trends; so, one of our important tasks is to visualize the trends as per our history data and forecasts.

Consider this example: we need to create a graph of the changing trends of heating-related service requests and noise-related service requests in NYC in 2013.

To produce this graph, we can use some simple code, as follows:

```
plot(Cmonth, HEATING_mean_month, main="% Heating and Noise
  Complains by Month", xlab="Month", ylab="% Complains", col="red")
points(Cmonth, Noise_mean, col="blue", pch=6)
```

The following screenshot shows the output of the preceding code:

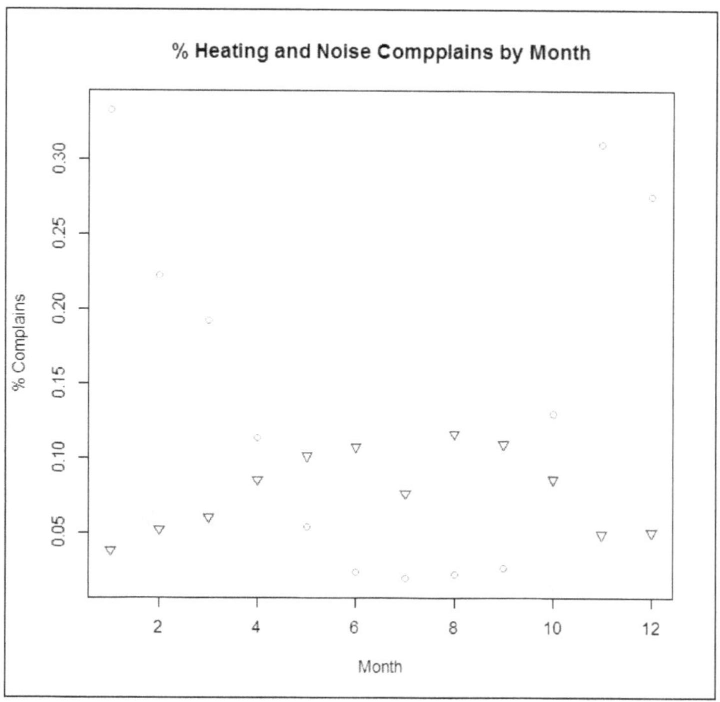

The preceding graph produced by our R notebook illustrates the changes over time in 2013 for, firstly, the noise-related service requests as denoted by blue triangles, and, secondly, heating-related service requests as denoted by red circles.

This graph shows a clear seasonal trend as there are a lot more requests for heating-related services in winter than in summer. As shown by this graph, there are a lot more noise-related service requests in summer than in winter.

Here's another example: a graph of sanitation requests from July 2010 to January 2015 in Los Angeles:

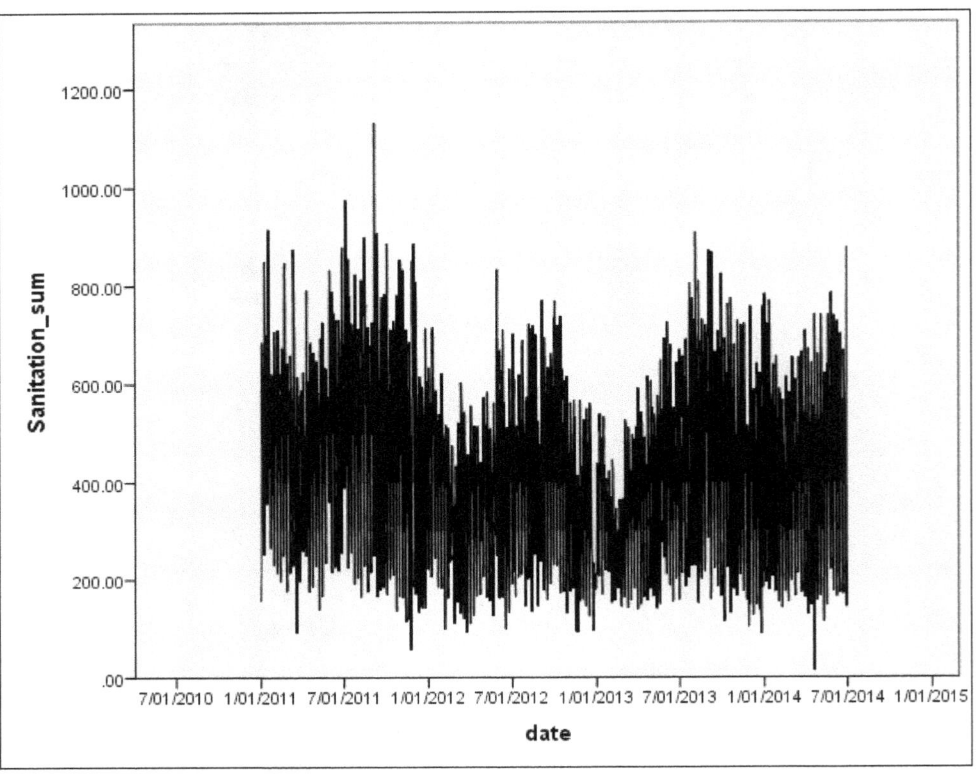

The preceding graph, also produced by our R notebook, shows a significant impact of seasons, but the trends may not be easily interpreted.

Let's take a look at yet another example: mapping out the high water usage areas per zip code in Los Angeles between 2012 and 2013.

In recent years, Los Angeles has been experiencing a water shortage problem, so the city government and several citizen groups are very interested in understanding the overall water usage as well as the impact of some of their interventions.

The following graph, again produced by our R notebook, identifies the high water usage per zip code zones denoted by blue dots:

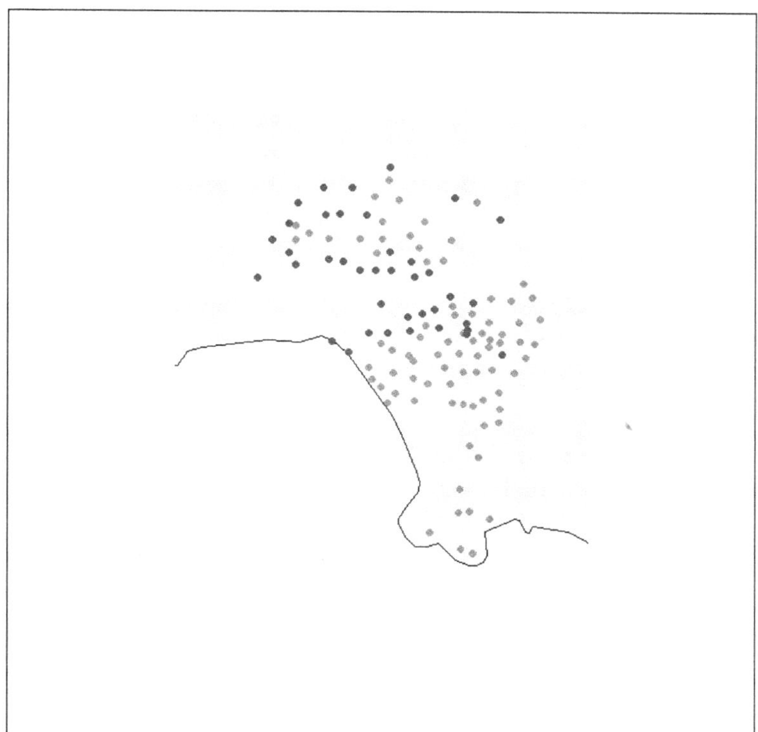

For the preceding visualization, we used the following code:

```
library(maps)
library(mapdata)
library(maptools)
library(scales)

map("worldHires", "usa", xlim=c(-119, -117), ylim=c(33.50, 34.50),
  col="gray95", fill=TRUE
l<-abs(long)

long1<--l
points(long1, lat, pch=19, col="red", cex=1)
points(long1[FY.12.13 > mean(FY.12.13)], lat[FY.12.13 >
  mean(FY.12.13)], pch=19, col="blue", cex=1)
```

As we can note here, we used a few packages, including `mapdata`, `maptools`, and `scales` to produce this graph.

So, as we experienced so far, R has many packages for visualization as well as forecasting, especially for time series data modeling. However, more may come soon for Spark MLlib deployment

One of the main purposes for this project is to produce good predictive models for the city to forecast the future service request volume on a daily basis per zip code using our developed regression models. This kind of forecasting is of value to various departments who use various kinds of software systems for decision making. As discussed before, MLlib supports model export to **Predictive Model Markup Language** (**PMML**). Therefore, we will export some developed models to PMML for this project.

In practice, the users of this project are more interested in rule-based decision making to use some of our insights and also in score-based decision making to evaluate their regional units.

Specifically, as for this project, the client is interested in applying our results to, firstly, decide when an alert may be sent out if the number of service requests forecasted is very high, for which rules should be established, and, secondly, develop scores and use these scores to rank regions, such as by zip code zones, so that the city could use these rankings to measure performance as well as to plan for the future.

Besides the preceding, clients are also interested in forecasting the services in general using time series models, for which R actually has a package called `forecast` that is ready to be used:

```
forecast(fit)
plot(forecast(fit))
```

To sum it up, for our special tasks, we need to turn some of our results into rules and to produce some performance scores for the client.

The rules of sending out alerts

As discussed before, for R results, there are several tools to help extracting rules out from developed predictive models.

For the decision tree model developed to model, whether or not the number of service requests exceeds a certain level, we should use the `rpart.utils` R package, which can extract rules and export them in various formats, such as RODBC.

The `rpart.rules.table(model1)*` package returns an unpivoted table of variable values (factor levels) associated with each branch.

However, for this project, partially due to the issue of data incompleteness, we need to use some insights to derive rules directly. That is, we need to use the insights discussed in the last section. For example, we can do the following:

- If a special event is to be held, our prediction will show certain service requests going up dramatically, and an alert will be sent out
- If weather conditions change for a certain area, some special service request will go up so that an alert needs to be sent out

From an analytical perspective, we face the same issue here to minimize false alerts while ensuring adequate warning.

The city government had a high false alert ratio from their past rules, and as a result of this, too many alerts were sent out that became a burden and also caused a lot of resource wasting.

Therefore, by taking advantage of Spark's fast computing, we carefully produced rules, and for each rule, we supplied false positive ratios that helped the company utilize the rules.

Scores to rank city zones

With our regression and time series modeling in place, we have two ways to forecast the number of service requests for each zip code zone at any specific time in the future.

For time series modeling, as discussed, we can have the R package of `forecast` and use the following code:

```
forecast(fit)
plot(forecast(fit))
```

With the regression models, we can use the estimated regression equations to perform the forecasting directly. Alternatively, we can use the following code:

```
forecast(fit, newdata=data.frame(City=30))
```

Once we have the forecasted service request number in hand, one way of creating scores is using the request number divided by the maximum number.

As long as we obtain the scores, we can classify all the zip code zones into several categories and also illustrate them on a map to identify special zones for attention, such as in the following graph:

Summary

In this chapter, using a service request forecasting project, we went through a step-by-step process of utilizing Big Data to serve city governments as well as related civic organizations, from which we processed open data on Apache Spark and then built several models, including regression and time series ARIMA models to predict service demands. With this, we then developed rules for alerts and scores for zip code zone ranking to help cities prepare resources to measure effectiveness and also rank communities.

Specifically, we first selected a supervised machine learning approach with a focus on time series modeling per use case needs after we prepared Spark computing and loaded in preprocessed data. Secondly, we worked on data and feature preparation by merging a few datasets together and selecting a core set of features from hundreds of features. Thirdly, we estimated model coefficients using the Zeppelin notebook with MLlib and the R notebook on Databricks. Next, we evaluated these estimated models mainly using RMSE. Then, we interpreted our machine learning results with graphs to show trends and tables to show the biggest predictors. Finally, we deployed our machine learning results with a focus on scoring but also used insights to develop rules.

The preceding process is similar to the process as described in the previous chapters. However, in this chapter, we worked on times series modeling, which is a new method. This enabled us to be able to deal with the data with time dimensions and develop insight over time.

After this chapter, readers should have gained a better understanding of how Apache Spark could be utilized not only for commercial use but also for public use to serve cities and universities.

As this is our last chapter, readers may use this real-life project of service request forecasting to review all the modeling methods, such as regression and decision tree, as well as all the Spark computing platforms, such as the Zeppelin notebook with Spark and the R notebook for the Databricks environment. For this purpose, we discussed more methods and platforms in this chapter than in the earlier ones.

10
Learning Telco Data on Spark

With a new approach different from the approaches in the previous chapters, in this chapter and the next chapter, we will start with a set of huge amount of data and then let the data lead us. In other words, we will apply Spark machine learning to certain types of Big Datasets, and then the data needs and new insights will guide our machine learning to result in useful and actionable insights, by taking advantage of the processes made easily and fast with Apache Spark. As for this chapter, we will work on telco data, and then, for the next chapter, we will work on open data made available by various levels of governments.

By following a similar process adopted in the previous chapters, in this chapter, we will first review machine learning methods and related Spark computing to use Telco Data to learn more about customer behavior insights. We will then discuss how Apache Spark comes in to make them easy as before. At the same time, with this real-life use case of customer behavior insight discovery, we will also follow our 4E process of working on equations selection, estimation, evaluation, and explanation to illustrate our step-by-step machine learning process of segmenting customers and scoring customers with this big Telco Data.

However, as you are expected to have gained knowledge of Spark computing and the related tools, including R and SPSS, at this stage, we will jump around the 4Es as the machine learning needs. We will also not be limited by working only on one project or on one model. Specifically for this chapter, we will work to discover insights, score customers, and then build predictive models of the newly developed scores to go deeper in solving clients' problems.

Here, we will use a real-life project to illustrate our technologies and processes, with a computing focus on customer scoring and explanation of the scores. However, what is described here is not limited to score customers, but can also be easily applied to other machine learning projects, such as marketing effectiveness or service quality studies. We will cover the following topics in this chapter:

- Spark for Telco Data learning
- Methods to learn from Telco Data
- Data and feature development
- Model estimation
- Model evaluation
- Results explanation
- Model deployment

Spark for using Telco Data

In this section, we will start with a real-life use case of learning from Telco Data and then describe how to prepare Apache Spark computing for this real-life project of Telco Data machine learning.

The use case

Telco companies in the United States and also in other regions have huge amounts of data in their hands now. Many telco companies have started considering this data as their most valuable asset. They have started utilizing the data not only for their own data-driven decision making, but also for their clients. Specifically, some telco companies started using Big Data analytics to differentiate their offerings and target customers more effectively, thereby generating greater customer loyalty as well as taking advantage of new innovative business models. They also used data to increase operational efficiencies and improve effectiveness of customer-experience management. To serve their corporate clients, some telco companies have used the data to help segment customers in better ways to increase marketing effectiveness.

As for this exercise, the telco corp. VRS provided us with a Big Dataset to start with. The dataset contains call data and other basic information about their millions of subscribers.

However, the raw data is just a collection of many codes, with things such as 1bbddf1... to represent IDs and 73de6rd... to represent location. So, we would need to utilize some subject knowledge to make use of them and then develop new features from the raw data.

The telco company is interested in learning any useful insights from the data. So, we were asked to explore any insights that could be learned from the data and then help them build some models to predict customer churn, Call Center calls, and purchase propensities, if possible. Once these scores get built, it is also helpful for the client to understand what affects these scores. So, the project is a very practical one. It is data driven and problems driven. We have strong interests to showcase our Apache Spark technologies, but the client is only interested in how the Apache Spark technologies can help discover new and useful insights faster and better.

Spark computing

As discussed in the *Spark computing* section of *Chapter 8, Learning Analytics on Spark*, you may choose one of the following approaches for our kind of projects: Spark on Databrick's platform, Spark on IBM Data Scientist Workbench, SPSS on Spark, or Apache Spark with MLlib alone. You have learned about all the details of utilizing them in the previous chapters, mainly from *Chapter 3, A Holistic View on Spark* to *Chapter 7, Recommendations on Spark*.

Either one of the previously mentioned four approaches should work very well for this project of learning from Telco Data. Especially, you may take the codes as developed in this chapter and put them into a separate notebook. You can then implement the notebook with an approach, as mentioned earlier. Using notebooks is preferred for all the approaches, except for SPSS on Spark.

As an exercise and also for the best to fit our data and project goals, we will focus on both the third approach and the fourth approach, which are to use SPSS on Spark and to utilize Apache Spark with MLlib. However, we will also use R notebook on Databrick's platform, as moving cleaned datasets around is not a difficult task.

To use SPSS on Spark, we will need IBM SPSS Modeler 17.1 and IBM SPSS Analytics Server 2.1, which has a good integration with Apache Spark. The following screenshot shows the SPSS Modeler for MLlib node creation:

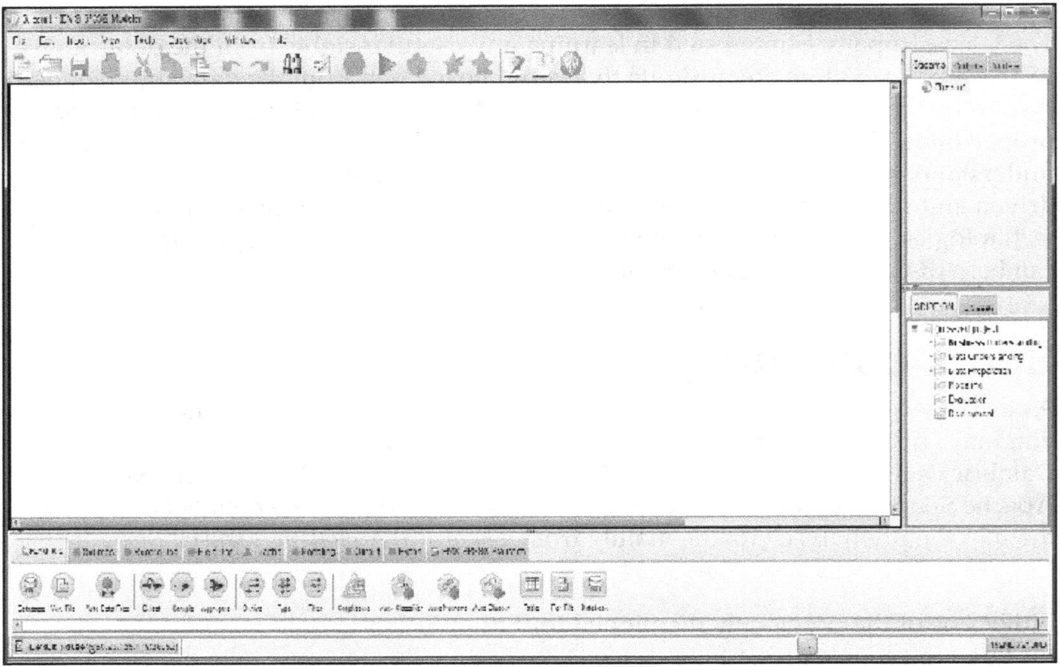

Through this good integration, data science users of SPSS Modeler can now create new Modeler nodes to exploit MLlib algorithms and share them so that we can combine the third and fourth approaches to implement them.

Methods for learning from Telco Data

In the previous section, we described our use case of learning customer insights from big Telco Data with a new dynamic approach and also prepared our Spark computing platform with SPSS on Spark and MLlib as the focus. By following the same process adopted in the previous chapters, as the next step for our machine learning, we now need to complete the task of mapping our use case to machine learning methods. We need to select our analytical methods or predictive models (equations) for this project of scoring customers with Big Data on Spark. Even during our machine learning, we may need to jump back to this stage. We shall still fully complete this stage and prepare all the needed knowledge and codes for jumping back here easily during our machine learning process.

As for the modeling part of our learning, that is, to model customer behavior with Big Data, which is either to depart or to call services, or to purchase for our case here, there are many suitable methods, including regression and decision tree. For this exercise, we will use both regression and decision tree. However, as both regression and decision tree have already been utilized many times in the previous chapters, we will spend more time to ensemble the estimated models for this chapter.

However, besides developing models for predictions, we are also asked for some exploratory work in which we can use some machine learning for descriptive statistics and insight visualizations.

As always, once we finalize our decision for analytical methods or models, we will need to prepare for coding, in MLlib, in SPSS, and in R, for this project.

Descriptive statistics and visualization

As one of our main tasks for this project is to explore the available data for useful insights, we will need to use descriptive statistics and visualization tools from R, SPSS, or MLlib.

One of the most basic methods for data exploration is to build cross-tabulation tables, for which we can use the following:

- The table function in R
- CROSSTAB in SPSS
- colStats in MLlib

As for visualizations, R has better plot functions for us to use from its ggplots package.

Linear and logistic regression models

For this project, in terms of creating predictions, we have two target variables: a binary variable about customer churn and a numeric variable about the number of calls made to the Call Center. As an exercise, we can build linear regression to predict Call Center calls and logistic regression models for customer churn.

So far, you must know very well that regression is most commonly used for prediction and has been utilized for various projects in this book so far.

For your convenience, in MLlib, for linear regression, we can use the following code:

```
val numIterations = 90
val model = LinearRegressionWithSGD.train(TrainingData,
  numIterations)
```

For logistic regression, we can use a line of different code as follows:

```
val model = new LogisticRegressionWithSGD()
  .setNumClasses(2)
```

In R, we can use the `glm` function of generalized linear regression to implement logistic regression, and the `lm` function to implement linear regression, while SPSS Modeler has a regression node for us to use.

Decision tree and random forest

Both decision tree and random forest aim to model ways of classifying cases into departed or not departed for our use case, in sequence with the results to be illustrated by trees.

Specifically, decision tree modeling uses a sequence of branching operations based on comparisons of some quantities such as number of calls and quality of services to illustrate the impact of predictors, which is relatively ease of use, robustness with missing data, and ease of interpretability, in comparison to regression modeling. Robustness with missing data has a big advantage for this use case, as data incompleteness is one of the biggest issues here.

Random forest comes from a set of trees, with good functions to produce scores and to rank predictors by their impact on target variables, which will be useful for us to help identify interventions to reduce subscriber churn. However, mean results of hundreds of trees somehow cover details so that a decision tree explanation can still be very intuitive and valuable. It is considered better than random forest.

Just like we did earlier, within MLlib, we can use the following code:

```
val numClasses = 2
val categoricalFeaturesInfo = Map[Int, Int]()
val impurity = "gini"
val maxDepth = 6
val maxBins = 32
val model = DecisionTree.trainClassifier(trainingData, numClasses,
  categoricalFeaturesInfo, impurity, maxDepth, maxBins)
```

For random forest and in MLlib, we can use the following code:

```
// To train a RandomForest model.
val treeStrategy = Strategy.defaultStrategy("Classification")
val numTrees = 300
val featureSubsetStrategy = "auto" // Let the algorithm choose.
val model = RandomForest.trainClassifier(trainingData,
  treeStrategy, numTrees, featureSubsetStrategy, seed = 12345)
```

More guidance about coding for decision tree can be found at `http://spark.apache.org/docs/latest/mllib-decision-tree.html` and for random forest at `http://spark.apache.org/docs/latest/mllib-ensembles.html`.

In R, we used the R package of `randomForest` and `rpart` to implement random forest and decision tree modeling with code similar to the following:

```
library(randomForest)
library(rpart)

Model2 <- randomForest(default ~ ., data=train, importance=TRUE,
  ntree=2000)
Model3 <- rpart(default ~ ., data=train)
```

For SPSS, the SPSS Modeler has a tree node and a random forest extension for us to use.

Data and feature development

In the *Feature extraction* section of *Chapter 2, Data Preparation for Spark ML*, we have reviewed a few methods for feature extraction and discussed their implementation on Apache Spark. All the techniques discussed there will be applied to our datasets here.

Besides feature development, for this project, we will also need to spend a lot of effort to merge various datasets together to obtain more features.

Therefore, for this project, we actually need to conduct feature development, then data merging and reorganizing, and then feature selection, which is to utilize all the techniques discussed in *Chapter 2, Data Preparation for Spark ML*, and also in *Chapter 3, A Holistic View on Spark*. A lot of work has been completed to produce several good datasets for this big project, with the techniques described earlier.

As an exercise, we will focus on some of the key tasks, which are to reorganize data per day, then merge datasets, and finally conduct feature selection to obtain a good set of features for machine learning.

Data reorganizing

To obtain more and good features to predict and use the data to serve the clients of the telco company, we need to add some external datasets, including customer purchase data and some open data.

In the *Joining data* section of *Chapter 2, Data Preparation for Spark ML,* we have described methods to join data with Spark SQL and other tools. All the techniques described there as well as the ones about identity matching and data cleaning techniques described in *Chapter 2, Data Preparation for Spark ML* could be used here.

As for this data-reorganizing task, the main focus in here includes (1) to aggregate data on date per day and (2) to aggregate data on location per zip code as well as per location types. That is, first, we reorganize all data into one dataset with features per day, which is to obtain the number of calls per day and other daily features. Then, the second task is similar, but to reorganize all the data into another dataset with features per location, here per zip code. It means to obtain features such as number of calls per zip code. About how to reorganize datasets, you may refer to the *Data reorganizing* section of *Chapter 2, Data Preparation for Spark ML.*

Specifically, all the tools to be used have good functions for data aggregation.

SPSS has a function of `aggregate`, for which we just need to specify the date or location as a break and specify the sum or mean as the function to create new data.

R also has a function of `aggregate`, for which we will need to use `by` to specify the date as a break and then use `FUN` to specify the function to create new data.

After we have these two datasets created, we can merge the first dataset with customer data.

Feature development and selection

After we merged location-related datasets and time-related datasets, as described in the previous section, we have more than 100 features ready to be used.

As for the feature selection for this project, we could follow what we used for *Chapter 8, Learning Analytics on Spark,* which is to utilize (**Principal Component Analysis** (**PCA**) and also to use subject knowledge to group features, and then apply machine learning for final feature selection. However, as an exercise, you will not repeat what you learned. We will try something different. That is, we will let the machine learning algorithms pick up the features most useful in prediction.

In MLlib, we can use the `ChiSqSelector` algorithm as follows:

```
// Create ChiSqSelector that will select top 25 of 400 features
val selector = new ChiSqSelector(25)
// Create ChiSqSelector model (selecting features)
val transformer = selector.fit(TrainingData)
```

In R, we can use some R packages to make computation easy. Among the available packages, CARET is one of the commonly used packages.

With all the work described in the preceding sections, *Data reorganizing* and *Feature development and selection*, is done, we end with a dataset with the following features to be used:

- **Basic info**: `location - state`, `account service length`, `area code`, `phone number`, `phone mftr`, `international call plan`, and `voice mail plan`
- **Usage info**: `number vmail messages daily`, `total day minutes`, `total day calls`, `total calls dropped`, `total day charge`, `total eve minutes`, `total eve calls`, `total eve charge`, `total night minutes`, `total night calls`, `total night charge`, `total intl minutes`, `total intl calls`, `total intl charge`, `number Call Center calls`, and `call locations`

Especially for our study, we also have a special feature that is about whether or not the subscriber churned, which will be the essential target variable for our core supervised machine learning. In the preceding list of features, the second to the last is `number Call Center calls`, which will be also used as a target variable for some of our supervised machine learning.

Model estimation

Once feature sets get finalized in our last section, what follows is to estimate all the parameters of the selected models, for which we have adopted an approach of using SPSS on Spark and also R notebooks in the Databricks environment, plus MLlib directly on Spark. However, for the purpose of organizing workflows better, we focused our effort on organizing all the codes into R notebooks and also coding SPSS Modeler nodes.

For this project, as mentioned earlier, we will also conduct some exploratory analysis for descriptive statistics and for visualization, for which we can take the MLlib codes and get them implemented directly. Also, with R codes, we obtained quick and good results.

For the best modelling, we need to arrange distributed computing, especially for this case, with various locations in combination with various customer segments.

For this distributed computing part, you need to refer to previous chapters, and we will use SPSS Analytics Server with Apache Spark as well as Databrick's environment.

As we discussed in the *Methods for service forecasting* section, we will use two methods, regression and decision tree, for the supervised machine learning part. From what you learned so far, for regression, you can complete the model estimation either with SPSS or with R. As for some modelling with random forest, it is better to use R so that you can implement the methods with R codes in the Databricks environment, for which we should refer to *Chapter 3, A Holistic View on Spark* and *Chapter 5, Risk Scoring on Spark.*

With the feature list we have from the previous section, we have our target variables of whether or not the subscriber departed and also another target variable of Call Center calls. When modelling subscriber churn, the variable of Call Center calls will also be used as one of the predictors.

For decision tree modelling, the following code in R is what is needed, as we need some R packages:

```
library(languageR)
library(rms)
library(Party)

data.controls <- cforest_unbiased(ntree=1000, mtry=3)
set.seed(47)
data.cforest <- cforest(CustomerChurn ~ x + y + z…, data =
  mob_churn, controls=data.controls)
```

Besides, we used R in the Databricks environment. At the same time, we used the SPSS Modeler to estimate these predictive models, for which we need to use the SPSS Analytics Server. The following screenshot shows the SPSS Modeler with nodes developed:

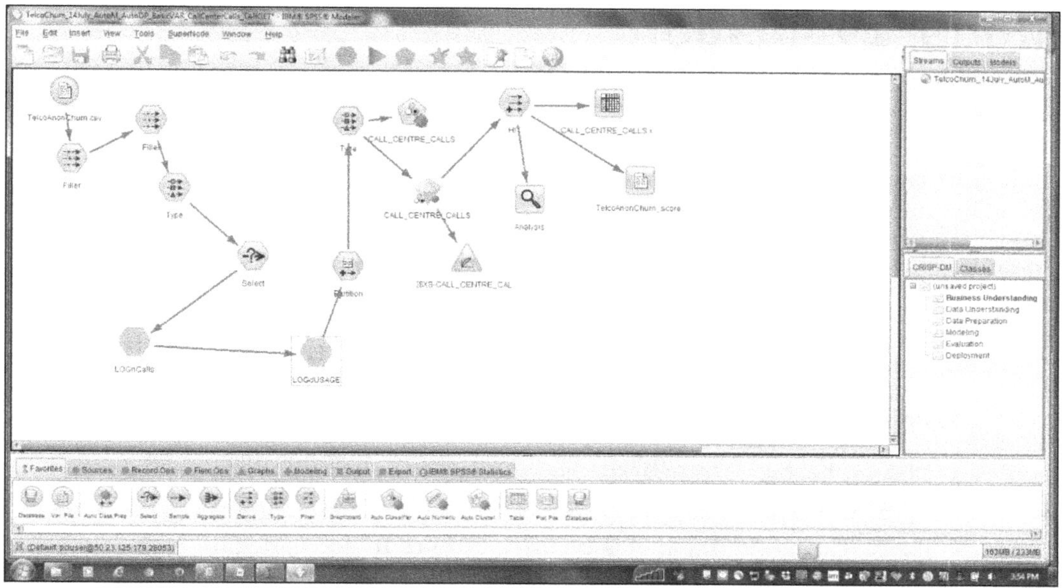

SPSS on Spark – SPSS Analytics Server

The IBM SPSS Modeler 17.1 and Analytic Server 2.1 offer easy integration with Spark, which allows us to easily implement the data and modeling streams built so far:

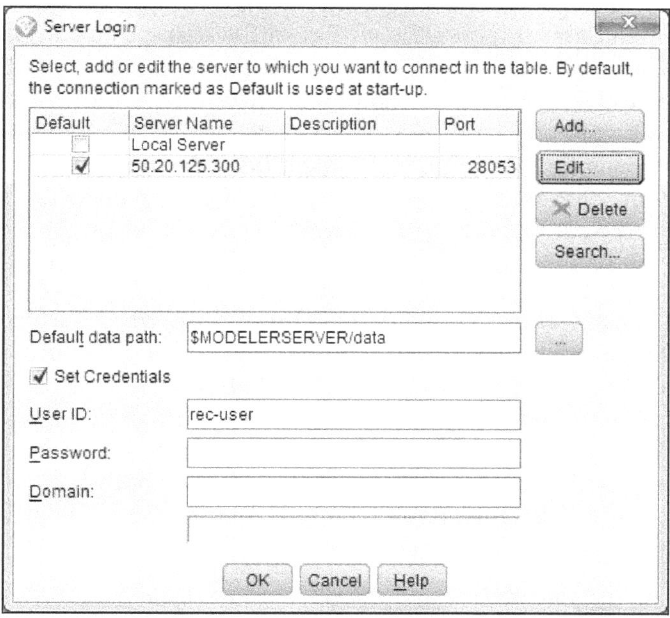

Model evaluation

In the last section, we summarized what is needed to complete our model estimation for our supervised machine learning. Now it is time for us to evaluate these estimated models to see if they fit the client's criterions so that we can either move to the results explanation stage or go back to some previous stages to refine our predictive models.

To perform our model evaluation, in this section, we will need to use **Root Mean Square Error** (**RMSE**) to assess our linear regression models of predicting Call Center calls, and use confusion matrix to assess our logistic regression model of predicting customer churn, for which the following numbers are often preferred:

- **True Positive (TP)**: Label is positive and prediction is also positive
- **True Negative (TN)**: Label is negative and prediction is also negative
- **False Positive (FP)**: Label is negative but prediction is positive
- **False Negative (FN)**: Label is positive but prediction is negative

Here, positive means the subscriber departed, and negative means the subscriber stayed.

The preceding four numbers are the building blocks for most classifier-evaluation metrics. A fundamental point in considering classifier evaluation is that pure accuracy (that is, was the prediction correct or incorrect) is not necessarily a best one, as a dataset could be highly unbalanced. For example, if a model is designed to predict fraud from a dataset where 95 percent of the data points are not fraud and 5 percent of the data points are fraud, then a naive classifier that predicts all as not fraud, regardless of the input, will be 95 percent accurate. For our case, the churn ratio is also not very high. For this reason, metrics for precision (positive predictive value) and recall (sensitivity) are typically used because they take into account the type of error. In other words, some balance between precision and recall is needed, which can be captured by combining the two into a single metric called the F-measure that will be calculated here with MLlib.

Just like for model estimation, to calculate RMSEs and to produce a confusion matrix, we need to use MLlib for regression modelling to be implemented with Apache Spark, which, as an exercise, can also be implemented with SPSS on Spark, when we take the MLlib codes to form a SPSS Modeler node. For logistic regression modelling, we will use R notebooks to be implemented in the Databricks environment for Apache Spark. In practice, we tried both MLlib and R for both calculating RMSE and calculating error ratios, because one of the main purposes for this project is to go beyond the limits of our tools of R and MLlib.

RMSE calculations with MLlib

In MLlib, we can use the following codes to calculate RMSE:

```
val valuesAndPreds = test.map { point =>
  val prediction = new_model.predict(point.features)
  val r = (point.label, prediction)
  r
}
val residuals = valuesAndPreds.map {case (v, p) => math.pow((v -
  p), 2)}
val MSE = residuals.mean();
val RMSE = math.pow(MSE, 0.5)
```

Besides the preceding code, MLlib also has some functions in the `RegressionMetrics` and `RankingMetrics` classes for us to use for the RMSE calculation.

RMSE calculations with R

In R, the `forecast` package has an `accuracy` function that can be used to calculate forecasting accuracy as well as RMSEs:

```
accuracy(f, x, test=NULL, d=NULL, D=NULL)
```

The measures calculated are:

- **ME (Mean Error)**
- **RMSE (Root Mean Squared Error)**
- **MAE (Mean Absolute Error)**
- **MPE (Mean Percentage Error)**
- **MAPE (Mean Absolute Percentage Error)**
- **MASE (Mean Absolute Scaled Error)**
- **ACF1 (Autocorrelation of errors at lag 1)**

To perform a complete evaluation, we need to calculate RMSEs for all the models we estimated. Then, we compare and pick up the ones with smaller RMSEs.

Confusion matrix and error ratios with MLlib and R

In MLlib, we can use the following code to calculate the error ratios:

```
// F-measure
val f1Score = metrics.fMeasureByThreshold
f1Score.foreach { case (t, f) =>
  println(s"Threshold: $t, F-score: $f, Beta = 1")
}

val beta = 0.5
val fScore = metrics.fMeasureByThreshold(beta)
f1Score.foreach { case (t, f) =>
  println(s"Threshold: $t, F-score: $f, Beta = 0.5")
}
```

In R, we have the following code to produce a confusion matrix, which can be included in our R notebook for implementation:

```
model$confusion
```

With what is described in the preceding paragraph, we selected our final linear regression models for Call Center calls prediction and our final logistic regression models for subscriber churns.

Results explanation

After we passed our model-evaluation stage and decided to select the estimated and evaluated model as our final models, our next task is to interpret the results to the telco company and their clients.

In terms of explaining the machine learning results, the telco company is particularly interested in understanding what influences the Call Center call volume as well as what impacts the subscriber churn. Of course, they are also open to other special insights.

We will work on these tasks, with our focus on big influencing features and some special insights.

Descriptive statistics and visualizations

With R or SPSS on Spark, as well as MLlib in place, one advantage is to obtain analytical results fast. So, quickly, we have obtained the following insights as summarized by the following tables.

For subscriber churn, we have the following two tables that summarize the subscriber churn ratios, per their phone manufactures and per our market segments of six main categories. Producing some customer segmentations is another task performed for the telco company, but we will not discuss this in detail as per the limitation of this book. You may just consider this as one of the taken features. The following table shows the subscriber churn ratios per phone manufactures:

:MFTR	Churn Rate
A	.09
H	.11
L	.11
M	.12
N	.08
R	.10
S	.10

The following table shows the subscriber churn ratios per market segment:

Segment	Churn Rate
DG1	.09
DG2	.05
HB	.13
NS	.10
NP	.10
UN	.10

For Call Center calls, we have the following two tables that summarize the average calls made by subscribers, per their phone manufactures and per our market segments. The following table shows the average calls made by the subscribers per phone manufactures:

MFTR	Average Call Center Calls
A	1.26
H	1.11
L	0.89
M	1.03
N	0.88
R	1.30
S	1.00

The following table shows the average calls made by the subscribers per market segment:

Segment	Average Call Center Calls
DG1	1.13
DG2	2.86
HB	0.50
NS	2.31
NP	1.12
UN	1.52

Furthermore, our results also map out stores per churn rate or per Call Center calls. Here is an example:

For this mapping task, we have used the R code.

The following is an example of R codes used to visualize store distribution:

```
library(maps)
library(mapdata)
library(maptools)
library(scales)

map("worldHires", "usa", xlim=c(-120, -70), ylim=c(25, 55),
  col="gray95", fill=TRUE)
points(lon, lat, pch=19, col="red", cex=1)
```

Biggest influencers

In terms of finding out the features with the largest impact on the target features of subscriber churn and Call Center calls, once our Spark computing is up, we can easily utilize algorithms for randomForest. Then, as we saw in *Chapter 8, Learning Analytics on Spark*, the randomForest algorithm can give us a list of all the features per their impact on the target variable and with nice visualization graphs.

However, for this project, with Call Center calls as a good target feature variable with continuous values, the linear regression results give us the insights directly. In other words, the features with larger coefficients in the linear regression have a larger impact on the target feature. Another way of assessing predictors is to use the associated R squared, which we also used when we conducted feature selection. In other words, this task may be performed together with the feature selection work as described in the *Data and feature development* section.

However, for impact on subscriber churns, we have used randomForest results, for which we have the following list of the five largest predictors in order:

- Call Center calls
- Quality of services
- Usage
- Manufacturer
- Customer segments

With the preceding results, it is easy and also not surprising to see the impact of Call Center calls as the biggest, which also indicates to the telco company about where they need to intervene to reduce subscriber churns.

For Call Center calls, we have the following list of the four largest predictors in order:

- Quality of services
- Usage
- Manufacturer
- Segments

Per the preceding results, the main drivers of Call Center calls are service quality and call usage, with actually the interaction of these two that needs to be further explored.

Special insights

As we see from the preceding section, quality of services has a very big impact on both customer churn and also on Call Center calls.

Therefore, the client is very interested in learning more about the relationship between QoS and churn, for which we use R to visualize their relationship. We found that there is more customer churn in the middle values of QoS.

This result may reflect a non-linear relationship between the two, and in our opinion, this calls for more data on the location's social and economic characteristics and about competition for us to explore the relationship deeper.

Visualizing trends

With our Spark computing in place, a lot of visualization can be produced, especially with R in place. The following image is one example. Here, data transforming success ratios over a year has been plotted to show service quality changes over the course of the year:

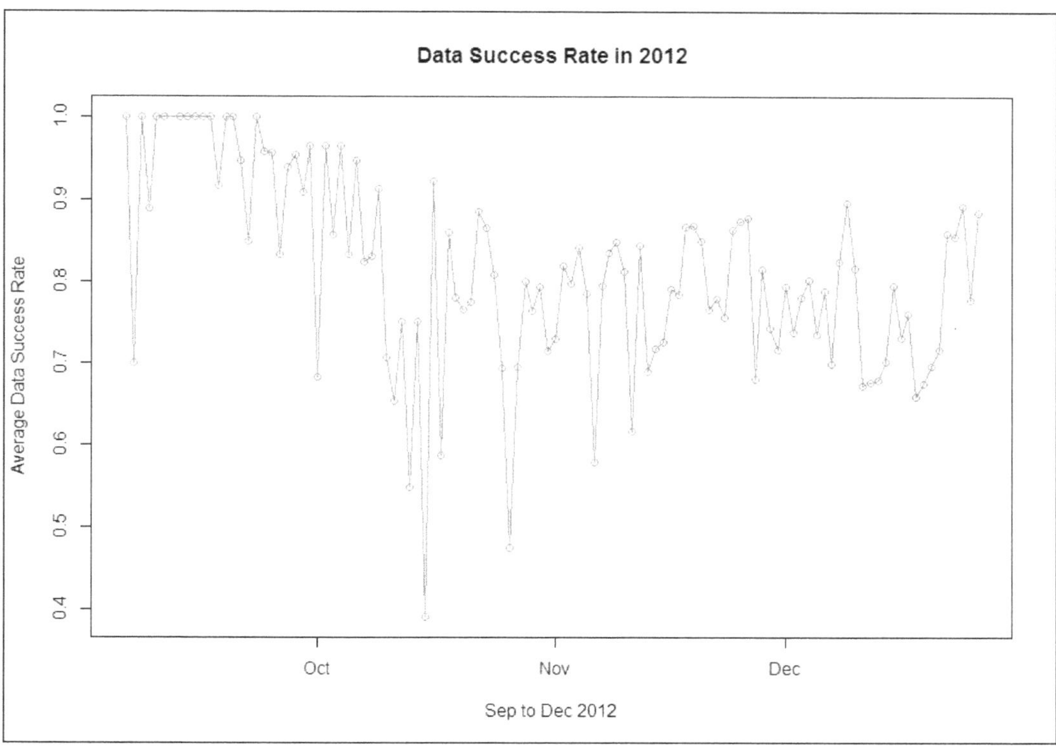

The following image shows the SMS success rate in 2012:

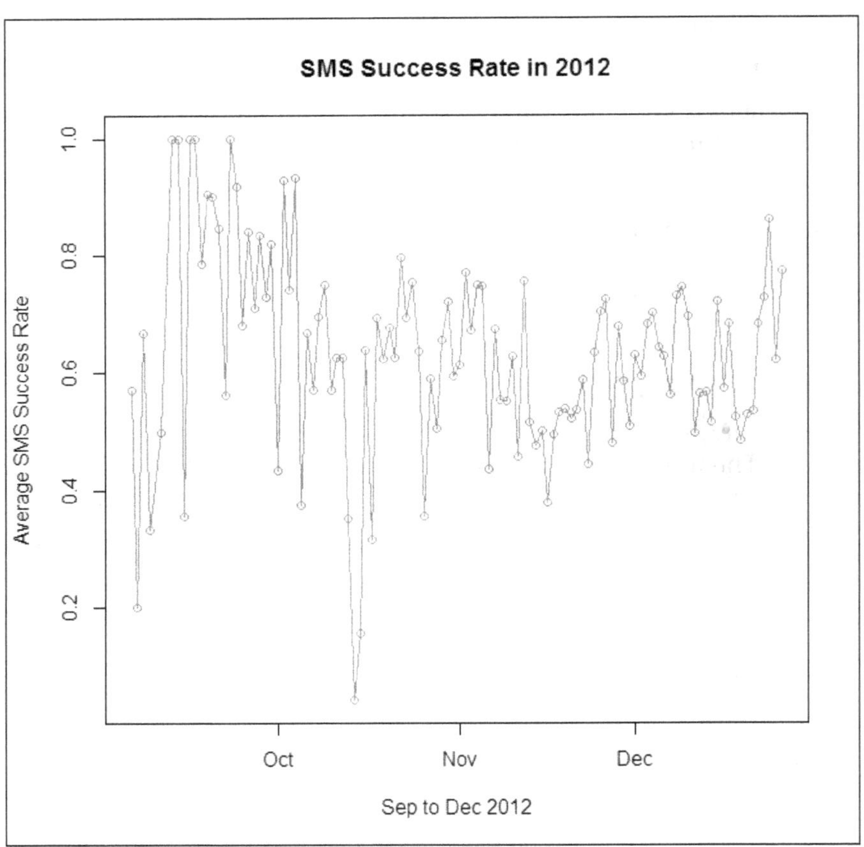

For this work, we used the following R code:

```
library(lubridate)
Rtime<-ymd(day1)
plot(Rtime[event_type == "SMS"],
event_success_mean[event_type == "SMS"], col="red",
main="SMS Success Rate in 2012",
xlab="Sep to Dec 2012", ylab="Average SMS Success Rate"
lines(Rtime[event_type == "SMS"],
```

```
event_success_mean[event_type == "SMS"],
col="red", main="SMS Success Rate in 2012",
xlab="Sep to Dec 2012", ylab="Average SMS Success Rate")
plot(Rtime[event_type == "Data"],
event_success_mean[event_type == "Data"],
col="red", main="Data Success Rate in 2012",
xlab="Sep to Dec 2012", ylab="Average Data Success Rate")
lines(Rtime[event_type == "Data"],
event_success_mean[event_type == "Data"], col="red")
```

Model deployment

One of the main purposes of this project is to produce good predictive models for the telco company to forecast Call Center calls on a daily basis and also to understand or even reduce subscriber churn, besides producing insights for some of the clients of this telco company. As discussed earlier, MLlib supports model export to **Predictive Model Markup Language** (**PMML**). Therefore, we export some developed models to PMML for this project so that the telco company can take them to integrate with their existing analytical and decision-making platforms.

In practice, the users for this project, executives of the telco company, are more interested in rule-based decision making to use some of our insights and also in score-based decision making to impact subscriber churns.

Specifically, as for this project, the client is interested in applying our results to (1) decide when an alert may be sent out if the number of service requests as forecasted will be very high, for which rules should be established, and (2) develop scores and use these scores to rank stores so that the company could use these rankings to measure performance as well as to intervene to get stores to work in reducing subscriber churns, besides changing the Call Center behavior.

To sum up, as for our special tasks, we need to turn some of our results into some rules and also need to produce some good scores for the telco company. To serve the clients of this telco company, we are asked to produce scores per purchasing propensity and to produce some better customer segmentations.

Rules to send out alerts

As discussed earlier, for analytical results produced with R, there are several tools to help extract rules from these developed predictive models with R.

For the decision tree model developed to model whether or not a subscriber left, we can use the `rpart.utils` R package, which will extract rules and export them in various formats such as RODBC. Specifically, `rpart.rules.table(model1)` will return an unpivoted table of variable values (factor levels) associated with each branch.

However, for this project, we will also utilize some insights to derive rules directly. That is, we need to use the insights discussed in the last section, *Results explanation*, as we have obtained very rich results, as described in the section.

From an analytical perspective, we face the same issue here: to minimize false alerts while ensuring adequate warning. In other words, if too many alerts were sent out, it will become a big burden and also will cause a lot of resource wasting, plus a lot of confusion.

Therefore, by taking advantage of Spark's fast computing, we carefully produced rules, and for each rule, we supplied false positive ratios that helped the telco company utilize these rules. Actually, for this stage of the work, some subject knowledge from the company experts has been used, and a good interaction is the key to ensure success.

Scores subscribers for churn and for Call Center calls

With our linear regression and logistic regression models in place, producing scores is easy.

For this project, we have used the churn probability as a score and then also used the predicted number of Call Center calls divided by the maximum calls as another score.

For MLlib, we used code similar to the following:

```
// Compute raw scores on the test set.
val predictionAndLabels = test.map { case LabeledPoint(label,
  features) => val prediction = model.predict(features)
  (prediction, label)
}
```

In R and SPSS, we also have easy methods to produce scores, for which you may refer to our previous chapters.

Scores subscribers for purchase propensity

After we merged our cleaned data with clients' transaction data, we used the same approach to develop models to predict purchases and other customer actions, as we do for predicting Call Center calls and churn, but with a different set of predictors.

With the predictive models developed, we can use MLlib, R, or SPSS to score new data, but for this project, we used SPSS nodes to do so.

Summary

This chapter constitutes an extension of what was described and discussed in the previous chapters (*Chapter 3, A Holistic View on Spark* to *Chapter 9, City Analytics on Spark*). Here, we took an approach driven by data and analytical needs rather than driven by predefined projects. We also developed some predictive models to score subscribers on customer churn, on Call Center calling probabilities, and even on purchasing propensity.

In this chapter, using a real-life project of learning from telco data, we have gone through a step-by-step process of utilizing Big Data to serve the telco company as well as their clients, from which we processed a large amount of data on Apache Spark. We then built several models, including regression and decision tree, to predict customer churn and Call Center calls and also purchasing, with which we then developed rules for alerts and also developed scores to help the telco company and its clients. At the same time, we completed some exploratory analytics by taking advantage of the Apache Spark fast computation.

Specifically, we first selected two supervised machine learning approaches after we prepared Spark computing and loaded in preprocessed data. Second, we worked on data and feature preparation by merging a few datasets together and further developing features. We then selected a core set of features for model building. Third, we estimated model coefficients by directly using MLlib and R notebooks on Databricks as well as SPSS. Fourth, we evaluated these estimated models, mainly using RMSEs and error ratios. Then, we interpreted our machine learning results with a focus on special insights and biggest predictors. Finally, we deployed our machine learning results by developing a few scores, but also used insights to develop rules for sending alerts.

This process is similar to the ones used in previous chapters. However, here, we take a more dynamic approach that we have used descriptive statistics and visualization for data exploratory work, and then work between SPSS and R and MLlib dynamically, as well as jump between the 4Es as needed.

After reading this chapter, you would have gained a better understanding about how Apache Spark could be used with MLlib, R, and SPSS to perform productive machine learning.

Specially, after reading this chapter, you will reach a new level of utilizing machine learning in a dynamic way to solve problems. That is, users are not limited to linearly progressing step by step to get a project done, but will go back and forth to achieve optimal results. They will also jump between MLlib, SPSS, R, and other tools to achieve the best analytical solutions.

11 Modeling Open Data on Spark

Following what we did in *Chapter 10, Learning Telco Data on Spark,* in this chapter, we will further extend our Apache Spark machine learning to a project of learning from open data. In *Chapter 9, City Analytics on Spark,* we already applied machine learning to open data, where we built models to predict service requests. Here, we will further move up into a new level where we will explore machine learning approaches of turning more open data into useful insights, as well as building models to score school districts or schools for academic achievements, technologies, and others. After that, we will build predictive models to explain what impacts the ranking and scoring of these districts.

To follow the good structure established early, in this chapter, we will still first review machine learning methods and related computing for this real-life project of learning from open data. We will then set up Apache Spark computing. At the same time, with our real-life learning examples, we will further illustrate our step-by-step machine learning process with Big Data. However, far beyond this, we will further demonstrate the benefits of our dynamic approaches as taken in the last chapter, *Chapter 10, Learning Telco Data on Spark,* which will allow us to generate results quickly. We will then quickly adjust ourselves to go deep in machine learning to generate even more insights. In other words, as you are expected to have already gained a much better knowledge of Spark computing and the related tools, including R and SPSS, at this stage, we will jump around the 4Es as needed. Also, we will not be limited by working only on one project or on one model or a specific process. Therefore, especially for this chapter, we will just work as needed to discover insights, score districts, and then build predictive models of the newly developed scores so that we can solve clients' problems better.

Here, we aim to illustrate our technologies and processes using these real-life projects of learning from open data. However, what is described in this chapter is not limited to district scoring and ranking, but can also be easily applied to other scoring and ranking projects, such as to score and rank corporations or countries. Also, they actually can be applied to various kinds of machine learning on various kinds of open datasets. In this chapter, we will cover the following topics:

- Spark for learning from open data
- Methods for scoring and ranking
- Data and feature preparation
- Model estimation
- Model evaluation
- Results explanation
- Model deployment

Spark for learning from open data

In this section, we will describe our real-life use case of learning from open data, and then describe how to prepare Apache Spark computing for our real-life projects.

The use case

As discussed in *Chapter 9*, *City Analytics on Spark*, in the United States and worldwide, more and more governments at various levels have made their collected data openly available to the public. As a result of expanding analytics of open data, many governmental and social organizations have used these open datasets to improve service to citizens, with a lot of good results recorded, such as in `https://www.socrata.com/video/added-value-open-datas-internal-use-case/`. Using data analytics for cities has a huge impact as more than half of us live in urban centers now, and this urban residence percentage is higher and higher every year.

Especially, using Big Data to measure communities is also favored by researchers and practitioners, as we can see at `http://files.meetup.com/11744342/CITY_RANKING_Oct7.pdf`. Many cities have policy initiatives to measure communities or even smaller units such as streets with good results and data available for public use, such as that from Los Angeles at `http://lahub.maps.arcgis.com/apps/MapJournal/index.html?appid=7279dc87ea9e416d9f90bf844505a54a`. Using available open data and computing tools just to create some measurements and rankings may be easy. However, creating an accurate and object ranking of certain properties of some communities is not an easy task. Here, we are asked to use available open data, in combination with other datasets, such as census data and social media data, to improve rankings of communities, with a focus on school districts or schools.

At the same time, we are also asked to explore the available open data and try to model it with available machine learning tools on Spark. In other words, for this project, besides developing a good score to measure and rank communities, we are also asked for special insights to be developed from our dynamic machine learning. Once the ranking is ready, we are even asked to explore the rankings with more machine learning, which makes this project really dynamic, as aided by the ease and speed of Spark computing.

However, everything starts from data, as we found out in *Chapter 9, City Analytics on Spark*. The datasets are not as good as we expected, and they have the following issues for us to deal with:

- Data quality is not as good as expected. For example, there are a lot of missing cases.
- Data accuracy is another issue to deal with.
- Data exists in different silos, which need to be merged together.

Therefore, we will still need to perform a big task of data cleaning and feature preparation. We are lucky that we already have a good process from data to equation, estimation, evaluation, and explanation.

For this work of learning from open data, as we took a dynamic approach, the research team became interested in educational data and gradually turned our focus to the work of ranking school districts with open data.

With regard to this subject, we found some open data about schools at `https://www.ed-data.k12.ca.us/Pages/Home.aspx`.

The state government of California also has some open data at `http://data.ca.gov/category/by-data-format/data-files/`.

Spark computing

As discussed earlier, like in the *Spark computing* section of *Chapter 8, Learning Analytics on Spark*, you may choose one of the following approaches for our kind of projects:

- Spark on Databrick's platform
- Spark on IBM DataScientistWorkbench
- SPSS on Spark
- Apache Spark with MLlib alone

You have already learned in detail about utilizing them one by one in the previous chapters, mainly from *Chapter 3, A Holistic View on Spark* to *Chapter 7, Recommendations on Spark*.

Either one of the preceding four approaches should work very well for our projects of learning from open data here. Specially, you may also take the codes as developed in this chapter, and put them into a separate notebook. You can then implement the notebook with one of the preceding approaches.

As an exercise and also for the best to fit our big amount of open data and project goals of fast ranking, we will need to work with the fourth approach, which is to utilize Apache Spark with MLlib. However, we will also need to use R programming a lot for better visualization and reporting, so that we will utilize our first approach of Spark in Databrick's platform as well. At the same time, to take advantage of some good PCA algorithms in SPSS and to easily develop related workflows, we will also need to use SPSS on Spark to practice a special dynamic approach of utilizing Apache Spark. Finally, to meet the needs of creating many data-cleaning workflows, we will also need to use the DataScientistWorkBench platform, with which we can use OpenRefine.

Let's review the approaches mentioned previously in brief to get us really prepared.

As we discussed in the *Spark computing for machine learning* section of *Chapter 1, Spark for Machine Learning*, Apache Spark has a unified platform that consists of the Spark core engine and four libraries, which are Spark SQL, Spark Streaming, MLlib, and GraphX:

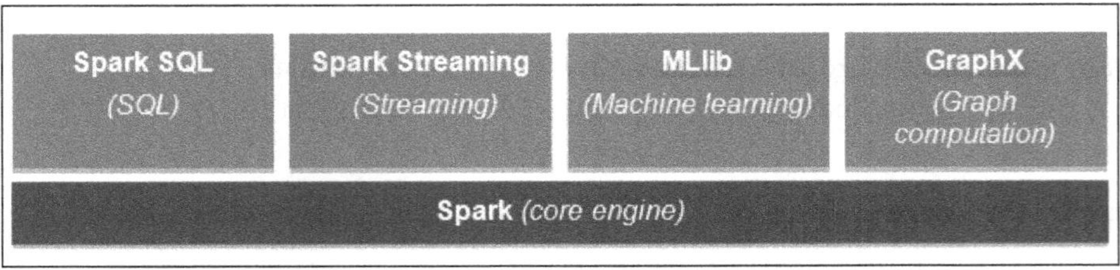

As MLlib is Apache Spark's built-in machine learning library, it is relatively easy to set up and scale for our project of learning from open data.

To work within the Databricks environment, we need to perform the following steps to set up clusters:

1. First, you need to go to the main menu and click on **Clusters**. Then, a window will open up for you to write a name for the cluster. You can select a Spark version and then specify the number of workers:

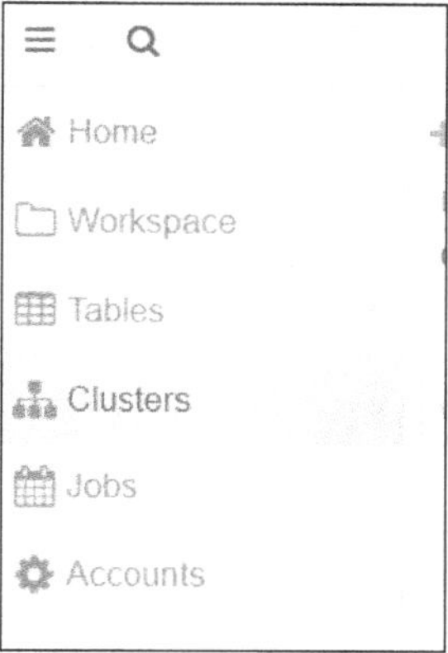

2. Once clusters have been created, we can go to the main menu, click on the down arrow on the right-hand side of **Tables**, and then choose **Create Tables** to import our open datasets that are cleaned and prepared, as shown in the following screenshot:

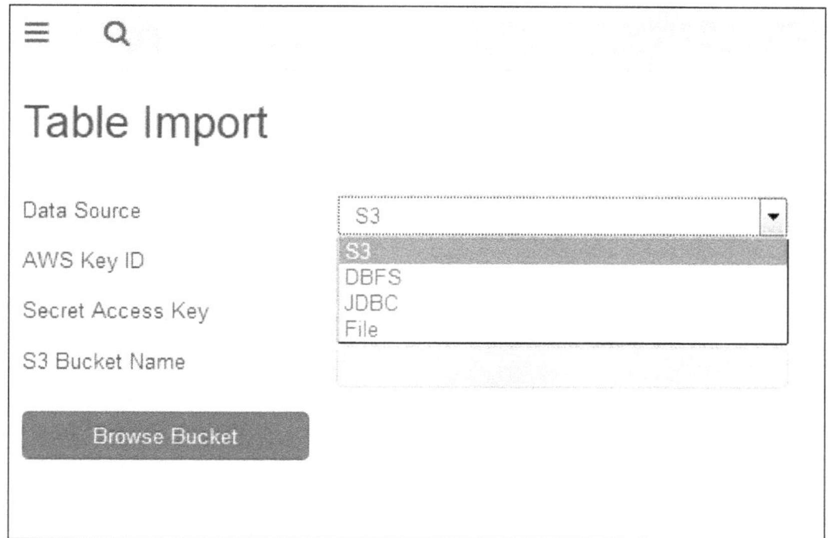

To utilize IBM Data Scientist Workbench, we need to go to `https://datascientistworkbench.com/`:

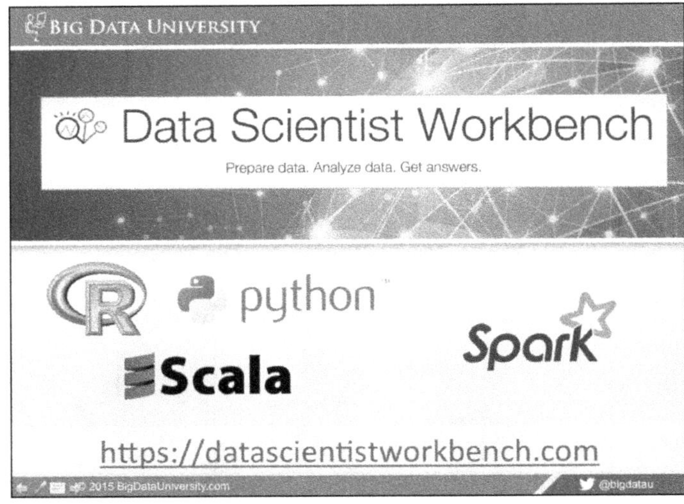

As shown in the preceding screenshot, Data Scientist Workbench has Apache Spark installed and also has a data cleaning system, OpenRefine, integrated so that our data preparation work can be made easier and more organized:

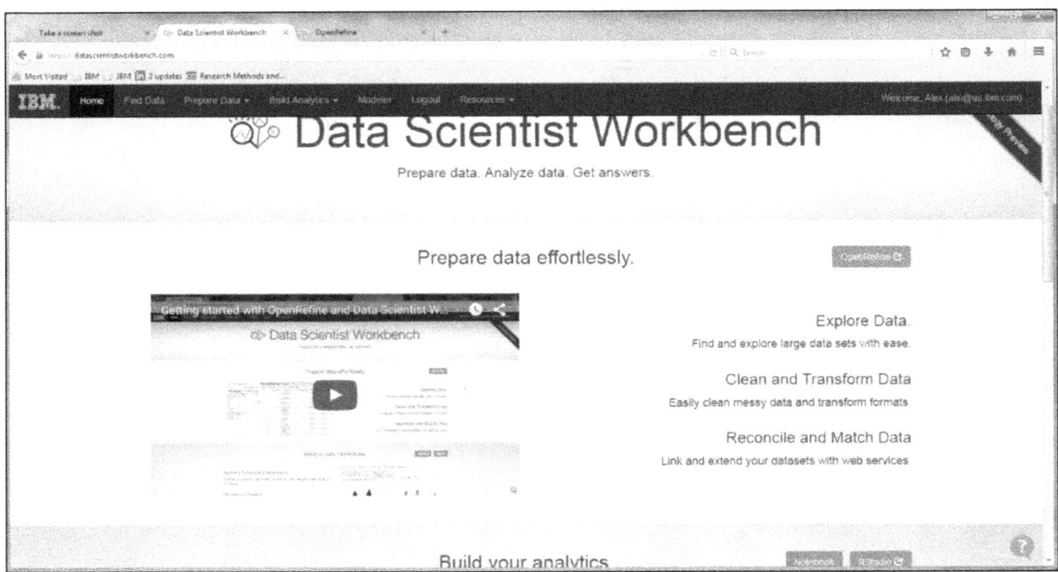

For this project, we will use Data Scientist Workbench for data cleaning and also a little for R notebook creation, as well as Apache Spark implementation. For this setup, some of the Apache Spark techniques described in the previous chapters should apply.

With regards to SPSS on Spark, we will use IBM SPSS Modeler 17.1 and IBM SPSS Analytics Server 2.1, which has a good integration with Apache Spark.

Methods for scoring and ranking

In the previous section, we described our use case of learning from open data, with a focus on using open data to score and rank communities, and also prepared our Spark computing platform with R notebooks, SPSS workflows, and MLlib codes to use. As the next step for our machine learning per our 4E framework, we need to complete a task of mapping our use case to machine learning methods, which is to select our analytical methods or predictive models (equations) for this project of scoring and ranking with open data on Spark.

To turn data into insights, we will need to explore many methods, for which our dynamic approach should work well. To develop scores and rankings, it is not a difficult task with our available analytical tools and fast computing. However, to obtain objective and accurate raking is not an easy job. One approach to achieve this is to ensemble many rankings together, as it will improve results dramatically per past research. Visit `http://www.researchmethods.org/Ranking-indicators` and `http://www.researchmethods.org/InnovativeAnalysisSociety` for more information.

Therefore, for this project, we will take a dynamic approach, with which we will explore our open data, with methods including cluster analysis and principal component analysis. We will then use this knowledge to build a few rankings and scores. After that, we will ensemble results to improve rankings and scores. Finally, we will develop models to explain the impact of various features on these rankings and scores. However, as we are taking a dynamic approach, we will jump between these stages to achieve optimal results. As always, once we finalize our decision for analytical methods or models, we will need to prepare the related dependent variable and also prepare for coding.

Cluster analysis

Both Spark MLlib and R have algorithms available for cluster analysis:

```
// Cluster the data into two classes using KMeans
val numClusters = 2
val numIterations = 20
```

```
val clusters = KMeans.train(parsedData, numClusters, numIterations)

// Evaluate clustering by computing Within Set Sum of Squared Errors
val WSSSE = clusters.computeCost(parsedData)
println("Within Set Sum of Squared Errors = " + WSSSE)
```

In R, we can use some R codes. Here is an example:

```
# K-Means Cluster Analysis
fit <- kmeans(schooldata, 5) # 5 cluster solution
# get cluster means
aggregate(schooldata,by=list(fit$cluster),FUN=mean)
```

For more about cluster analysis with Spark MLlib, go to `http://spark.apache.org/docs/latest/mllib-clustering.html`.

Principal component analysis

Both Spark MLlib and R have algorithms available for **principal component analysis (PCA)**:

```
// Compute the top 10 principal components.
val pc: Matrix = mat.computePrincipalComponents(10) // Principal
components are stored in a local dense matrix.

// Project the rows to the linear space spanned by the top 10
principal components.
val projected: RowMatrix = mat.multiply(pc)
```

In R, we can use the `prcomp` function from the `stats` package.

For more on PCA with Spark MLlib, go to `http://spark.apache.org/docs/latest/mllib-dimensionality-reduction.html`.

Besides cluster analysis and PCA, we will also use regression modelling and decision tree modelling to help us understand more about how communities fall into one category or one rank rather than others.

Regression models

So far, you must know that regression is among the most commonly used models for prediction, and has been utilized for various projects so far.

As we discussed, there are two kinds of regression modeling that are suitable for various kinds of predictions. One is linear regression and another is logistic regression. For this project, linear regression can be used when we take daily service request volume as our target variable, while logistic regression can be used if we want to predict whether or not a certain type of service is requested in a certain location at a certain time period.

For your convenience, in MLlib, for linear regression, we have the following code to be used:

```
val numIterations = 90
val model = LinearRegressionWithSGD.train(TrainingData,
  numIterations)
```

For logistic regresssion, we can use these following code:

```
val model = new LogisticRegressionWithSGD()
.setNumClasses(2)
```

In R, as we did earlier, we will use the GLM and LM functions for linear regression modeling and logistic regression modeling.

Score resembling

Once the scores get developed, one of the easy ways of resembling them is to construct a linear combination with special weighting for each. The weights can be developed with subject knowledge or with machine learning.

Besides the preceding things, there are also a few R packages for score ensemble.

Data and feature preparation

Everyone who has worked with open data will agree that a huge amount of time is needed to clean datasets, with a lot of work to be completed to take care of data accuracy and data incompleteness.

Also, one main task is to merge all the datasets together, as we have separate datasets for crime, education, resource usage, request demand, and transportation from the open datasets. We also have datasets from some separate sources, including census.

In the *Feature extraction* section of *Chapter 2, Data Preparation for Spark ML*, we reviewed a few methods for feature extraction and discussed their implementation on Apache Spark. All the techniques discussed there can be applied to our data here.

Besides data merging, we will also need to spend a lot of time on feature development, as we need features to develop our models to obtain insights for this project.

Therefore, for this project, we actually need to conduct data merging, and then feature development and selection, which is to utilize all the techniques discussed in *Chapter 2, Data Preparation for Spark ML*, and also in *Chapter 3, A Holistic View on Spark*.

Data cleaning

To obtain good datasets to use, a lot of work needs to be completed to clean our data, especially in taking care of the data accuracy issue and missing values.

Due to the big demand for data cleaning, we have adopted a few special approaches and actually also a dynamic approach for us to use a few tools in cleaning the datasets and then combine them for our machine learning. Specially, we have also used OpenRefine as discussed in *Chapter 5, Risk Scoring on Spark*. OpenRefine, formerly *Google Refine*, is an open source application for data cleaning.

Some of our team members have also used OpenRefine directly. For more information on for using OpenRefine directly, go to `http://openrefine.org/`.

To use OpenRefine on Data Scientist WorkBench, first go to `https://datascientistworkbench.com/`.

After login, we will see the following screenshot:

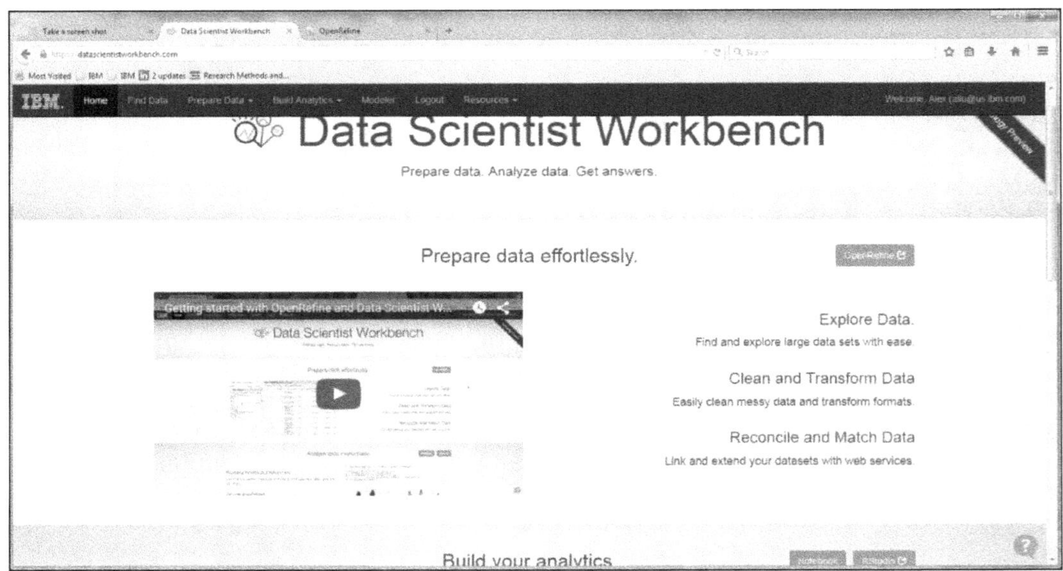

Then, click on the **OpenRefine** button in the top-right corner:

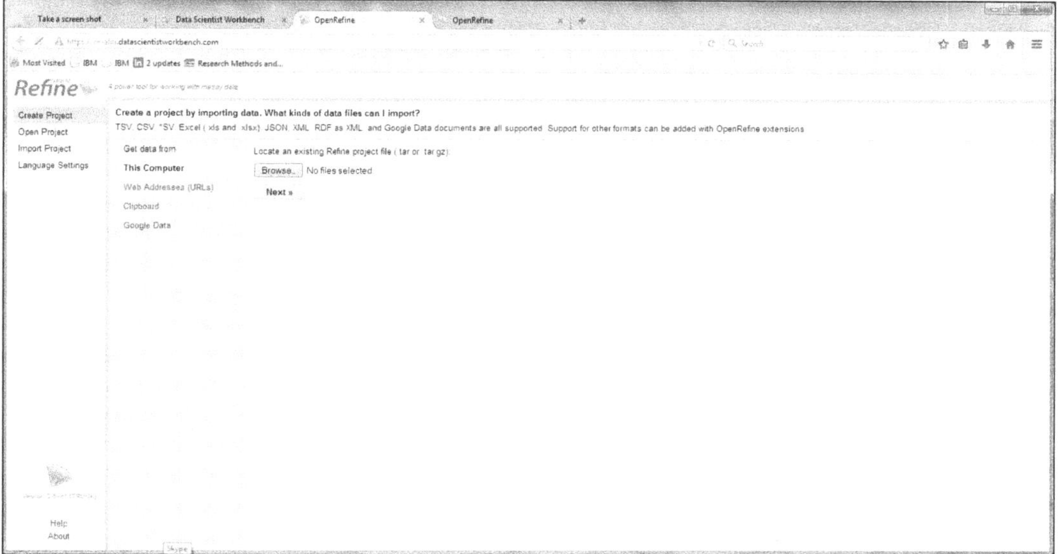

From here, we can import datasets from your computer or from a URL address.

Then, we can create an OpenRefine project to do data cleaning and preparation. After that, we can export the prepared data or send the data to a notebook by drag and drop.

For this project, we especially used OpenRefine for identity matching (reconciliation), duplicates deleting, and then a little bit of dataset merging.

Besides using OpenRefine, some of our members have cleaned sample data. They have then programmed the procedures for distributed computing for data cleaning, especially for taking care of some data mistakes.

Data merging

In the *Joining data* section of *Chapter 2, Data Preparation for Spark ML*, we described methods to join data together with Spark SQL and other tools. All the data techniques described in *Chapter 2, Data Preparation for Spark ML*, as well as the ones about identity matching and data cleaning techniques will be used.

As for this data merging task, the main focus is to merge data on location per zip code and also per school districts. That is, first, we need to work on identity analytics to ensure that we have good IDs for matching.

Then, we merge datasets.

After that, we reorganize datasets into a format suitable for the methods we selected in the previous section.

For information about how to reorganize datasets, you may refer to the *Data reorganizing* section of *Chapter 2, Data Preparation for Spark ML.*

Specifically, we start with simple data at `https://www.ed-data.k12.ca.us/Pages/Home.aspx`.

Then, we merge a few datasets, such as weather data, census data, and city educational datasets, into it.

After that, we reorganize all the data to obtain features per school district and per academic term.

Feature development

As an exercise, we have also used some social media data and worked to develop features from it.

One easy feature for social media is the social influence score for the principal of the school, which I suspect is not very useful. However, to obtain the social influence scores for all the students or for all the teachers is difficult.

As for the web data, we obtained some log data for each school's website. Using some similar methods to those used in *Chapter 4, Fraud Detection on Spark*, we extracted some features from the web log data. Specifically, to parse them and to make sense of them, we used some subject knowledge. With that, our team worked manually with some sample data. Then, they used the patterns discovered to develop codes in R to parse and turn extracted information into features. These features include the number of clicks, time between clicks, type of clicks, and other features, which were used to construct interaction features for the schools.

Feature selection

After the work mentioned in the preceding section, we have more than 100 features ready to be used.

As for the feature selection for this project, we could follow what we used for *Chapter 8, Learning Analytics on Spark*, which was to utilize PCA and also to use subject knowledge to group features, and then apply machine learning for its final feature selection. However, as an exercise, you will not repeat what you learned, but will try something different. That is, we will let the machine learning algorithms pick up the features most useful in prediction.

In MLlib, we can use the `ChiSqSelector` algorithm as follows:

```
// Create ChiSqSelector that will select top 25 of 400 features
val selector = new ChiSqSelector(25)
// Create ChiSqSelector model (selecting features)
val transformer = selector.fit(TrainingData)
```

In R, we can use some R packages to make computation easy. Among the available packages, CARET is one of the commonly used packages.

After this, we will end with a large amount of data with the following list of our sample features:

- School name
- School ID
- Graduation ratio
- Dropout ratio
- Average score from state exam 1
- Average score from state exam 2
- Social media participation score
- Web interactions
- Parent participation
- Outdoor activities
- Mobility
- Technology usage
- College connection

Besides this, we have also obtained a dataset with a school district as a unit, for which school averages were calculated as each district has more than one school.

So, besides the preceding features, we also have data for school district for the following features:

- Economics
- Crime
- Business

We have all the data from 2000 to 2015.

Model estimation

Once the feature sets get finalized in our last section, what follows is to estimate all the parameters of the selected models, for which we have adopted a dynamic approach of using SPSS on Spark, R notebooks in the Databricks environment, and MLlib directly on Spark. For the purpose of organizing workflows better, we focused our effort on organizing all the codes into R notebooks and also coding SPSS Modeler nodes.

For this project, as mentioned earlier, we need to conduct some exploratory analysis for descriptive statistics and for visualization. For this, we can take the MLlib codes and implement them directly. Also, with R codes, we obtained quick and good results.

For the best modelling, we need to arrange distributed computing, especially for this case, with various locations in combination with various customer segments per parents. In the United States, there are 13,506 school districts in 50 states. The difference between states is quite big. For this distributed computing part, you need to refer to the previous chapters. We will use SPSS Analytics Server with Apache Spark as well as the Databricks environment.

As we discussed in the *Spark for learning from open data* section, we mainly use regression for the supervised machine learning part. From what you have learned so far, for regression, we can complete the model estimation either with SPSS or with R. In order to implement them in the Databricks environment, we should refer to *Chapter 3, A Holistic View on Spark* and *Chapter 5, Risk Scoring on Spark.*

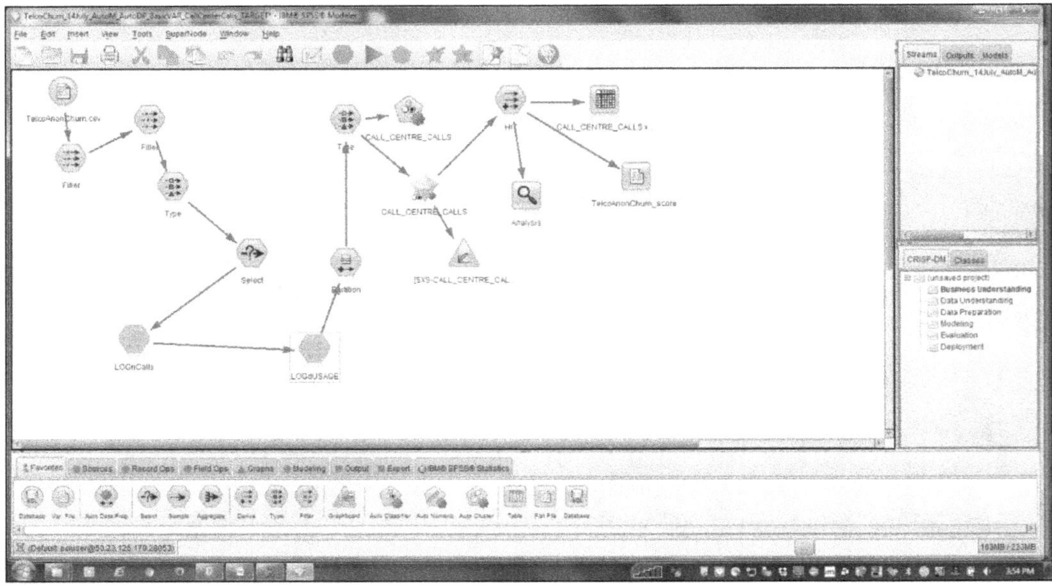

SPSS on Spark – SPSS Analytics Server

The IBM SPSS Modeler 17.1 and Analytic Server 2.1 offer easy integration with Spark, which allows us to implement the data and modeling streams built so far easily.

Besides using SPSS Modeler to estimate these predictive models, for which we need to use SPSS Analytics Server, we have also used R notebook in the Databricks environment and Data Scientist WorkBench.

With this, as an example, we have obtained a cluster analysis plot as follows:

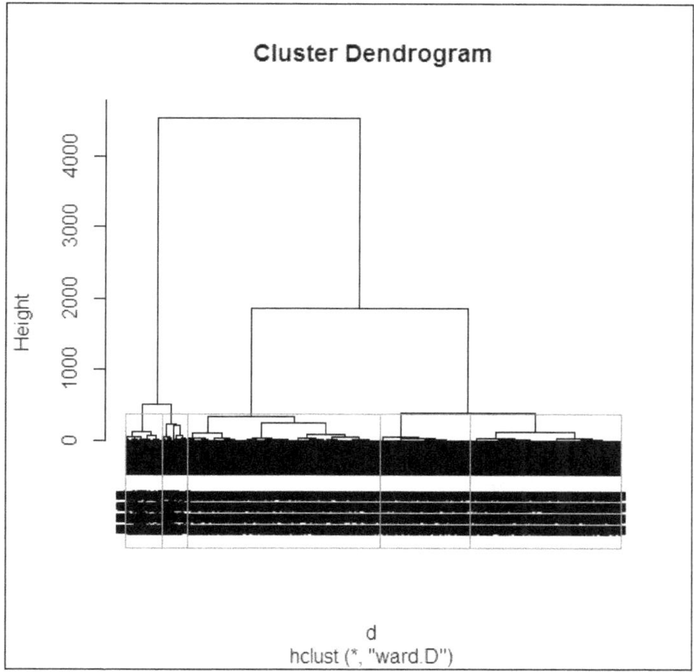

As an example, with R, we have obtained a PCA plot as follows:

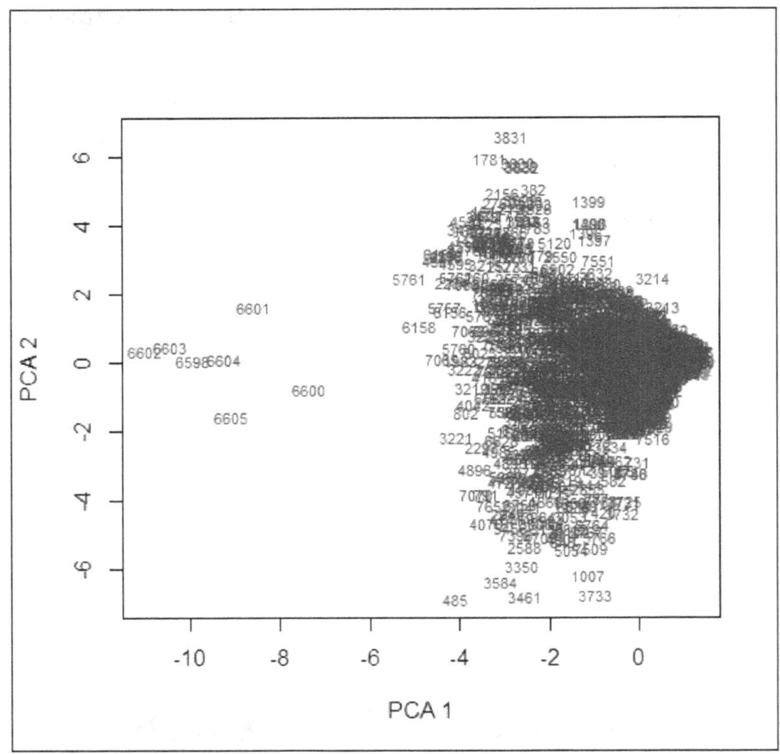

Model evaluation

In the previous section, we completed our model estimation as well as some exploratory work. Now it is time for us to evaluate these estimated models to see if they fit our criteria so that we can either move to our next stage for results explanation or go back to some previous stages to refine our predictive models.

To perform our model evaluation, in this section, we have conducted evaluations for cluster analysis and also for PCA. However, our focus is still on assessing predictive models, the regression models with rankings as our target variables. For this task, we will mainly use **Root Mean Square Error** (**RMSE**) to assess our models, as it is good for assessing regression models.

Just like we did for model estimation, to calculate RMSEs, we need to use MLlib for regression modeling on Spark. At the same time, we will also use R notebooks to be implemented in the Databricks environment for Spark. Of course, we also used an analytical server for SPSS, as we have adopted a dynamic approach here.

RMSE calculations with MLlib

As used with good results in the past, for MLlib, we can use the following code to calculate RMSE:

```
val valuesAndPreds = test.map { point =>
  val prediction = new_model.predict(point.features)
  val r = (point.label, prediction)
  r
}
val residuals = valuesAndPreds.map {case (v, p) => math.pow((v -
  p), 2)}
val MSE = residuals.mean();
val RMSE = math.pow(MSE, 0.5)
```

Besides the preceding code, MLlib also has some functions in the `RegressionMetrics` and `RankingMetrics` classes for us to use for the RMSE calculation.

RMSE calculations with R

In R, the `forecast` package has an `accuracy` function that can be used to calculate forecasting accuracy as well as RMSEs:

```
accuracy(f, x, test=NULL, d=NULL, D=NULL)
```

The measures calculated also include the following:

- **ME (Mean Error)**
- **RMSE (Root Mean Squared Error)**
- **MAE (Mean Absolute Error)**
- **MPE (Mean Percentage Error)**
- **MAPE (Mean Absolute Percentage Error)**
- **MASE (Mean Absolute Scaled Error)**
- **ACF1 (Autocorrelation of errors at lag 1)**

To perform a complete evaluation, we calculated RMSEs for all the models we estimated. Then, we compared and picked up the ones with smaller RMSEs.

Results explanation

Per our 4Es framework used for this book, after we passed our model evaluation stage and selected the estimated and evaluated models as our final models, our next task for this project is to interpret the results to our clients.

In terms of explaining the machine learning results, the users of our project are particularly interested in understanding what influences the known rankings that are widely used. Also, they are interested in how new rankings are different from others and how the new rankings can be used.

So, we will work on their requests, but will not cover all of them as the purpose here is mainly to exhibit technologies. Also, for the confidentiality issue and also space limitations, we will not go into the details too much, but will focus more on utilizing our technologies for better explanations.

Overall, the interpretation is straightforward here, which include the following three tasks:

- Present a list of top-ranked schools and school districts
- Compare various lists
- Explain the impact of factors such as parent involvement and economy on the rankings

One of the main achievements of this project is for us to obtain a better and more accurate ranking with our ensemble methods as well as good analytics, but it is very challenging to explain it the users, and it is also beyond the scope of this book here.

Another big improvement achieved here is the capability for us to quickly produce rankings per various requirements, such as to rank per academic performance or per future employment or per graduation rate, which is interesting to users, but seems still take time for adoption. However, users understand the benefits of fast-producing rankings, as made possible using Apache Spark.

So, as a result, we have delivered a few lists, and reported on ranking comparison and on factors influencing rankings.

Comparing ranks

R has some packages that help us analyze and compare rankings, such as pmr and Rmallow. However, for this project, the users preferred simple comparison, such as a direct comparison of the top 10 schools and the top 10 school districts, which made our explanation a little easier.

Another task of the explanatory works is to compare our list to others, such as the one at `http://www.school-ratings.com/schoolRatings.php?zipOrCity=91030`, or the one provided by the LA Times at `http://schools.latimes.com/`, or the one by SchoolIE. They claimed to be using Big Data to evaluate schools from many perspectives, rather than by one angle, at `http://www.schoolie.com/`.

As a result, we found ours to be closer to the one created by SchoolIE.

R has some algorithms to compute similarity or distance between rankings, which we explored, but have not used to serve the clients. This is because we adopted an approach with simple comparison that our clients preferred, and it is still very effective.

Biggest influencers

As people are interested in how some schools are on top and other schools are not, our results about the biggest predictors are of great interest.

For this part, we use results from our estimated predictive models of regression, for which we have used our own rankings as the target variable, and also some well-known rankings such as those provided by the US News and World Report and those by some state organizations.

For this task, we have just used the coefficients in our linear regression models to tell us which one has a bigger impact. We also used the `RandomForest` function to rank features per their impact on moving schools into the top 100. In other words, we split the list into "top 100" and "the rest." We then ran the decision tree modeling and random forest modeling on it, and then used the Random Forest's feature `importance` function to obtain a list of features as ordered by their impact on the target variable of whether the school is in top 100. In R, we need to use the function of `importance` in R's `randomForest` package.

Per our results, the economic status of the community, parents' involvements, and college connections are among the factors having the biggest impact for some coast schools. However, technology use has not had as much impact as expected.

Deployment

In the past, rankings were mostly reviewed as a reference by users. With this project, we found we are also in a position to assist our users in integrating our results with their decision-making tools, to help them utilize rankings better and also make their lives easier. For this, producing rules from rankings and also making scores behind rankings easily accessible became very important.

Because of the preceding reason, our deployment is still on to develop a set of rules and also to make all the scores available for decision makers, which include schools and some parents. Specifically, the main task of sending out a rule to alert users when some ranking changes dramatically, especially when a ranking drops down dramatically. Users of this project also have a need to obtain all the scores and rankings for their management performance.

Another purpose for this project is to produce good predictive models for the users to forecast possible changes of school rankings as per population changes using our developed regression models.

All the three needs for rankings, scores, and forecasting, mentioned in the preceding paragraph, are of value to various kinds of users who use various kinds of software systems for decision making. So, we need a bridge such as **Predictive Model Markup Language** (**PMML**), which is adopted as the standard by many systems. As discussed before, MLlib supports model export to PMML. Therefore, we export some developed models to PMML for this project.

In practice, the users for this project are more interested in rule-based decision making to use some of our insights and also in score-based decision making to evaluate their regional units' performance. Specifically, for this project, the client is interested in applying our results to (1) decide when an alert may be sent out if rankings have been changed or ranking changes will likely occur in the future, for which rules should be established, and to (2) develop scores and use them scores to measure performance as well as to plan for the future.

Besides this, clients are also interested in forecasting the attendance and other requests per ranking changes, for which R actually has a package called `forecast` that is ready to be used for this purpose:

```
forecast(fit)
plot(forecast(fit))
```

To sum up, for our special tasks, we need to turn some of our results into some rules and also need to produce some performance scores for the client.

Rules for sending out alerts

As discussed earlier, for R results, there are several tools to help extract rules from developed predictive models.

For the decision tree model developed to model whether or not a service request level exceeds a certain level, we should use the `rpart.utils` R package, which can extract rules and export them in various formats such as RODBC.

The `rpart.rules.table(model1) *` package returns an unpivoted table of variable values (factor levels) associated with each branch.

However, for this project, partially due to the data incompleteness issue, we will need to utilize some insights to derive rules directly. That is, we need to use the insights discussed in the last section. For example, we can do the following:

- If big mobility occurred and also parents' involvement dropped, our prediction shows rankings will go down dramatically and so an alert will be sent out

From an analytical perspective, we face the same issue here, to minimize false alerts, while ensuring adequate warning.

Therefore, by taking advantage of Spark's fast computing, we carefully produced rules, and for each rule, we supplied false positive ratios that helped the client utilize the rules.

Scores for ranking school districts

With our regression modeling in place, we have two ways to forecast the ranking change at a specific time.

One is to use the estimated regression equations to do forecasting directly. Alternatively, we can use the following code:

```
forecast(fit, newdata=data.frame(City=30))
```

As long as we have obtained the scores, we can classify all the districts or schools into several categories and also illustrate them on a map to identify special zones for attention, such as the graphs as produced by R:

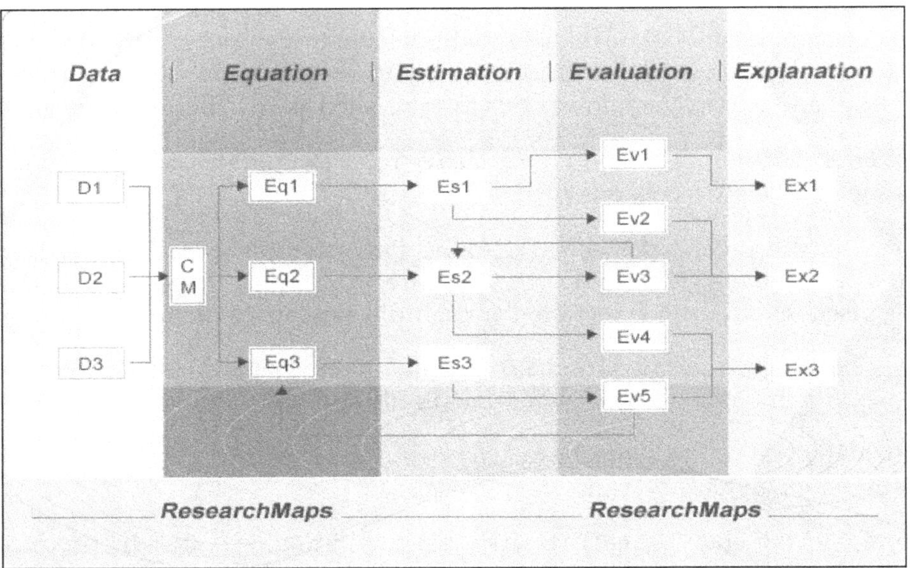

Summary

The work presented in this chapter is a further extension of *Chapter 10, Learning Telco Data on Spark,* as well as *Chapter 9, City Analytics on Spark*. It is a very special extension of *Chapter 9, City Analytics on Spark,* as both chapters are using open datasets. It is also an extension of *Chapter 10, Learning Telco Data on Spark,* as both chapters take a dynamic approach so that readers can take advantage of all the learned techniques to achieve better machine learning results and also to develop the best analytical solutions. Therefore, this chapter may be used as a review chapter, as well as a special chapter for you to synthesize all the knowledge learned.

In this chapter, with a real-life project of learning from open data, we have repeated the same step-by-step RM4Es process as used in the previous chapters, from which we processed open data on Apache Spark and then selected models (equations). For each model, we estimated their coefficients and then evaluated these models against model performance metrics. Finally, with the models estimated, we explained our results in detail. With this real-life project of learning from open data, we further demonstrated the benefit of utilizing our RM4Es framework to organize our machine learning processes.

A little different from the previous chapters, specifically, we first selected a dynamic machine learning approach with cluster analysis and PCA plus regression. Then, we prepared Spark computing and loaded in preprocessed data. Second, we worked on data and feature preparation using cleaned open datasets, by reorganizing a few datasets together, and by selecting a core set of features. Especially, in dealing with open datasets, a lot more work is needed to clean the data and reorganize it, as demonstrated here, which should be a special learning for anyone using open data. Third, we developed measurements and estimated predictive model coefficients using MLlib, R, and SPSS on Spark. Fourth, we evaluated these estimated models, mainly using RMSEs. Then, we interpreted our machine learning results with lists and ranking comparisons, as well as the biggest predictors for top rankings. Finally, we deployed our machine learning results with a focus on scoring and rules.

The preceding process is similar to the process described in the previous chapters. However, in this chapter, we focused our effort on a dynamic approach, which give you opportunities to combine what you have learned so far for the best analytical results. Especially, for this project, we explored the datasets and built several measurements and rankings of districts, with which we then developed rules for alerts and scores for performance, to help schools and parents for their decision making and performance management.

After reading this chapter, you would be completely ready to utilize Apache Spark for dynamic machine learning so that you can quickly develop actionable insights from a large amount of open data. By now, users will have mastered our process, our framework, and various approaches. Rather than being limited by any of them, users will be able to fully take advantage of all of them or any combination of them for optimal machine learning results.

Index

A

B

C

D

E

F

N

O

S

T

Z

www.ingramcontent.com/pod-product-compliance
Lightning Source LLC
Chambersburg PA
CBHW060540060326
40690CB00017B/3556

* 9 7 8 1 7 8 5 8 8 0 3 9 1 *